FOR ONE WEEK ONLY!

FOR ONE WEEK ONLY!

THE NORFOLK AND NORWICH OPERATIC SOCIETY
1925–2025

Adrian Wright

THE BOYDELL PRESS

© Adrian Wright 2025

All Rights Reserved. Except as permitted under current legislation no part of this work may be photocopied, stored in a retrieval system, published, performed in public, adapted, broadcast, transmitted, recorded or reproduced in any form or by any means, without the prior permission of the copyright owner

The right of Adrian Wright to be identified as the author of this work has been asserted in accordance with sections 77 and 78 of the Copyright, Designs and Patents Act 1988

First published 2025
The Boydell Press, Woodbridge

ISBN 978 1 83765 215 0

The Boydell Press is an imprint of Boydell & Brewer Ltd
PO Box 9, Woodbridge, Suffolk IP12 3DF, UK
and of Boydell & Brewer Inc.
668 Mt Hope Avenue, Rochester, NY 14620–2731, USA
website: www.boydellandbrewer.com

A CIP catalogue record for this book is available
from the British Library

The publisher has no responsibility for the continued existence or accuracy of URLs for external or third-party internet websites referred to in this book, and does not guarantee that any content on such websites is, or will remain, accurate or appropriate

This is for everyone who stayed in the wings

Contents

Illustrations	xi
Foreword	xv
Preface and Acknowledgements	xvii
Opening Night	xix
Beginnings	xxi

The 1920s

Dorothy	2
Les Cloches de Corneville	8
The Gondoliers	11
The Little Michus	14

The 1930s

The Marriage Market	20
Sybil	22
The Mikado	28
The Yeomen of the Guard	32
The Rebel Maid	34
Iolanthe	38
The Gondoliers	40
Trial by Jury/H. M. S. Pinafore	42
Merrie England	45

The 1940s

Iolanthe	50
The Mikado	52
Ruddigore	54

The 1950s

The Gondoliers	59
Trial by Jury/H. M. S. Pinafore	60
The Pirates of Penzance/Cox and Box	62
The Yeomen of the Guard	65
The Maid of the Mountains	67
Iolanthe	71
The Quaker Girl	74
The Belle of New York	76
White Horse Inn	79
Show Boat	82

The 1960s

The Desert Song	90
The Gypsy Princess	93
The Student Prince	96
Oklahoma!	98
Pink Champagne	100
The Merry Widow	103
Brigadoon	106
Song of Norway	109
Rose Marie	111
Kismet	113

The 1970s

White Horse Inn	118
Annie Get Your Gun	122
Carousel	124
The Dubarry	126
Hello, Dolly!	128
King's Rhapsody	131
South Pacific	136
Camelot	137
Gigi	140
The Merry Widow	142

The 1980s

Fiddler on the Roof	146
Kiss Me, Kate	147
Die Fledermaus	149
Oklahoma!	151
The Most Happy Fella	152
The King and I	155
My Fair Lady	157
Guys and Dolls	159
Brigadoon	160
The Sound of Music	163

The 1990s

Annie Get Your Gun	169
The Music Man	170
Oliver!	173
42nd Street	175
Meet Me in St Louis	177

CONTENTS

Barnum	178
Hello, Dolly!	181
Carousel	183

The 2000s

Me and My Girl	186
Mack and Mabel	188
South Pacific	190
My Fair Lady	192
Kiss Me, Kate	193
Jesus Christ Superstar	196
Oklahoma!	199
42nd Street	201
Titanic	203
West Side Story	206

The 2010s

The Producers	212
Fiddler on the Roof	216
Hello, Dolly!	217
Sweeney Todd	219
Anything Goes	222
Sister Act	224
Sunset Boulevard	225
The Witches of Eastwick	228
Top Hat	229
Guys and Dolls	231

The 2020s

Made in Dagenham	234
The Sound of Music	236
Kinky Boots	239
Betty Blue Eyes	241

Envoi	245
Appendix 1: The Norwich Amateur Operatic Company	249
Appendix 2: Directors and Musical Directors	253
Notes	255
Select Bibliography	259
Index of N&N Productions	261

Illustrations

1. Theatre programme cover for *Dorothy* (1925). Courtesy of NNOS Archive — 3
2. The Society's first producer, director and musical director Henry Butcher. Courtesy of NNOS Archive — 6
3. Ruth, Lady Ballance in 1929 © National Portrait Gallery, London — 7
4. Percy Winter and the girls of *Les Cloches de Corneville* (1926) Courtesy of NNOS Archive — 9
5. Vignettes from *The Gondoliers* (1927). Courtesy of NNOS Archive — 12
6. *The Little Michus* (1929). Courtesy of NNOS Archive — 15
7. Flooding the stage in *The Marriage Market* (1930). Courtesy of NNOS Archive — 22
8. Madeleine Back and Neville Howlett larking about in *Sybil* (1931). Courtesy of NNOS Archive — 23
9. W. B. Davies as Petrov and Phyllis Duncan as Sybil in 1931. Courtesy of NNOS Archive — 24
10. 'Three little maids from school' from *The Mikado* (1932). Courtesy of NNOS Archive — 30
11. A. G. Whittle and Harry G. Cook looking over the script for *The Rebel Maid* (1934). Courtesy of NNOS Archive — 36
12. A dashing Clement Smith and Percy Woods in *The Gondoliers* (1937). Courtesy of NNOS Archive — 41
13. Roy Thurston and Clement Smith with an ingénue Ivy Oxley at a trial by jury in 1938. Courtesy of NNOS Archive — 44
14. Prominent officers of the Society in 1939. Courtesy of NNOS Archive — 46
15. An urgent need for crowd control for the 1947 fairies of *Iolanthe*. Courtesy of Jarrolds Ltd, Norwich — 51
16. 'Everybody on stage!' for *The Mikado* (1948). Courtesy of NNOS Archive — 53
17. Ghostly remains of the haunted *Ruddigore* (1949). Courtesy of Jarrolds Ltd, Norwich — 55
18. *The Pirates of Penzance* in 1952 © Eastern Daily Press, Norwich — 63
19. *The Yeomen of the Guard* in 1953 © Eastern Daily Press, Norwich — 66
20. *The Maid of the Mountains* in 1954 © Eastern Daily Press, Norwich — 68

21. 'I am generally admired!' Private Willis meets the fairies in the 1955 *Iolanthe* © Eastern Daily Press, Norwich — 72
22. *The Quaker Girl* (1956) © Eastern Daily Press, Norwich — 75
23. *The Belle of New York* (1957) © Eastern Daily Press, Norwich — 77
24. *White Horse Inn* (1958) © Eastern Daily Press, Norwich — 80
25. Joyce Johnson, keeper of the Society's archive, waiting to board the 1959 *Show Boat* © A. R. Miller Photography, Bungay — 81
26. A melodramatic moment in *Show Boat* (1959) © Eastern Daily Press, Norwich — 83
27. Patricia Michael as Polly in *Divorce Me Darling!* (1964). Courtesy of Josh Siegel. — 89
28. Norma Wick (centre) with girlfriends in *The Desert Song* of 1960. Courtesy of NNOS Archive — 91
29. Lynn Wardle depending on the ladies in *The Gypsy Princess* (1961), another operetta from a bygone age © Eastern Daily Press, Norwich — 94
30. The male chorus insisting on 'Drink, Drink, Drink' and holding their patently empty tankards aloft for *The Student Prince* of 1962. Courtesy of NNOS Archive — 97
31. Ersatz operetta? The 1964 *Pink Champagne* © A. R. Miller Photography, Bungay — 101
32. *The Merry Widow*. Four principals pose for the 1965 theatre programme © Montague, St. John Maddermarket, Norwich — 104
33. 'Come to Me, Bend to Me': Margaret Elliott and supporters in *Brigadoon* (1966) © Eastern Daily Press, Norwich — 107
34. Sylvia Dix and her Mounties in the 1968 *Rose Marie* © Eastern Daily Press, Norwich — 112
35. *Kismet* (1969). Courtesy of NNOS Archive — 114
36. An unjustly unappreciated gem from 1962. Thank heaven for its original London cast recording LP! © PYE Records, Printed and made by Garrod & Lofthouse Ltd — 115
37. Milkmaids await their moment at the White Horse Inn (1970) Courtesy of NNOS Archive — 119
38. George Baker and company in the 1970 version of *White Horse Inn* © Eastern Daily Press, Norwich — 119
39. Margaret Elliott and John Dunsire book into the White Horse Inn in 1970 © Montague, St. John Maddermarket, Norwich — 120
40. Margaret Elliott, Pip Jenkinson and Norma Wick (1970). Courtesy of NNOS Archive — 120

ILLUSTRATIONS

41. A change in the weather: *White Horse Inn* (1970) © Eastern Daily Press, Norwich — 121
42. Ready to say 'Hello, Dolly!' in 1974 © Eastern Daily Press, Norwich — 129
43. Adrian Wright and Coral Newell awaiting *King's Rhapsody* (1975). Courtesy of NNOS Archive — 132
44. L-R: Norma Wick, Adrian Wright, Ivy Oxley and Coral Newell in *King's Rhapsody* (1975) © Eastern Daily Press, Norwich — 133
45. The *Camelot* company of 1977 © Eastern Daily Press, Norwich — 138
46. Gordon Canwell, Christopher Speake and Coral Newell looking over *The Merry Widow* in 1979 © Alan Howard Photography, Norwich — 143
47. Robin Baines, David Ivins, John Bill and Adrian Wright 'Standing on the Corner' in *The Most Happy Fella* of 1984 © The Cameo Photographic Studio and Frame Boutique, Norwich — 153
48. Della Stone and John McInnes in the 1998 *Brigadoon* © Peter King Photography — 161
49. Dancing mistress Michelle Neave with Norma Wick during *The Sound of Music* (1989). Courtesy of NNOS Archive — 165
50. *42nd Street* (1995) © Peter King Photography — 176
51. Handover of Presidency from Desmond Elliott to Charles Roberts, July 2000. Courtesy of NNOS Archive — 195
52. Steve Jones, Stephanie Moore and Chris Dilley, *Jesus Christ Superstar* (2005). Courtesy of David Pulling — 197
53. *42nd Street* Theatre programme cover (2007). Courtesy of NNOS Archive — 202
54. Ian Chisholm, Josh Lincoln, Sarah Browne and Christine Mullord set sail on the ill-fated *Titanic* (2008). Courtesy of David Pulling — 204
55. The Jet Boys and Jet Girls of *West Side Story* (2009). Courtesy of David Pulling — 207
56. The Shark Boys and Girls of *West Side Story* (2009). Courtesy of David Pulling — 208
57. Little old ladies out on their zimmers in *The Producers* (2010). Courtesy of David Pulling — 213
58. Roger de Bris (Adrian Wright) and his team 'Keep it Gay' in *The Producers* (2010). Courtesy of David Pulling — 213
59. Roger de Bris overcome by finding stardom in 'Springtime for Hitler' in *The Producers* (2010). Courtesy of David Pulling — 214
60. Hatching a plot: Lawrence Guymer, Holly Graham and Nick Bird in *The Producers* (2010). Courtesy of David Pulling — 214

61. Holly Graham as Ulla in *The Producers* (2010). Courtesy of David Pulling 215
62. Andy Gledhill and Stephanie Moore: *Sweeney Todd* (2013). Courtesy of David Pulling 220
63. Stephanie Moore and Gary Higgs in *Sweeney Todd* (2013). Courtesy of David Pulling 221
64. Linda Campbell as Norma Desmond in *Sunset Boulevard* (2016) © Jaz Instone-Brewer 227
65. *Top Hat:* Christopher Penn, Linda Campbell, Adrian Wright, Ian Chisholm and Alex Green (2018). Courtesy of David Pulling 230
66. *Top Hat*: Alex Green and Kathryn White in *Top Hat* (2018). Courtesy of David Pulling 231
67. *Made in Dagenham,* yet another musical about striking workers (2020). Courtesy of David Pulling 235
68. *The Sound of Music* 2022: The von Trapp Family. Courtesy of David Pulling 237
69. *The Sound of Music* The escape to the mountains (2022). Courtesy of David Pulling 237
70. 'I'm Not My Father's Son': Dominic Sands and Akeem Ellis-Hyman from the 2023 *Kinky Boots* © Richard Jarmy Photography 240
71. *Betty Blue Eyes* A Private Function (2024) © Richard Jarmy Photography 242
72. The finale of *Betty Blue Eyes* (2024) © Richard Jarmy Photography 243

The author and publisher are grateful to all the institutions and individuals listed for permission to reproduce the materials in which they hold copyright. Every effort has been made to trace the copyright holders; apologies are offered for any omission, and the publisher will be pleased to add any necessary acknowledgement in subsequent editions.

Foreword

The Norfolk and Norwich Operatic Society (N&N) is one hundred years old in 2025, and as Chairman I am delighted that Adrian Wright agreed to get involved in the production of this book. He has devoted much of the past two years to researching and writing and has produced an authoritative record of the musical history of the Society for which I will be eternally grateful.

The second half of the nineteenth century saw a rise in the popularity of amateur theatre. Operetta was the most common genre with Gilbert and Sullivan prompting the formation of many amateur groups. Today, it is difficult to say how many groups exist across the country but with 2000 registered with the National Operatic and Dramatic Association the total must be well over that figure. Some societies, of course, will have celebrated their centenaries before now and will appreciate the great sense of achievement in reaching that milestone. This book was originally intended solely as a permanent record of the achievements of the N&N over the past hundred years, but has grown to highlight the development of musical theatre throughout the century and explore the history of the N&N and its ongoing contribution to the arts in Norfolk.

I first saw Adrian Wright at Norwich's Maddermarket Theatre in 1977. I was a volunteer, helping out in the bar, the lighting box or selling programmes. He, as a young entertainer, trod the boards with panache in its annual New Year's Eve Music Hall. I always thought him a talented and entertaining person and was in complete awe. So much so that it was not until I developed a love of Musical Theatre and joined what was then called the Norfolk and Norwich Amateur Operatic Society in 1994, some 17 years later, that I felt "entitled" to actually get to know Adrian. It wasn't until my chairmanship started in 2009 and Adrian was cast as Roger De Bris in our production of *The Producers* that I came to know him as a fellow performer and author with a knowledge of all things Musical Theatre, especially British Musical Theatre, unsurpassed amongst those that have become my friends and acquaintances over the years.

I am fortunate to hold the archives of the Operatic Society and, as much as my committee were happy that we commission Adrian to write this book in celebration of our Centenary, neither my committee nor I realised the importance of the extensive archive of material that we had amassed over the 100 years until Adrian had the opportunity of seeing what we had collected. A complete archive of every show that we have produced and minutes of almost all meetings that the Committee has had since 1924 – it was invaluable in Adrian's research for this book.

Since being elected as Chairman I have tried to steer the Society through ever difficult times to ensure that the aims of its founders are met and the Society grows to become more professional as each decade passes, surely the aims of all chair-people of every society across the country. The problems we face today are really no different from those that Ruth, Lady Ballance, had when she started the Society in 1924. Choosing the right show, attracting those talented enough to perform and selling enough tickets at the right price to cover the costs. Ruth and her committee were not as good at it then as we are now but, without doubt, there was a similar amount of enthusiasm amongst the local population to both get up and audition and/or to buy tickets to watch then as there is now. It bodes well for the future.

2025 sees the start of the next century and the N&N has been chosen as one of only 11 lead societies to produce "Les Misérables" in July 2025 as part of Cameron Mackintosh's "Let the People Sing" celebrations for the 40th anniversary of that show's first opening in the West End – the world's longest running musical. We are proud to represent the East of England in this huge community project.

We are eternally grateful for the help and support of the management and staff of the Theatre Royal over the century. Without it we would have struggled to deal with the introduction of new technology as it was introduced into the theatre. Indeed, even in 1936, as the Theatre was being rebuilt after a great fire forced its closure, the then owner, Jack Gladwin, almost paid the N&N to return to the 'new' Theatre Royal rather than the Hippodrome Theatre in Norwich, threatening: "if the Society plays the Hippodrome then they'll never play the Royal again". The N&N returned to the Royal with their 1937 production of "Gondoliers".

Amateur theatre in Norfolk is flourishing through the hard work and dedication of countless volunteers and I am blessed with the support of a loyal and hardworking committee. Adrian's book is testament to not only their work but that of all past holders of the Chair and their Committees and the countless members of the N&N who have trodden the boards and worked backstage over the past one hundred years.

The aims of the NNOS are simply to provide as many local amateur performers as possible with an opportunity to work with industry professionals, to perform in East Anglia's premier Theatre, in as professional an environment as possible and to allow our audiences to see top quality productions at as reasonable a cost as possible. I believe that we have been doing so for the past one hundred years. May it continue for the next hundred.

David Pulling
September 2024

Preface and Acknowledgements

My first thank you must be to the late Joyce Johnson, a staunch member of the Society who for many years maintained an archive of the Society's activities, mainly consisting of theatre programmes, newspaper reviews and photographs, and ultimately donated the archive to the Society. Despite her industriousness there remain many omissions, especially from the Society's earliest years. The problem was highlighted at the time of the Society's 50th anniversary in 1975, when Margaret Elliott, one of the Society's most prominent performers of that time, became its honorary archivist. It was pointed out that when the time came to celebrate the 100th anniversary of the Society there would be a serious paucity of material to exhibit, and a public appeal was made to boost the archive. This seems to have mostly fallen on deaf ears, but the archive does contain a great number of photographs of Miss Elliott.

Writing about long gone theatrical productions is a challenging business; writing about 100 years of them is daunting. It is a simple matter of how to bring those evenings and matinees back to life, to make them seem in any way relevant to the job in hand. We are, after all, principally concerned with illusion, the lack of reality, and people in many cases long gone into the wings. 'Make believing' is a common denominator of theatrical life.

Take, for example, the matter of matinees, with that thrilling promise of going through the same process all over again that evening. I have always had a special fondness for matinees. I hasten to add that I have only a vague recollection of that splendid event when you attended a matinee performance, the thing one looked forward to with such anticipation: The Interval. In those civilised, halcyon days of theatre-going, the usherette had taken your order for afternoon tea, including a slice of Fuller's fruit cake, brought to you via your neighbouring patrons who passed the tea-tray along the row until it reached its final destination: yourself. Nowadays, it is down to wrestling with an overpriced tub of ice-cream that cunningly conceals a little wooden spoon about its person, the sound of scalding hot tea being poured into fine china cups having long ago been consigned to history.

Make no mistake: there is something special about theatrical matinees. Perhaps it is simply the knowledge that outside the theatre, in the streets and shops, in our homes and workplaces, ordinary life goes on through all sorts of weather while on stage real life is suspended, the sense of artificiality accentuated. Let us recall the discipline of the great music hall performer Hetty King who always insisted on being in her dressing room at least four hours before curtain-up. 'I like to get everything ready' she explained. Her regime meant that for a 2.30 pm matinee she was facing her dressing room mirror at 10.30 am. It was a matter of excluding the real world. Musical theatre is very good at that.

My first reaction to being asked by David Pulling, the chairman of the Norfolk and Norwich Operatic Society, to write a book to mark the Society's 100th birthday, was that it needed to be a celebration of its past and, somehow, a marker to the future. It is not, and is not intended to be, a history of the N&N (as the Society is sometimes known). The private meetings of its committee remain private. We only here and there take a peep into its ponderings and decision-making, and then quietly withdraw. Here and there we may have information about the Society's finances and associated facts. Artificial intelligence has not been involved in the book's compilation. Indeed, on seeing the author's name, some will feel that intelligence of any kind is sadly lacking. *For One Week Only!* may not be a nuts and bolts history of the company but endeavours to supply a passage through time via individual essays on the company's productions throughout the last 100 years.

Sympathetic readers will understand that the author cannot be expected to be equally enthusiastic about every one of the Society's productions, throughout almost 100 years. Those essays do not follow any strict form. As a general rule I have paid little attention to the plots. I always find these the most tedious aspect of reviews, and have not lingered with them. On occasion the essays stray from the show in question to more discursive consideration. Some of the essays may seem to be as much about unassociated matters as the production under review.

Each essay has the date of production, its authorship, director and musical director, followed by a full cast list. It is inevitable that personal taste will have its effect as it considers each production. In this way, the essay for *Sunset Boulevard* presented a challenge compared to that for *The Maid of the Mountains.*

My grateful thanks to Josh Siegel for providing the photograph of Patricia Michael in the leading role of Sandy Wilson's *Divorce Me, Darling!* and to Miss Michael for her comments on amateurism. The film historian and biographer Roger Mellor has been staunchly encouraging throughout. I am grateful to the theatre critic Neville Miller for discussing his career, and to Christine Mullord and to the various performers who have appeared with the Society over many years.

My thanks are due to Maria Andrew, the archivist of Norwich Theatre Royal, for her kind assistance with research. I am also grateful for the permission to use material published in the *Eastern Daily Press* and *Norwich Evening News*, and to James Goffin for allowing me to quote from his reviews. The assistance of Helen McDermott was much appreciated. I am of course grateful for the continuing support of my editor Michael Middeke and the team at The Boydell Press.

Opening Night

It is November 1925, a cold month for East Anglia, with frequent fogs. In its last week, there are severe frosts with Norwich recording seven inches of snow. Arctic winds blow across the city. It is Tuesday 8 December when Ruth, Lady Ballance, well-wrapped against the night, leaves her house in All Saints Green. She probably does not want to turn out, and is possibly nervous about what lies ahead, but there is a reason so important that, had she not been involved in it, her name might now be all but forgotten.

She steps gingerly into the street. She will not want to falter, not this evening. It is downhill from All Saints Green, and the paths may be slippery and wet in the dwindling light. A short journey of a minute or so, down the hill past All Saint's Church and immediately in the heart of the city before climbing gently uphill to the Theatre Royal, St Stephen's Church on her left, the magnificence of St Peter Mancroft on her right.

Tonight, the Royal is the destination not only of her ladyship but the company of unpaid players, and audience members who will be watching her on stage, the great and good and the more numerous anonymous of Norfolk and Norwich, the well-heeled patrons who can afford a private box (28s 9d), a seat in the stalls (4s 3d), and the less affluent in the gallery (1s 3d). At 7.30 pm the curtain will rise on the Norfolk and Norwich Amateur Operatic Society's debut production, *Dorothy*. And Lady Ballance *is* Dorothy for one week only (in fact, only half the week as there is a double cast).

Tonight, she knows that Norwich's other theatre, the Hippodrome, originally grandiloquently named the Grand Opera House, is presenting the sort of touring show for which it has become renowned. More than a few involve women on the verge of nudity. This week it is a variety revue called *High Life* with 'book and lyrics' by Con West, whose reassuring credits involve writing films for Old Mother Riley and Her Daughter Kitty. The *High Life* company includes several now forgotten artistes, among them Henry and Edgar Martell, Nina Leon and Her Imperial Trio, and the enticing promise of 'The Eight Shurley Girls'.

High Life and those eight dancing girls are merely passing through, but at the Theatre Royal, where hopefully they have already turned on the heating in Lady Ballance's dressing room, a much more local affair, a theatrical institution, is about to begin. There must be a bouquet or two awaiting her arrival at the stage door. From the moment she enters the building and makes her way to her dressing room, she is aware of being in a strangely different country from which the real world has, temporarily, been expunged.

Two printed programmes are available to the patrons who will soon be taking their seats in the auditorium: the stylish basic version and the illustrated souvenir programme designed and printed by A. E. Soman and Co., publicity specialists in St Andrew's Street. Most of the businesses advertising in the programme work within a stone's throw of the theatre; this is after all a local affair. No doubt some of the representatives of those companies will be watching this evening's entertainment. Perhaps some of the employees of Madame Pfob 'Chiropodist, Hair and Skin Specialist' from the Royal Arcade, and some of the waitresses from The Popular Restaurant attached to the Haymarket Picture House, offering afternoon teas from 3 to 6 pm during which customers are entertained by the Restaurant Orchestra, and a five-course dinner costing 5/6d including coffee.

Will some of the staff of Willmotts in Prince of Wales Road be in the audience? It is a wonderland of a shop where 'Gramophone and Record Service Is Unequalled'. This is no mere boast. As their advertisement claims 'You have at your disposal private Audition Lounges to hear any record made by Columbia'. Willmotts is also the sole distributor for Selecta Gramophones, surely a bargain at £1.15, with easy terms available. Much mourned, Willmotts (until its very last day of business offering sanctuary to your schoolboy author, happily letting him listen to gramophone recordings in one of those snug audition lounges) will close down in 1966.

Perhaps Mrs Pillow, the restful-sounding proprietress of Princes Tea and Luncheon Rooms in nearby Castle Street ('Wedding Cakes and Invalid Jellies a speciality') is excitedly waiting for the curtain to rise. We should be grateful for Mrs Pillow and the shopkeepers of Norwich who gather together this evening to see *Dorothy*, a 'pastoral comedy opera', performed by the newly formed Norfolk and Norwich Amateur Operatic Society. It is the beginning of just another performance of Alfred Cellier's then hugely popular and best-known work, but – even more remarkably – the beginning of a theatrical history that has endured for 100 years.

Beginnings

The first entry in the minute book of the Norfolk and Norwich Amateur Operatic Society is written in a fine looping hand. It tells us that:

> At the kind invitation of Lady Ballance the following met at 41 All Saints Green on 26th January 1925 to discuss the formation of a Norfolk and Norwich Amateur Operatic Society: The Lord Mayor of Norwich (Dr. G. S. Pope), Ruth Lady Ballance, Lady Morse, Miss Wise, Mrs Winder, Mrs Thompson, Mrs Meiklem, Sir Hamilton Ballance, Mr Bachelor, Mr Henry Butcher and Mr Thompson

It was not a particularly original idea. Such societies flourished throughout the country, and Norwich had already had one of its own: the Norwich Amateur Operatic Company, operating between 1901 and 1913. Its termination may have been influenced by the fact that some of its male members (always more difficult to recruit than their female counterparts) were all too soon catapulted into World War I, but financial problems played their part in its failure.

Now, at All Saints Green, perhaps among the tinkle of china cups and saucers and apostle spoons and refreshments offered by a maid imitating a Lyons House nippy

> it was agreed that in the first place a Provisional Committee should be appointed in order to carry out the necessary preliminary arrangements. The following were to be asked to serve on the committee: the Lord Mayor of Norwich (Dr. G. S. Pope), Lady Ballance, Lady Morse, Mrs Astley, Mrs Winder, Mrs Cicely Gurney, Capt. J. H. Mander, Mr Ivan Spain, Mr J. Thompson and Mr Henry Butcher.

Two years later, in the light-hearted 'Who's Who in the Society' pages found in its theatre programme for *The Gondoliers,* Butcher is described as 'a live wire, every inch of him, and there are some! A dynamic personality who combines with endless energy and remarkable vitality the gift of promoting and maintaining a cheery good-fellowship in the Company.'

The Norfolk and Norwich Amateur Operatic Society was formed because its originators considered that there was ample talent in the county and city for the making of a first-rate company. Its object would be 'to discover and promote local talent and also to provide entertainment and thereby to increase the opportunities of hearing light opera'. Among its stipulations was that 'All acting members will be expected to sing a song at a private audition.'

It made clear that 'Members shall attend all practises – in case of illness or other adequate reason for non-attendance written notice is imperative' and that 'Principals shall send notice to their understudies when unable to attend'. Furthermore, 'The Producer shall have the right to withdraw the part from any member in case of the said member being found unsuitable vocally or histrionically'.

On 9 March 1925 Ruth, Lady Ballance, proposed that Henry Butcher, A.R.A.M. 'of Ipswich' should be engaged as the society's first producer. Asked for his opinion as to the choice of opera, Butcher suggested Gilbert and Sullivan's *The Gondoliers* or Alfred Cellier's *Dorothy*. Arrangements were made for Butcher to see a current production of *Dorothy*.[1] Butcher wasted no time. By mid-April 1925 he had already arranged for the hire of costumes, wigs and scenery from that production. On rehearsal days in Norwich, the committee paid 5s for his overnight accommodation at the Bell Hotel, plus his supper and breakfast.

At the inaugural meeting of the Society at the Royal Hotel Norwich on 16 March 1925, Lady Ballance's husband, Sir Hamilton Ballance, was elected temporary chairman. From the beginning, the local press, notably the *Eastern Daily Press* and *Eastern Evening News*, encouraged the venture:

> It seems a strange thing that the musical and dramatic talent of Norwich has so rarely, and then only to a limited degree, found expression in opera. There has never, we believe, been an operatic society in the city of a standard comparable with that of the Choral or Philharmonic Society [...] Many places much smaller than Norwich have excellent operatic societies, and there seems no reason why Norwich should not be equally as successful in opera as it is in the repute it has gained in music and the drama. This can only be proved by experience, and it may be found that perfection is by no means easily attained.[2]

As a one-time president of the Society, Desmond Elliott explained that in the early days 'a few well-known people of wealth, style and rank, who it was thought might be interested in light opera and musical theatre, were invited to become Vice Presidents, to add stature, substance and respectability to this fledgling group of amateur performers'.[3]

At which of the three Norwich theatres would the company perform? The Society considered the options for its first production: the Theatre Royal on Theatre Street, the Hippodrome on St Giles Street, and F. H. Cooper's Regent Theatre, opened in 1923 on Prince of Wales Road. Consultations with the Theatre Royal and the Regent resulted in the committee offering to rent the Regent for 'Takings up to £400–50% with a diminishing scale of 5% for each £100 above the first £400'.

The original preference was for the Hippodrome, a fine Edwardian theatre opened as the Grand Opera House in 1903. But when it transpired that the management could not accommodate the Society's first production between

14 and 19 December, an agreement was reached with the Theatre Royal to present it between 7 and 12 December. At the committee meeting at All Saints Green on 6 April, it was decided that the company would make its debut in Alfred Cellier and B. C. Stephenson's 'pastoral comedy opera' *Dorothy*.[4]

Rehearsals would be on Monday evenings between 7.30 and 9.30pm, with Miss Channell paid 2 guineas as accompanist for the season. It was suggested that Butcher's fee as producer should be £84; that fee was agreed by late September. He was asked to interview Madame Baird of 10 Linden Gardens, W.2, engaged as dancing mistress for 10 guineas, her duties to commence in October. She offered to bring her own troupe of dancing girls, a gesture rejected by the committee. Rehearsals would take place at the Church of England Young Men's Society. It was then decided that the first performance would take place not on Monday 7 December, but on Tuesday 8 December , allowing for a dress rehearsal on the Monday.

Conflicting dates, with a municipal popular concert scheduled for 12 December, had to be sorted, not least because some members of the Norwich Festival chorus were now also members of the new Operatic Society. Along the way, Madame Baird seems to have been discarded. At only 7 guineas, the engagement of Miss Ida Ransome of Bracondale as dancing mistress was confirmed. Meanwhile, Mr Ivan Spain would collaborate with the producer on engaging an orchestra, with Butcher now officially recognised as the Society's first producer and conductor. In July, the committee set up a guarantee fund to underwrite any losses the company might incur, with the Ballances and Captain Mander leading the way with £10 each.

By August, Miss Ransome was asking if her agreed fee of 7 guineas might be increased. Ominously, the committee passed her request to Butcher for his comments. The possible engagement of a perruquier was held over to the next meeting. Could some rehearsals be switched to Thorpe Mental Hospital? More significantly, in September the committee decided that any profits from the production should be passed to the Norfolk and Norwich Hospital, for which reason the secretary was tasked with obtaining exemption from any entertainments tax. Mrs Winder arranged to hire some of the principal's costumes from Nugent Monck of the Maddermarket Theatre and set about finding a perruquier. Discussions between the committee and one of the Theatre Royal's managers Mr Fitt, resolved that prices of admission would be the same as those in place when the D'Oyly Opera Carte Company played at the theatre.[5]

Dress Circle and Stalls	4s 3d
Pit	3s 6d
Balcony	2s 4d
Gallery	1s 3d
Boxes	28s 9d

Meanwhile, fortune smiled on Miss Ransome, whose fee was upped to 12 guineas. When Monck decided he could not supply costumes, Mrs Winder suggested the principals' costumes should be made specially. Ultimately, they were hired.

In late October, plans were afoot to emphasise the purpose of the Society at the next committee meeting. The alterations in wording are subtle. It was now proposed that 'The objects of the Society shall be the study and performance of Operas and Plays and the raising of funds for Charitable and Philanthropic purposes' and that 'The Net proceeds of all entertainments given by the Society shall be devoted to charitable and philanthropic purposes'.[6]

Members of the company and their audiences were treated with consideration. A room in the Scottish Presbyterian Church opposite the Theatre Royal was thought suitable as a place where the company might be refreshed between matinee and evening performances, while Mrs Spain would look after the company in the Green Room at the theatre. Howes and Co. Ltd would keep their nearby garage open during the evening performances. The secretary asked the railway company to provide cheap return fares on the days when matinees were given. As the time for rehearsal dwindled and the day of theatrical reckoning approached, the cast (split into two companies) learned when they would be on stage. It was perhaps inevitable that the dress rehearsal fell to Cast B, with the opening night awarded to Cast A. Cast B returned for Wednesday evening and Thursday matinee, with Cast A on Thursday evening, Friday evening and Saturday matinee, Cast B rounding the week off on Saturday evening.

The scene is set and the curtains about to rise. It is a convenient moment for us to tiptoe away, gently closing the door on the hard-working committee with its ever-ready officers grappling with the decisions and arguments involving the Society for the next 100 years. With, naturally, occasional breaks for comfort and refreshment.

The 1920s

The decade opened hard upon the beginning of the hyphen between the wars. Few yet thought seriously of another war; the world in recovery was expanding; there were changes in life and manners that would have seemed crazy during the long early summer of 1914. Naturally the theatre reflected this age of relaxed conventions, of fervid good cheer and questing experiment. It was a decade ever ready to look at the new thing, to open astonished and delighted eyes at any fresh ideas, and at the same time to be just as delighted if an old idea were suitably dressed up.[1]

In a way, those words of the celebrated theatre critic J. C. Trewin sum up the time lapse that has characterised the amateur operatic movement throughout its long career. *Dorothy*, the company's first production, had been a substantial and unexpected commercial West End success almost 40 years earlier in 1886, an example of late Victorian musical theatre. The time lapse between a work's professional debut and its amateur successor persists to this day. A model of propriety, *Dorothy*'s genteel inoffensive charm at least suggested the serious intent of the new company.

Planquette's *Les Cloches de Corneville* indicated the preference for European operetta that characterised the Society's work up until 1932. Arguably this was one of the most exhilarating and ambitious periods of the company's history. The last of the best of Gilbert and Sullivan resurfaced in *The Gondoliers* before a return to European operetta with its less-corseted *esprit* and deep romanticism (qualities rarely associated with the Savoy operas) in a work long since removed to the shadows, Planquette's *The Little Michus*. There was no musical production in 1929. Instead, A. A. Milne's play *The Dover Road* was staged at the Agricultural Hall Assembly Rooms from 31 October to 2 November. The experiment was considered an artistic rather than commercial success, and was not repeated. Meanwhile, musical works considered for production in 1930 were Victor Jacobi's *The Marriage Market*, Howard Talbot's *The Belle of Brittany* and Gilbert and Sullivan's below-par *Utopia Limited*.

1925
DOROTHY

Norwich Theatre Royal, 8–12 December
Music: **Alfred Cellier**
Book and lyrics: **Benjamin C. Stephenson, revised by Avalon Collard**
Producer and Musical Director: **Henry Butcher**

First produced by George Edwardes at the Gaiety Theatre London in September 1886, the success of *Dorothy* was so great that it paid for the building of the Lyric Theatre on Shaftesbury Avenue, where it finished its record-breaking run of 931 performances, far outstripping anything by Gilbert and Sullivan. This lightest of confections, tastefully and delicately orchestrated by the now almost forgotten Alfred Cellier, seemed unlikely to achieve long life when it opened, *Punch* declaring that 'speaking for myself, I was quite pleased when it was all over', while the *Stage* lamented that 'Mr George Edwardes has not been fortunate in his choice of a new piece'.[2] Cellier's other stage works include *The Foster-Brothers* (1869), *The Sultan of Mocha* (1874), *The Tower of London* (1875), *Nell Gwynne* (1876) and *Charity Begins at Home* (1883), a body of work almost totally forgotten.

The longevity of *Dorothy* was made possible by the fact that, after its London premiere and lukewarm critical reception, the show was wrested from Edwardes by the theatrically-minded chartered accountant Howard Leslie, who rejuvenated the production by bringing in Marie Tempest and Ben Davies, and accentuated the presence of one of light opera's most popular British tenors, Hayden Coffin, giving him the show's outstanding ballad 'Queen of My Heart', twice encored on the revised *Dorothy*'s opening night. The music had originally been used for another Cellier ballad 'Old Dreams', now redressed with new lyrics by Benjamin C. Stephenson that emphasised romantic urgency: 'Why should we wait till tomorrow? You are Queen of my Heart Tonight!' Oddly, there is no solo for Dorothy herself, but the score is rich in its abundance of charmingly concerted if not particularly muscular numbers.

For Thomas S. Hischak, Cellier's score 'went beyond the competent. At times vivacious and bubbly, other times felicitous and tender, the songs were delightful interruptions in the silly plot'.[3] That meticulous chronicler of operetta Richard Traubner regards *Dorothy* as 'a comic opera with a derivative, though tuneful score that not unsuccessfully smacked of both the Savoy [the theatrical home of Gilbert and Sullivan] and the 'period' works [such as *Merrie England*] that Edward German would compose. However, it lacked any truly memorable songs'.[4] The *Eastern Daily Press* (the *EDP*) informed its readers that Cellier and Stephenson's light opera plot 'is borrowed from *She Stoops to*

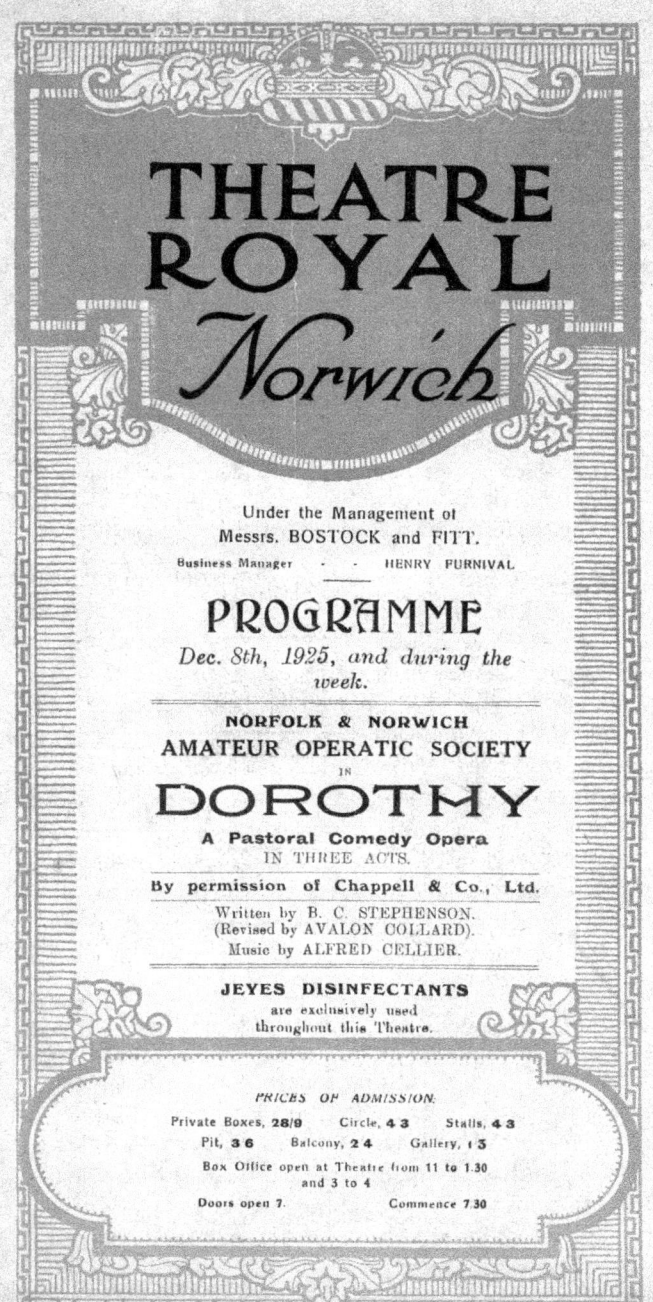

1. Theatre programme cover for *Dorothy* (1925). Courtesy of NNOS Archive.

Conquer, and although it affords scope for some amusing and pretty scenes it is not the work of a genius, while as regards the dialogue, B. C. Stephenson, the librettist, cannot wear the mantle of either Burnand or Gilbert.'[5] Raymond J. Walker notes that 'One is conscious of a rustic, idyllic innocence in the melodies and rhythms that conjure up thoughts of a "Constable" background.'[6]

The Society's production of *Dorothy* was subjected to considerable critical scrutiny in the press (predominantly the *EDP*) with both Cast A and B each given 16 inches of very small print. The reviewer was J. E. H. B., sympathetically emphasising that 'to put a company of over seventy strong on the boards of the Theatre Royal, many of whom for the first time in their lives, with only one rehearsal on the stage, is a task that would daunt many a producer'. Justly, the enigmatic J. E. H. B. explained that 'I have not hesitated to point out blemishes where necessary'. He began with chorus and orchestra.

> The chorus were excellent, and though the tone was not quite as full as one might have expected from such a large number it was pleasant in quality. Their words were distinct and their intonation good. I am afraid I cannot give the same praise to the orchestra, who were at times rather ragged.

The seven principals were dealt with in admirable detail. As Geoffrey Wilder, John Thompson displayed a 'breezy manner, a sense of humour' and 'a pleasant light tenor voice which would be more effective if not somewhat strained, while he has a slight difficulty in bridging the gap between his two registers'. Reginald Winder as Harry Sherwood used his 'full baritone of excellent quality' to win an encore for the standout ballad 'I Stand at Your Window' (better known as 'Queen of My Heart'). However, 'he has still to learn to sing sostenuto singing and not to drop his voice until the note should finish, and though the pronunciation of the beginning of his words is very clear one fails to hear the final consonant'. Percy Winter's performance as Lurcher was 'immense ... both in facial expression and as a real humourist'. Perhaps most notable of the artistes was J. J. Manning's performance as Sherwood, a role he had played in 1905 with the Norwich Amateur Operatic Company directed by Jerrold Manville.

And so to the leading ladies. Dora Robinson as Phyllis Tuppitt was 'engaging' and 'was of valuable assistance in the concerted music'. She may or may not have been grateful for J. E. H. B.'s warning that 'She must be careful of her intonation, being a little sharp in her last song'. Rosemary Mander as Lydia possessed 'a small voice, but she knows how to use it'. Perhaps, if Mr B's judgement can be relied on, Ruth, Lady Ballance in the title role was the first of some of the Society's sopranos who have become favourites with Norwich audiences. Her voice was 'not of great volume' but 'remarkably clear, and she has acquired the art of getting it over the footlights. She has also good control over her top notes, which she takes without effort, being also able to sing them softly.'

Exhaustive as his comments were, J.E. H. B. was not done, promising readers that 'I hope to say more about the concerted numbers to-morrow, when I shall be able to deal in more detail with many other good points in the general performance than those I have already noted.' True to his promise, another 16 inches of small print followed the next morning, firstly dealing with some of those who appeared in both Cast A and B. Top of his list was Hazel Wilson as Mrs Privett. Her comedy sequences 'in the true vein of comedy [...] brought down the house'. No doubt Mr B. retired to bed exhausted by his demanding critical obligations but, punctilious to the end, he apologetically returned to the *EDP* on 11 December:

> I much regret to find that I failed to include in either of my notices any mention of the extremely beautiful dresses both for the men and women in the third act. I doubt if such a display of sartorial splendour has ever been seen on any provincial stage before. The utmost praise is due to the honorary wardrobe mistress, Mrs Winder, for her artistic taste and judgment. All the costumes were true to period and formed a scheme of purest harmony of colour. No less excellent, if not so gorgeous, were the dresses in the other two acts.

Cast A (Tuesday, Thursday, Friday evenings, Saturday afternoon)
Sir John Bantam (W. R. Beard), Geoffrey Wilder (John Thompson), Harry Sherwood (Reginald Winder), John Tuppitt (Harry G. Cook), William Lurcher (Percy Winter), Tom Strutt (Herbert Alford), Parson (Herbert Dakin), Blacksmith (J. Nevil Gee), Ostler (A. E. Sandys Winsch), Darby (Herbert Dakin), Joan (Maie MacKinnon), First Page (Rita Skoyles), Second Page (D. Clotilde Griffin), Footman (A. E. Sandys Winsch), Dorothy Bantam (M. Ruth Ballance), Lydia Hawthorne (Rosemary Mander), Phyllis Tuppitt (Dora Robinson), Lady Betty (G. K. Dupuis), Mrs Privett (Hazel I. Wilson)

Cast B (Wednesday evening, Thursday afternoon, Saturday evening)
Sir John Bantam (W. R. Beard), Geoffrey Wilder (A. S. H. Dicker), Harry Sherwood (J. J. Manning), John Tuppitt (Harry G. Cook), William Lurcher (A. G. Whittle), Tom Strutt (Herbert Alford), Parson (Herbert Dakin), Blacksmith (J. Nevil Gee), Ostler (A. E. Sandys Winsch), Darby (Herbert Dakin), Joan (Maie MacKinnon), First Page (Rita Skoyles), Second Page (D. Clotilde Griffin), Footman (A. E. Sandys Winsch), Dorothy Bantam (Irene L. Gaze), Lydia Hawthorne (Ethel V. Dewhurst), Phyllis Tuppitt (Dorothy M. Master), Lady Betty (G. K. Dupuis), Mrs Privett (Hazel I. Wilson)

Gentlemen of the Chorus Herbert Alford, Alec T. Balls, W. R. Beard, J. S. Bishop, Stanley W. Blofield, Ernest Booth, George B. Boyes, Joseph F. Brundell, Frank Bryant, Louis W. Bullock, Harry G. Cook, E. G. Cooper, Herbert Dakin,

2. The Society's first producer, director and musical director Henry Butcher. Courtesy of NNOS Archive.

3. Ruth, Lady Ballance in 1929 © National Portrait Gallery, London.

J. H. V. Daynes, A. S. H. Dicker, S. F. Durrant, G. H. Gedge, J. Nevil Gee, P. F. George, John H. R. Green, H. W. King, J. J. Manning, F. M. Nunn, R. J. Raby, H. A. Roberts, Wilfred Robinson, A. C. Thirtle, John Thompson, J. A. Underhill, A. G. Whittle, Reginald Winder, A. E. Sandys Winsch, Percy Winter, Ivan G. Wright

Ladies of the Chorus Gladys K. Arnold, M. Ruth Ballance, Minnie Bolton, Kathleen Bremner, Daphne Buxton, E. Carter, Bea Chanteri, M. C. Denny Cooke, Gertrude E. Crotch, Dorothy Curl, Edith F. Daynes, Ethel V. Dewhurst, G. K. Dupuis, Joyce English, Irene L. Gaze, Constance Greenham, D. Clotilde Griffin, M. Willoughby Hall, Lottie Hallam, Lena Jacobs, Rosemary D. E. Mander, Dorothy M. Master, Marjorie Matthews, Margaret Meiklem, V. Miller, Dora Robinson, Stella M. Rudd, Thelma M. Rudd, Katherine R. Scott, Rita Skoyles, Ada Taylor, Hazel E. Underdown, Sybil Wetherall, Hazel L. Wilson, Barbara Sandys Winsch, Flora J. Winter

1926

LES CLOCHES DE CORNEVILLE

Norwich Theatre Royal, 26–30 October
Music: Robert Planquette
Book and lyrics: Original libretto by Jules Clairville and Charles Gabet
English version: H. B. Farnie, R. Reece and Alexander Henderson, revised by H. Simpson
Director and Musical Director: Henry Butcher

We should not underestimate the challenge that faced any amateur company undertaking Planquette's natty 1877 operetta. The demented and scheming miser Gaspard, in the employ of the Comte de Lucenay, agrees to look after his master's money and daughter Lucienne when the Comte flees to France. Gaspard brings up the girl as his own daughter, now called Germaine, and secretes the Comte's treasure in the Marquis of Corneville's abandoned chateau. Cunningly, Gaspard wheels 'spectres' through the chateau, convincing the curious that it is haunted. Dashing and splendidly bewigged, young Henri, heir to the Corneville estate, returns, rumbles Gaspard's scheme, and inevitably falls for Germaine, although Gaspard's adopted child Serpolette hopes to ensnare the unexpected hero. As almost always in a copper-bottomed costume piece of frivolity, a satisfactory conclusion is reached when Henri and his pals, dressed as the ghostly spectres of Corneville, confront Gaspard. The legend has come true; when the bells of Corneville ring its rightful master will have returned. Wedding bells await.

In London, the opera was a sensation, running for 705 performances. It was first professionally performed in Norwich in February 1881 by Mr C. Bernard's company, 'never flagging in merriment, and the songs and chorus being given with much taste and spirit'.[7] Gervase Hughes, one of the most acerbic of commentators on operetta, almost chastises Planquette for the fact that 'apart from a few ballads and comic songs his output consisted entirely of operettas, and he only wrote about twenty'.[8] Hughes maintains that 'not for twenty years did he write anything better'. For Hughes 'Not only the sparkling overture but at least one of the entr'actes and much of the dance music (especially the delightful 'kissing polka') had a touch of originality and refinement worthy of Delibes'. For Traubner, 'Planquette's score is rarely lacking in spirit, the songs have considerable movement to them, and each character has his or her opening song to distinguish themselves'. Furthermore, 'several numbers are undeniably irresistible, no matter how musically boring, thanks to their virulently catchy refrains'.[9] Here was a work 'which in aggregate number of performances worldwide may well be the most popular French operetta ever

MR. PERCY WINTER as "Gaspard," The Miser

MRS. E. M. CARTER   MISS S. WEATHERALL   MISS R. D. MANDER   MISS V. MILLER   MRS. L. JACOBS   MISS. D. M. MASTER
as   as   as   as   as   as
"Catherine"   "Jeanne"   "Gertrude"   "Marguerite"   "Susanne"   "Manette"

4. Percy Winter and the girls of *Les Cloches de Corneville* (1926).
Courtesy of NNOS Archive.

written'.[10] It was however a 'throwback to the past', a 'cliché-ridden, sentimental opéra-comique that Offenbach and Hervé had tried to kill off by inventing the modern operetta'.[11]

The *EDP* congratulated the Society for doing good service to rescuing from wholly underserved oblivion the charming and melodious *Les Cloches*, 'a romantic opera bouffe, a class of work that appears to have lost favour in England, having given place to musical comedy, which from a musical point of view is a great advance on *Dorothy*'. Henry Butcher had wisely not given unlimited rope to the comedians of the company. The reviewer had seen the original French production, and looked on the N&N's efforts with a gimlet but sympathetic eye. The Serpolette of Gertrude Crotch was 'admirably presented in the same style as that adopted [in the original French production] by Mlle Simone Girard – that is pert and not vulgar but refined and dainty'. Her singing of 'Just Look at That, Just Look at This' made one of the hits of the evening'. Mr Dicker as Grenicheux had 'an easy and attractive manner' despite 'suffering from a kind of flu and could hardly speak on Monday, so faulty intonation should be refused on this occasion'.

There was praise for Gerald Whittle's 'delicious performance', and versatility, for 'Not long on stage, he made the small part probably the most prominent part of the evening'. In Norwich, some of the principal roles were shared, with Ruth Ballance (suffering from a severe cold) and Mrs M. Meiklem taking turns as Germaine, Mr P. F. George and Mr A. W. Babstock as the fantastically-wigged Marquis de Corneville, Miss E. V. Dewhurst and Miss G. E. Crotch as Serpolette, and Mr H. Alford and Dicker singing Planquette's touching barcarolle 'Go, Little Cabin Boy'.

Cast

Marquis de Corneville (P. F. George / A. W. Babstock), Germaine (Lady Ballance) / Margaret Meiklem), Gaspard (Percy Winter), Serpolette (E. V. Dewhurst / G. E. Crotch), The Bailie (Harry Cook), Grenicheux (A. S. H. Dicker / H. Alford), Christophe (Joyce English), Gobo (A. G. Whittle), Catherine (E. M. Carter), Jeanne (S. Wetherall), Gertrude (R. D. Mander), Marguerite (V. Miller), Susanne (L. Jacobs), Manette (D. M. Master)

Gentlemen of the Chorus Herbert Alford, Albert Babstock, Alec T. Balls, W. R. Beard, Stanley W. Blofield, Ernest Booth, G. B. Boyes, Frank Bryant, Louis W. Bullock, Cyril G. Butcher, G. H. Gedge, C. F. B. Healls, F. M. Nunn, W. Douglas Reeks, H. A. Roberts, Wilfred Robinson, A. C. Thirtle, J. A. Underhill, Douglas Watson, A. G. Whittle, Leslie C. Willis, Reginald Winder, Percy Winter

Ladies of the Chorus M. Ruth Ballance, Minnie Bolton, Irene Booth, Kathleen Bremner, E. Madeleine Carter, Stelle D. Coleman, Phyllis I. Cook, M. C. Denny Cooke, Pearl Cross, Gertrude Crotch, Dorothy Curl, Edith Daynes,

Ethel Dewhurst, Joyce English, Irene L. Gaze, M. Willoughby Hall, Lottie Hallam, Marion Little, Lena Jacobs, Marion Little, Maie MacKinnon, Rosemary Mander, Dorothy M. Master, Marjorie Matthews, Margaret Meiklem, V. Miller, Ivy M. Normington, Dora Robinson, Stella Rudd, Thelma M. Rudd, Katherine R. Scott, Rita Skoyles, D. M. Smith, Ada Taylor, Vera M. Tudor, Sybil Wetherall, Sophy A. Wilson, Flora J. Winter

1927
THE GONDOLIERS

Norwich Theatre Royal, 12–17 December
Music: **Arthur Sullivan**
Book and lyrics: **W. S. Gilbert**
Director / Musical Director: **Henry Butcher**

It was inevitable that, during its long history, the Society would at some time turn to the Savoy operas of Gilbert and Sullivan. On the heels of *Les Cloches de Corneville*, the first to be produced was their sunniest, first seen in London in 1889, now reproduced and musically directed by Henry Butcher. It was five years later that Gilbert and Sullivan returned with *The Mikado*, followed by the 1933 *The Yeoman of the Guard* and *Iolanthe* (1935) before reviving *The Gondoliers* in 1937. By now, the Society might almost have been regarded as the East Anglian branch of the D'Oyly Carte Opera Company. From 1938 through 1953 the Norwich company presented wall-to-wall Gilbert and Sullivan, with Edward German's *Merrie England* sneaking in for 1939.

It was only with their 1955 *Iolanthe* that the company turned its back on Savoy operas. The only Gilbert and Sullivan operas not performed by the Society were the less popular *The Sorcerer*, the three-act *Princess Ida*, *Patience*, and the generally considered inferior late works *Utopia Limited* and *The Grand Duke*, by which time the collaborators had run out of steam. In fact, this NNAOS production of *The Gondoliers* did not draw the crowds. According to the *EDP* the first night's house was 'far from full'. It seemed that 'Norwich playgoers notoriously fight shy of a first night partly through waiting to hear the public verdict before they decide to go'. Thankfully, the reviewer reported that the evening showed 'full evidence of careful rehearsals and was played throughout with spirit', and Lady Ballance's fans would have been delighted that she danced the role of Gianetta 'with charm and grace'.

Nevertheless, nightly average attendance at the Theatre Royal was a mere 578, total attendance for the week being 4,045. The problematic expense of performance rights at a time when Gilbert and Sullivan's works were rigorously

Mrs. M. Back as "Tessa"
Mr. R. Winder as "Guiseppe"

Miss J. English
as "Fiametta"

Mr. D. Watson
as "Antonio"

Mr. A. G. Whittle as "The Duke"

Mr. R. Winder
as "Guiseppe"

Mr. W. H. Pursehouse
as "Marco"

5. Vignettes from *The Gondoliers* (1927). Courtesy of NNOS Archive.

controlled by the D'Oyly Carte management (a stranglehold only released when the company's copyright expired in the early 1960s) was another factor.

Elegantly costumed by wardrobe mistress Mrs Winder, and with the 45-strong ensemble well-rehearsed by the Society's accompanist Gladys Channell, and choreography by Ida Ransome, the company was not short on talent. Two elder members, A. G. (Gerry) Whittle and Bea Chanteri, played the Duke and Duchess of Plaza-Toro, accompanied by their daughter Casilda (Phyllis Duncan) and factotum Luiz (W. B. Davies). If the programme's photographs are to be believed, Reginald Winder and W. H. Pursehouse personified the principal dashingly handsome Venetians Giuseppe and Marco, with Marco probably encoring the hit of the evening with his stand-out solo 'Take a Pair of Sparkling Eyes'. Their girlfriends Gianetta and Tessa were represented by Lady Ballance and Madeleine Back, while the arrival of Percy Winter as Venice's Grand Inquisitor Don Alhambra Del Bolero unleashed considerable Gilbertian wit. Subsequently, Butcher informed the committee that he was willing to remain as the Society's director but would no longer be musical director.

Cast
Duke of Plaza-Toro (A. G. Whittle), Duchess of Plaza-Toro (Bea Chanteri), Casilda (Phyllis Duncan), Luiz (W. B. Davies), Marco (W. H. Pursehouse), Guiseppe (Reginald Winder), Tessa (Madeleine Back), Gianetta (Lady Ballance), Don Alhambra del Bolero (Percy Winter), Fiametta (Joyce English), Vittoria (M. Willoughby Hall), Giulia (Ada Taylor), Antonio (Douglas Watson), Francisco (Herbert Alford), Giorgio (A. C. Thirtle), Annibale (J. H. V. Daynes), Inez (Minnie Bolton)

Gentlemen of the Chorus Alec T. Balls, Stanley W. Blofield, Ernest Booth, G. B. Boyes, Frank Bryant, Louis W. Bullock, H. W. Cleland, Harry G. Cook, E. G. Cooper, Ray Davies, H. J. Eastick, Frederick Fitch, G. H. Gedge, P. F. George, C. F. B. Healls, Louis W. Lambert, H. A. Roberts, Wilfred Robinson, J. Gordon Ward, Leslie C. Willis, A. E. Sandys Winsch

Ladies of the Chorus Irene Booth, Kathleen Bremner, E. Madeleine Carter, R. Chamberlin, M. C. Denny Cooke, Pearl Cross, Gertrude E. Crotch, Ethel V. Dewhurst, Vera Emms, Irene L. Gaze, Lottie Hallam, Barbara Higgs, Lena Jacobs, Dorothy Master, Marjorie Matthews, Ivy M. Normington, Dora Robinson, Rita Skoyles, Kathleen Vincent, Ethel C. Ward, Sybil Wetherall, Flora J. Winter

There was no musical production in 1928.

1929

THE LITTLE MICHUS

Norwich Theatre Royal, 8–13 April
Music: Andre Messager
Book and lyrics: A. Vanloo and G. Duval
English version: Henry Hamilton
Lyrics: Percy Greenbank
Director and *Musical Director*: Henry Butcher
Conductor: B. K. Wilson

As Michael Booth has written in his beguiling homage to melodrama:

> Nothing is harder to bring to life for a modern reader than the theatre of the past. To recreate vanished playhouses, to populate them once again with noisy audiences, and to light them with flickering candles, harsh hissing gas, and soft multi-coloured pools of limelight picking out actors long forgotten, acting in old-fashioned ways in front of creaking flats and jerking wings, is to make dead eyes see and dead ears hear.[12]

Theatre is essentially fleeting. Any attempt to revive it is fraught with difficulty. Essentially, through 100 years of its existence, the Society is and has been a repertory company of non-professional – otherwise amateur – performers, whom the celebrated critic Caryl Brahms once indelicately described as 'orphans of the theatrical storm'. She would surely at least have appreciated the Society's persistence.

The earliest works produced by the company set the bar high, with *Les Cloches de Corneville*, *The Little Michus*, *The Marriage Market*, *Sybil* and, to a lesser extent, the very British *Dorothy*. They had selected *The Little Michus* in favour of Messager's more well-known *Veronique* and Emmerich Kálmán's *A Little Dutch Girl* (*Das Hollandweibchen*). It seemed that the company shunned lighter material of the musical comedy genre that in 1929 was more familiar to West End audiences, the only exception that year being Noël Coward's operetta *Bitter-Sweet*.

One of the most charming items of that opening salvo of the Society was Messager's enchanting *The Little Michus*, originally premiered as *Les P'tites Michu* at the Bouffes-Parisiens in 1897. Audiences were delighted. Described by one critic as 'a feminine version of *The Gondoliers*', it told the story of two female babies (Blanche-Marie and Marie-Blanche) being given a shared bath 'with the result that their identities became hopelessly muddled, and ever since there has been a doubt as to which was which'.[13] Inevitably, the confusion

Douglas Watson as "Bagnolet"   "Madame Michu"   Neville Howlett as "Gen. Des Ifs"
A. G. Whittle as "Michu"   Kathleen Vincent as "Marie-Blanche"
Marjorie Aylen as "Blanche-Marie"

A. G. Whittle
as "Michu"

W. B. Davies
as "Gaston"

6. *The Little Michus* (1929). Courtesy of NNOS Archive.

complicates their love lives. The situation could hardly be more Gilbertian: think Little Buttercup's admission in *H. M. S. Pinafore* that in her baby-farming days she made the same mistake ('I mixed those children up, and not a creature knew it'), and Inez confessing to just such a lamentable error in *The Gondoliers*. The link with that work was accentuated when Messager incorporated a game of Blind Man's Buff into *The Little Michus*, just as played by flirtatious Marco and Giuseppe in Gilbert and Sullivan's Venice.

In his highly recommended survey of operetta, Richard Traubner celebrates 'one of those unusual works that begins well enough and gets better and better' with its 'surely outstanding' third act in the bustling Les Halles with market traders 'bearing flowers, accompanied by one of music's most florid arrangements'. Traubner appreciates Messager's

> distinctly personal style. Tripping, gay, never heavy, and perfectly written for the voice, it is his gracious, well-mannered, craftsman-like approach which makes Messager's style so inimitable. He is thus able to take a sentimental waltz so typical of the turn of the century – which in other hands would be a run-of-the-mill *café-concert* number – and transform it into something much more symphonic.

Gervase Hughes agrees that 'The tunes, though inevitably not all of equal merit, were consistently suave and graceful; the ensembles were superbly well-constructed; the orchestration was masterly'.

Assiduously reviewed in the manner of the day, the *EDP* was full of praise. The conductor B. K. Wilson 'has never before attempted the task of the musical direction of an opera' and despite the fact that 'once or twice there was some slips' could be 'heartily congratulated'. Of the comics, Neville Hewlett and A. G. Whittle drew 'roars of laughter'. In the small role of Madame du Tertre, Phyllis Duncan delighted with her 'Miss Nobody from Nowhere', and there was 'a really comic sketch' from Lottie Hallam as a market woman. Lady Ballance's daughter Rosemary showed 'hereditary talent' as the dancing Mdlle St Cyr. If the leading ladies as Blanche-Marie and Marie-Blanche were even half as enchanting as their theatre programme photographs suggest, audiences must have been captivated. The reviewer especially enjoyed Vincent's 'I Would Like to be a Grand Lady' and was so impressed by Aylen that he wished Messager had written another number for her. No doubt exhausted from his labours he regretted that 'At this late hour it is impossible to name the rest of the cast'.

At least his few words give us a glimpse of that evening, as if we had just for a moment or two peeped at the stage from the wings.

We are unlikely to see much revival of Messager's *The Little Michus*, whose operas *Veronique* and *Fortunio* (the latter with one of the most thrilling and uplifting final moments of any opera) have long been discarded from the British repertoire.

Cast

General Des Ifs (Neville Howlett), Gaston Rigaud (W. B. Davies), Pierre Michu (A. G. Whittle), Aristide Vert (Herbert Alford), Bagnolet (Douglas Watson), Man (C. L. Ashurst), Footmen (W. R. English, C. F. B. Healls), Gardener (C. L. Ashurst), Madame Du Tertre (Phyllis Duncan), Madame Rousselin (Ivy Normington), Madame de Saint Phar (M. Willoughby Hall), Madame d'Albert (Ethel C. Ward), Mdlle. St Cyr (Rosemary Ballance), Mdlle Herpin (Lena Jacob), Mdlle Julie (Ethel V. Dewhurst), Claire (E. Madeleine Carter), Loie (Sybil Wetherall), Ernestine (Dora Robinson), Pamela (Margaret Meiklem), Ida (Irene Gaze), Francine (Vera Emms), Estelle (Joyce English), Palmyre (Marjorie Matthews), Market Woman (Lottie Hallam), Madame Michu (Bea Chanteri), Blanche-Marie (Marjorie Aylen), Marie-Blanche (Kathleen Vincent)

Gentlemen of the Chorus Phil. Back, Ernest Booth, J. H. Brand, Louis W. Bullock, Harold Chapman, Harry G. Cook, E. Forster, G. H. Gedge, P. F. George, Robert Gilchrist, J. Loynes, Wilfred Phillips, H. A. Roberts, Wilfred Robinson, A. W. Vincent, J. Gordon Ward

Ladies of the Chorus Ida Armes, Madeleine Back, Muriel Bacon, M. Ruth Ballance, Irene Booth, Pearl Cross, Doris Eastcott, K. R. H. Hannent, Rita Skoyles, Ada Taylor, Jean Winder, Joy Woodhouse

The 1930s

This was a decade when the N&N stage was mostly given over to Gilbert and Sullivan, as noted by Ian Bradley reminding us that 'It was, indeed, Gilbert and Sullivan's operas, with their wholesome and family appeal, which really gave birth to the whole amateur operatic movement on both sides of the Atlantic'. NODA (the official umbrella organisation for the amateur operatic societies) recommends the Gilbert and Sullivan works as :

> Relatively easy to stage. With a good variety of parts, plenty of chorus work and box office appeal, they became instant favourites. No works have played a more important role in developing and sustaining the amateur movement and Gilbert and Sullivan remain the only artists to whose works numbers of societies are specifically designated.

In fact, the N&N's most interesting offerings of the 1930s came at the very beginning of the decade, with two excellent pieces by the Hungarian Victor Jacobi, the highly agreeable and frolicsome *The Marriage Market* and, most notably, *Sybil*, a remarkable work that deserves to be much better known. Its glorious mix of gymnastic high jinks and sumptuous melody single *Sybil* out as something patently unBritish. Emotionally, it eclipses anything Gilbert and Sullivan ever wrote. It demands direction and singing and acting of the highest order to emphasise the wealth of theatrical brilliance it offers. It is probably one of the most theatrically thrilling works ever produced by the Society, written by people who knew how to blend tragedy and comedy and how to bring a curtain down. It is also forgotten.

From 1932 to 1938 the revolving door of Gilbert and Sullivan remained open, only interrupted by the 1934 *The Rebel Maid*, a work that already seemed to belong to an earlier age. It was not a commercial success for the Society and is little remembered. It is fustian stuff, a costume piece, probably remembered only for its rousing paean to 'The Fishermen of England'. As much may be said of Edward German's celebratory *Merrie England*, in its way a cousin to *The Rebel Maid*, although it may have seemed an appropriate balm to the troubled atmosphere in 1939. *Merrie England* (belonging to a period that was redolent of very little merriness) has sometimes been revived professionally, but its reputation has not flourished. Thus the curtain temporarily fell on the N&N until 1947 when the company resumed productions. A second version of *The Gondoliers* ushered in another Gilbert and Sullivan fest that kept the company afloat until, in 1954, it summoned *The Maid of the Mountains* (one of the most resilient leading ladies of her period) to free it from Savoy opera bondage.

1930

THE MARRIAGE MARKET

Norwich Theatre Royal, 28 April–3 May
Music: Victor Jacobi
Book: Miklós Bródy and Ferenc Martos, adapted by Gladys Unger
Lyrics: Arthur Anderson and Adrian Ross
Director: Henry Butcher
Musical Director: R. J. Maddern Williams

We cannot hear the singing of Marjorie Aylen as San Francisco heiress Mariposa Gilroy, or see the dancing of Kathleen Vincent as her best friend Kitty Kent, or tell whether on stage W. B. Davies as hero Jack Fleetwood (known more popularly as Slippery Jack) was as vital as he appears in the theatre programme; the passage of time denies us that privilege. We may, however, confidently applaud the costuming. The plentiful studio portraits are made the more appealing by the period dresses, their effect the responsibility of wardrobe mistress Mrs Winder. With its colourful characters, that responsibility is considerable, involving its chorus of Spanish and American cowhands, assorted sailors and 'middies' (midshipmen) and miners. *The Marriage Market* inhabits a world where (according to the *EDP*'s critic C. L. A.) 'strong rough men take what they mean to hold'. Here was 'a most delightful entertainment, and 'it would be Norwich's fault if it missed the show, 'a most capital amateur presentation of a musical melange of dancing, humour and romance'. At curtain-up, some may have wondered if they had slipped mistakenly into a production of Puccini's 'cowboy' opera *The Girl of the Golden West* (Puccini's favourite, as it happens).

Premiered in Budapest in 1911 and in London 1913, *The Marriage Market* (originally *Leányvásár*) is in its way cousin to Emmerich Kálmán's *Die Herzogin von Chicago* (*The Duchess of Chicago*), in which Kálmán pitches conventionally romantic operetta-type musical numbers against the Charleston. Victor Jacobi's career was fruitful but all too brief. He died aged only 37, having moved (via the *Lusitania*) from Hungary to New York in 1915. Jacobi happily assimilated jazz and ragtime and the rhythms of Broadway into his scores, as evidenced in the frequently exuberant *Marriage Market*. Audiences warmed to a work that

> remains immediately delightful – a profusion of charming waltzes and irresistible up-tempo comic duets and couplets with chorus [just as they] relished the lariats, shoot-outs, and the yip-yip cowboy number 'The Mendocino Stroll', as well as a second Act on board a ship anchored off San Francisco. The Wild West plus naval manoeuvres proved a potent draw.[1]

The Society was sufficiently satisfied with the piece that they decided on another Jacobi opera, *Sybil*, as their next production, having turned down Gilbert and Sullivan's *Princess Ida* and *Utopia Limited* and Ivan Caryll's operetta *The Duchess of Dantzic* (1903).

The sense of the Society being a coming together of friends can be found not only in the severely overcrowded group photograph printed as a postcard but in the theatre programme's 'Who's Who in *The Marriage Market*' in which every member of the company involved in the production is biographed. At this early moment in the Society's history, the sense of comradeship rings true. For example:

> Miss IDA ARMES One of the 'Middies'. Proves the saying that small parcels contain the most valuable articles.
> LADY BALLANCE 'Maimie'. Where would the Society be without her? 'Anne' of the Dover Road.
> MR E. G. CODLING. Sailor. A new member, but we wish we'd had him before.
> MR W. B. DAVIES 'Jack'. Has the luck always to be the lover of lovely ladies.
> MISS RUTH MORSE. Understudying 'Kitty'. As charming as possible, perhaps morse-o.
> MRS WINDER. Wardrobe Mistress. Her motto is definitely not 'sew sew'. Absolutely indispensable. Possesses unbounded energy and tact.

Cast

Jack Fleetwood (W. B. Davies), Lord Hurlingham (Neville Howlett) Blinker (Douglas Watson), Senator Abe K. Gilroy (A. G. Whittle), Bald-Faced Sandy (Harry G. Cook), Mexican Bill (Herbert Alford), Shorty (Ernest Booth), Tabasco Ned (J. Gordon Ward), Cheyne Harry (G. H. Gedge), Hi-Ti (Alec T. Balls), Captain of the Mariposa (R. McD. Winder), Middy (Joyce English), Kitty Kent (Kathleen Vincent), Mariposa Gilroy (Marjorie Aylen), Emma (Madeleine Back), Pansy (Rita Skoyles), Peach (Ethel V. Dewhurst), Dora (Peggy Castle), Clara (M. Willoughby Hall), Sadie (Barbara Sandys Winsch), Mamie (M. Ruth Ballance), Dolores (Bea Chanteri)

Gentlemen of the Chorus P. G. Back, J. H. Brand, Louis W. Bullock, G. P. Burroughs, Harold Chapman, E. G. Codling, W. R. English, E. Forster, C. F. B. Healls, J. Loynes, Wilfred Phillips, H. A. Roberts, Wilfred Robinson, A. D. Ward

Ladies of the Chorus Ida Armes, Ursula Back, Muriel Bacon, Irene Booth, Bea Chanteri, Vera Emms, Mavis Hill, Marjorie Matthews, Ruth Morse, Olive Notley, Dora Robinson, A. D. Ward

7. Flooding the stage in *The Marriage Market* (1930). Courtesy of NNOS Archive.

1931
SYBIL

Norwich Theatre Royal, 13–18 April
***Music*: Victor Jacobi**
***Book and Lyrics*: Miklós Bródy and Ferenc Martos**
***Director / Musical Director*: Henry Butcher**

The famed London impresario George Edwardes hoped to present the Hungarian operetta *Sybil* following his successful production of Victor Jacobi's earlier *The Marriage Market*, a winner at 423 performances, but abandoned the project at the beginning of World War I. *Sybil* opened on Broadway in 1916 with the *New York Times* declaring the score was 'no matter for enthusiasm'.[2] It went on to even greater success in the 1921 London production starring the legendary José Collins, the West End's famed 'Maid of the Mountains'.

Whether opera, operetta or, as the Theatre Royal programme has it, 'a Musical Comedy', *Sybil* is a work of enormous charm and romantic drama. There is comedy aplenty, with Jacobi frequently kicking up a vocal and orchestral storm, but its central theme of undying love draws from him a deeply expressed passion that blazes intermittently into life. The emotions in this piece are not those genteel, polite acknowledgements of something approaching physical desire that

8. Madeleine Back and Neville Howlett larking about in *Sybil* (1931)
Courtesy of NNOS Archive.

permeated *Dorothy*; with Jacobi, passions seep into the music. At the heart of it is the bewitching 'Love May Be a Mystery' ('Ilúzió a szerelem'), at first a duet for the troubled lovers Sybil and her Captain of the Imperial Guard Lieutenant Paul Petrov, and repeated by Sybil in the work's final thrilling moments. Jacobi and his collaborators may not be well remembered, but we cannot question his grasp of musical theatre. There can be no doubt of Traubner's claim that 'Ilúzió', with its moments of silence interrupting the rise and fall of the melody is 'one of the loveliest slow waltzes of the Hungarian repertoire'.[3]

With no evidence, we cannot know to what extent Butcher's interpretation of the piece dealt with *Sybil*'s tragic elements. These were surely crucial to any understanding of the material, and they are at least recognised as being so in the fascinatingly detailed *EDP* review by C. L. A. The quality of his response reminds us how essential the local press, specifically the *EDP* and *Eastern Evening News* (*EEN*) and *Norwich Evening News*, has been to the Society's existence. C. L. A.'s ebullient response to seeing a Hungarian opera on an evening in Spring 1931 is given in full as it is not only a model of thoughtful reflection, but raises many issues that remain pertinent to the Society a century later.

9. W. B. Davies as Petrov and Phyllis Duncan as Sybil in 1931. Courtesy of NNOS Archive.

Amateurs in *Sybil*

There is an intriguing and fascinating series of articles running in a well-known Sunday paper under the title of 'What the Stars Foretell.' Happening to glance at the astrological prediction for the 13th, I found nothing but import of misfortune, with an impressive admonition to all and sundry to attempt nothing of importance on this date. Last evening, at the Theatre Royal Norwich, the Norfolk and Norwich Amateur Operatic Society attempted something of extreme importance to them – and incidentally to the local theatre-going public – and I am pleased to chronicle that Professor Naylor has in this particular case failed miserably to read aright the portent of the heavens – or, perhaps, the sweet cause of charity has confounded superstition.

Our local Amateur Operatic Society have created in their last two productions quite a respectable and well-earned reputation for musical comedy, produced and put over with finish and effect almost professional in its detail and cumulative effect, and in attempting the more pretentious proportions of 'Sybil 'they have challenged the strength of their reputation gained by the experience derived from their excellent work in 'The Little Michus 'and 'The Marriage Market.' 'Sybil', the most ambitious of the three musical comedies Mr. Butcher has now produced for us, is also distinctly heavier in type than either of its two predecessors, and although fun abounds at fairly frequent intervals the story of the play, set in serious strain and sometimes reaching dramatic intensity, is unwoven to the accompaniment of music and recitative singing which demands almost faultless execution to develop and sustain the required strength of effect.

The story of the play does not apparently pretend to dazzle by its originality. Set in the picturesque Russia of the musical stage it is the old story of conveniently mistaken identity to save two young lovers, with the inevitable trail of complications and jealousies spreading behind the initial idea, through the second to the final act where everything is made straight, and, as we expect from musical comedy, the lovers are reunited. Last evening's production was enthusiastically received by a well-filled house, but frankness compels me to state that it did not appear such a spontaneous and tuneful piece of business as last year's 'Marriage Market.' To begin with, unless the dramatic value of the more serious passages in the play be given their due emphasis the effect of light and shade is apt to become a trifle shadowy; and whereas fooling amid the antics of the comedian can cover a host of lapses or inconvenient drags, there must not be a loss of tempo in the dramatic side of the production otherwise the situation hangs fire, interest wanes, and the atmosphere becomes unduly heavy and non-effective. The amateur status of the venture of course demands special treatment in review, and before bestowing praise on those who helped to make last night's premiere the success it was, it is only just to interpolate the hope that a judicious speeding up of the action would, especially in the first act, and one period in the middle act, cause a considerable increase in the tonic effect of what is after all a very jolly business, despite its love story.

Mrs. Phyllis Duncan [Sybil] has an exacting part in *Sybil*, but she seizes this great chance of exploiting her undoubted vocal and histrionic talents with a sureness which is at once compelling, and in some of the sterner passages of the play when her happiness and the life of her lover are at stake, she appeared to carry almost the entire burden of the theme on her own shoulders. Her outbreak before the Grand Duchess [Anna Pavlovna, played by Marjorie Aylen] in the closing moments of the story showed her to be an emotional actress capable of unexpected depth of feeling. Mrs. Duncan's voice was in perfect pitch throughout her performance, and her rendering of the martial Crimson Hussar number made a virile patch of colour during a period when the action of the play seemed to demand some such enlivening effect. Mr. Neville Howlett has only to step upon the local boards, and with characteristic poise utter an inanity or skilfully cover up and improve upon a lost line, to create a roar of laughter. His rendering of Poire, forcibly reminding me of last year's Lord Hurlingham but with an added roundness of effect which just separated the two characters, is, as expected, a joyous and energetic piece of first class and polished fooling. I do not think there is the humour in his lines which he merits, nor has the opportunity been taken of introducing a topical song number, in the manner of delivering which Mr. Howlett excels. But this is not his fault, and with what he has to handle he makes an admirable contribution to the evening's feast.

Mrs. Madeleine Back as Poire's wife, Margot, is excellently cast, and she makes him an extremely clever dancing partner in crime and song. Mr Herbert Alford has been granted a good opportunity this year in the character of the Grand Duke, and his tenor voice, of exceptional purity and sweetness, is admirably suited for the tender passages in the love theme which develops between him and Sybil. He would improve his performance with the addition of controlled dramatic utterance in the spoken word, even at the expense of incurring the risk of artificiality. After all, the character of the Grand Duke Constantine is essentially a stagey one, and the introduction of the braggadocio of the musical comedy hero would undoubtedly help to give his performance increased colour. Mr. A. G. [Gerry] Whittle's portrayal of the Governor of Bomsk is one of the outstanding performances of the evening. The interest invariably quickened when he was on the stage, and it was not so much what he had to say, but the manner in which he said it, which makes his characterisation of the amorous Russian swash buckler a cameo which 'gets over' in every detail. A most comfortable, mature, piece of work.

Mrs. Marjorie Aylen is, to my mind, far better cast as the Grand Duchess than she has ever been. Her imperious bearing combined with a voice which again declares its strength and quality are factors which make her part in the play a most successful one. Mr. W. B. Davies has little opportunity as Lieut. Petrov, but what he has to sing he accomplishes in faultless style, and his acting is very well sustained. Mr. Leon Bailey, a newcomer to the Society, creates a favourable first impression as Bortschakow, the Hotel Manager. There are two dance numbers which deserve special praise, and Miss Lily Gayford is to be congratulated upon so successfully arranging them. I refer to the Russian Dance in the Governor's Palace, a splendidly executed and well-dressed item, and the pyjama dance in the final act. This latter number, with its note of piquancy, its exhilarating speed, and the flicker light effect on the dancers, created the most applause of the evening and had to be repeated several times.

Reviewed in its entirety I cannot regard 'Sybil' as seen last night as the best thing the Amateur Operatic Society has given us. Speed will come as the week progresses, but the work is not so rich in ear-haunting melodies as one would desire, and some of the dramatic episodes require more punch in order to create contrast. It is an ambitious production to attempt, and despite everything the company have made an enthusiastic and by no means unsuccessful attempt to give local audiences an opportunity of witnessing a very well dressed and well-put-on musical. C. L. A.

Cast

Grand Duke Constantine (Herbert Alford), Grand Duchess Anna Pavlovna (Marjorie Aylen), Governor of Bomsk (A. G. Whittle), Captain Dologow (G. H. Gedge), Lieutenant Koyander (J. Gordon Ward), Count Milowski (Harry G. Cook), Sybil Renaud (Phyllis Duncan), Charles Poire (Neville Howlett), Margot (Madeleine Back), Lieutenant Paul Petrov (W. B. Davies), Bortschakow (Leon Bailey), Hall Porter (H. A. Roberts), Hussar Officer (Douglas Watson), Life Attendant (Ruth Morse)

Gentlemen of the Chorus D. R. Anderson, Ernest Booth, J. H. Brand, Louis W. Bullock, Harold Chapman, W. Chapman, Ray Davies, A. A. Emmett, W. R. English, E. Forster, R. W. Garrett, P. F. George, E. J. King, Y. E. Thompson

Ladies of the Chorus Ida Armes, Ursula Back, Muriel Bacon, Irene Booth, Bea Chanteri, E. M. Carter, Peggy Castle, Ethel V. Dewhurst, Doris Eastcott, Joyce English, M. Willoughby Hall, Lottie Hallam, Sybil Hambling, Marjorie Matthews, E. Minns, Ivy Normington, Olive Notley, Constance Robins-Billing, I. Scott, Rita Skoyles, A. Taylor, Vera Tudor, Kathleen Vincent, Nancy Walker, Ethel C. Ward

1932

THE MIKADO

Theatre Royal, Norwich, April 4–9
Music: Arthur Sullivan
Book and lyrics: W. S. Gilbert
Director: Harry Briden
Musical Director: R. J. Maddern Williams

The fulsomeness of C. L. A's comprehensive review in the *EDP* for 5 April 1932 is evidence of how seriously the local press took the Society.

> For the past four years the Norfolk and Norwich Amateur Operatic Society has adopted a policy of presenting, with varying success, a series of musical comedies, the modern and topical appeal of which it was hoped would prove to popularise the annual Norwich festival of local amateur talent. The policy of the society has shown marked, even striking, departures from the practice of past years during the last twelve months, however perhaps the most outstanding of these alterations in principle, certainly the most welcome to a large section of the musical fraternity of the neighbourhood, is the reversion to a Gilbert and Sullivan opera.

Henry Butcher would probably not have been thrilled to learn that

> Another important line of demarcation which has been made by the Operatic Society is the changing of its producer, and a great deal of the success of last night's brilliant opening performance can he traced not only to Mr. Harry W. Briden's skill in production. It was noticed at once that Mr. Briden has embraced the invaluable help which top direct lighting can give – even one arc is worth a dozen meaningless side-floods – and while on this subject of lighting, may it be said how capital was the green lighting effect through an otherwise complete black-out, during the rendering of the trio between Ko-Ko, Pooh-Bah, and Pish-Tush? This was lighting with a meaning.

C. L. A. reminded readers that it was always advisable to readjust one's attitude from the outset when approaching the review of an amateur production, insisting that 'a first-class amateur is better than a third rate professional, and this can be heartily endorsed, but nevertheless it must be acknowledged and appreciated that amateurs are not expected to beat professionals at their own game, and a Savoyard is apparently born, not made'. In fact, Briden's company had the benefit of 'one or two remarkable surprises in the direction of individual performances that will rank with many and beat not a few professional characterisations'. These included Ernest Booth in 'a highly coloured and courageous piece of work, taken with both hands by Mr. Booth and executed to a point of excellence which would seem to imply that here is a man with dramatic talent left too long languishing in the ranks of the chorus'. This must have perked Ernest up, even if it did not enchant those already 'languishing' in the chorus!

E. Hudspith had joined the cast when rehearsals were already advanced, but his Nanki-Poo was a 'delicate, melodious, and sentimental study' blossoming into 'a pure if not markedly' strong tenor voice. A. G. (Gerry) Whittle's Ko-Ko was 'one of the high-water marks of the production, and everything he does from facial expression and sprightly dance to his capital rendering of the famous "Tit Willow" number is a safe, polished, one might say a professional piece of first-class tomfoolery'.

Apparently, the best acting came from T. G. Woolley's Pooh-Bah, 'a very joyful piece of work'. The harshest verdict was passed on Percy Winter's Pish Tush which was 'not the convincing affair expected, and apart from his singing, especially in the quartet in the last act, he appeared too stage conscious to give comfort to his part'.

The three little maids from school – Phyllis Duncan, Marjorie Matthews and Joyce English – were 'not only charming to gaze upon, but exceedingly sweet to listen to'. Duncan's Yum-Yum was enhanced by her feeling singing 'so splendidly characterised by her ability to adapt and pursue change of tempo without leaving the beat of her conductor. Miss Matthews deserves special mention for a vivacious little study of Pitti-Sing' and the sophisticated outlook of Peep-Bo 'was well caught by Miss Joyce English'. In the manner of Gilbert's lifelong depiction of ladies of a certain age obsessed with breaking into contralto arias, Bea Chanteri satisfied requirements and 'has never given us anything finer'.

C. L. A. signed off with a final endorsement of the Society and its progress, urging prospective patrons to rush to the box office:

> All those who do not usually care for amateurs should go to the Theatre Royal this weekend and forget the fact that they are witnessing unpaid artists. In most cases it will not be a difficult thing to forget – and the chorus would be the envy of many touring musical companies.

The production had total attendance of 5,526, compared to 4,023 for the previous year's *Sybil*, thus breaking the Society's record. The company returned to *The Mikado* in 1948. Between 1927 and 1955 it spent 15 years presenting Gilbert and Sullivan operas.

Ko Ko's 'little list' song was probably updated for the 1932 production: certainly, a revised lyric appears in the theatre programme (and was probably used on stage).

> As some day it may happen that a victim must be found
> We've got a little list. We've got a little list
> Of members, friends and others who'd be better underground,
> Who Gilbert somehow missed, so we've added to his list.

PHYLLIS DUNCAN as "Yum-Yum"   MARJORIE MATTHEWS as "Pitti-Sing"   JOYCE ENGLISH as "Peep-Bo"
ALL—"Three little maids are we."

10. 'Three little maids from school' from *The Mikado* (1932)
Courtesy of NNOS Archive.

There's the member of the Company who always turns up late;
When called for 7.30 he arrives at half past 8.
All ladies who will chatter when they really didn't ought
And never pay attention when the cast is being taught –
They flick their fans with vigour when the order is 'Desist'
They'd none of 'em be missed, They'd none of 'em be missed.
There are folks who won't support us, and who always stay away
And our appeals resist, we've got them on the list,
And those who don't subscribe, but who think the show should pay
They never would be missed, They never would be missed.
There's the highbrow individual who elevates his nose,
And says he can't stand amateurs, and so he never goes,
And the chap who once saw Grossmith, and who says that after that
All other funny fellows are funereally flat
And vows that in these dismal days comedians don't exist,
We don't think he'd be missed, We're sure he'd not be missed.

Cast

Mikado (Ernest Booth), Nanki-Poo (E. Hudspith), Ko-Ko (A. G. Whittle), Pooh-Bah (T. G. Woolley), Pish-Tush (Percy Winter), Yum-Yum (Phyllis Duncan), Pitti-Sing (Marjorie Matthews), Peep-Bo (Joyce English), Katisha (Bea Chanteri), Sword-Bearer (Mary Maddern Williams)

Gentlemen of the Chorus Herbert Alford, B. R. Anderson, J. H. Brand, W. Chapman, Harry G. Cook, Stanley J. Cross, A. A. Emmett, E. Forster, Harold G. Godbold, C. D. Houghton, E. J. King, Sidney Lessiter, C. G. Lufkin, A. S. Mansfield, J. S. Rippier, Wilfred Robinson, Maurice J. W. Taylor, Brian Wicks, D. J. Williams

Ladies of the Chorus Babs Bacon, Ivy Bundey, Barbara Bunting, Annie Callis, E. M. Carter, Peggy Castle, Gwen Coltman, Pearl Cross, Ethel V. Dewhurst, Irene L. Gaze, M. Willoughby Hall, Lottie Hallam, Dorothy Imrie, Margaret Meiklem, Ruth Morse, Beatrice Miller, Ivy Normington, Dora Robinson, Ethel C. Ward, Flora J. Winter

1933

THE YEOMEN OF THE GUARD

Norwich Theatre Royal, 24–29 April
Music: Arthur Sullivan
Book and lyrics: W. S. Gilbert
Producer: Harry W. Briden
Musical Director: R. J. Maddern Williams

The Society followed *The Mikado* with Gilbert and Sullivan's romance set around the Tower of London. As Arthur Jacobs understood in his brilliant biography of Sullivan: 'For librettist and composer *The Yeomen of the Guard* was a reaching-out, and from Gilbert's point of view a halt. It marked the furthest point that he permitted himself to go towards "serious" opera.'[4] *The Era* recognised 'an altogether soberer style of opera, approaching more closely than they have done before the old school of "English opera"'.

Exhausted and ill, Sullivan conducted the first performance at the Savoy in 1888. His diary records that there were nine encores. He wrote: 'I think its success is even greater than *The Mikado*.' The score has Sullivanesque quality, with a drama that used elements of Gilbert's 1875 play *Broken Hearts*. Gilbert reins in his tendency to parody human emotion, an essential of his work that is generously displayed in his other librettos then offered to Sullivan. *The Yeomen of the Guard* frames an essentially tragic story involving Jack Point, a wandering minstrel very different from *The Mikado*'s Nanki-Poo. The brilliance of Gilbert's lyric for the duet for Sergeant Meryll and Dame Carruthers in act two could never be mistaken for the work of any other Victorian librettist. In her first entrance matronly Carruthers vividly sings of the brutal history enacted within the Tower; as she explains 'Men may bleed and men may burn'. Compare this to the Mikado and Katisha's talent for bloodthirstiness (boiling oil being one of their most enjoyed). Gilbert clearly understood the British passion for bloodlust, and exercises it with considerable relish in several of his librettos.

The *EDP*'s reviewer C. L. A. gave his carefully considered reaction to the production's first night at the Theatre Royal. He preferred it to any of the Society's previous productions, although he thought none of the actors outstanding, except perhaps for the 'safe hands' of T. G. Woolley in 'a very finished, amusing, yet individual performance', notably when Woolley was joined by Marjorie Matthews as Phoebe in 'Were I Thy Bride'. Matthews was remarked for her 'daintiness and charm' and her 'marked ability for acting', while Bea Chanteri was a shoe-in for Carruthers, very much in the manner of the middle-aged contralto roles that Gilbert seemed incapable of excluding from anything he wrote. She is in the long line of such characters as Little Buttercup in *H. M. S. Pinafore*, Ruth in *The Pirates of Penzance* and Queen of the Fairies in *Iolanthe*. Phyllis Duncan's Elsie Maynard was much-praised, despite a shaky start, but went on to give a 'well-sustained and highly-coloured temperamental study'.

In Sergeant Meryll, Harry Cook found 'a part after his own heart'. C. L. A's comments suggest that James H. Lee, making his debut with the company as Fairfax, may not have been a natural actor, but he was a fine tenor, probably making the most of his 'Is Life a Boon?'. It may be charitable to feel some sympathy with the gentlemen of the company: the beefeater costume is not especially flattering to the male figure. This at least was no problem for the travelling entertainer Jack Point as played by A. G. Whittle, although his jester's costume was not flattering. The role was, of course, 'a wonderful opportunity for a player', but C. L. A. sorrowfully reported that 'Frankness compels me to state I do not think this is a part for which Mr. Whittle is best suited'.

On the whole this was a production that 'impresses by reason, not of any outstanding principal performances but because it possesses the saving grace of clever uniform and efficient production, helped by sound team-work and definitely aided by excellent orchestral co-operation'. Much of the credit went to its producer Harry Briden and musical director R. J. Maddern-Williams, but 'we have rarely received from our local amateur society such a uniform offering denoting efficiency in general ... such an excellent example of polished technique'. The last night's audience demanded several encores and, at curtain fall, the company was almost overwhelmed with bouquets and presents and tributes. The Society's much-admired secretary explained that 'it did not ask the public to patronise these shows for charitable purposes. They gave them the best show they could'. The lord mayor reminded the audience that 'it was out of their genuine love for the arts of music and drama that the members gladly sacrificed their leisure for such a production'.

The wet April weather materially affected attendance, with disappointing take-up of unreserved seats. Total attendance for the seven shows was 4,894, the receipts amounting to £625.8s.8d. Payment to charities since the Society began were £872, but Nugent Monck had something to say about this. He acknowledged that societies often had financial difficulties. A great many societies gave their performances for charities and he was not sure whether that was not fundamentally wrong. They probably gave a performance not for the charity but for the sake of the audience which the name of that charity would bring, and there was no reason why people should try to buy their way into heaven by paying for an entertainment. If the Society wanted to be charitable they could give a lump sum after everything had been paid for, quietly and anonymously. When they were bringing a certain joy and enthusiasm to a work it was a pity it should not be made to pay.[5]

Cast

Sir Richard Cholmondeley (Robert Brown), Colonel Fairfax (James H. Lee), Sergeant Meryll (Harry G. Cook), Leonard Meryll (Herbert Alford), Jack Point (A. G. Whittle), Wilfred Shadbolt (T. G. Woolley), Headsman (A. A. Emmett), First Yeoman (E. Forster), Second Yeoman (Wilfred Robinson), First citizen (Brian Wicks), Second Citizen (E. J. King), Elsie Maynard (Phyllis Duncan), Dame Carruthers (Bea Chanteri), Kate (Annie Callis)

Gentlemen of the Chorus B. R. Anderson, Stanley W. Blofield, William Boatwright, J. H. Brand, Louis W. Bullock, Maxwell Carter, W. Chapman, Ernest G. Codling, Stanley J. Cross, F. T. Cushing, W. R. English, P. F. George, S. D. Houghton, Sidney Lessiter, Donald Miles, Geoffrey Miles, I. Moore, James Warden, G. Watling, D. J. Williams

Ladies of the Chorus Babs Bacon, Irene Booth, Evelyn Boatwright, Lillie Burgess, E. M. Carter, Joan Clutten, Gwen Coltman, Joyce English, Doreen George, Doris Gowing, Enid Habberfield, M. Willoughby Hall, Lottie Hallam, Dorothy Imrie, Margaret Meiklem, Beatrice Miller, Audrey Payne, Sybil Phillips, D. Reid, Mollie Rippier, Dora Robinson, Peggy Walpole, Ethel C. Ward, Dorothy Warden

1934

THE REBEL MAID

Norwich Theatre Royal, 9–14 April
Music: **Montague Phillips**
Book: **Alex M. Thompson and Gerald Dodson**
Additional dialogue: **Bertrand David**
Lyrics: **Gerald Dodson**
Producer: **Harry W. Briden**
Musical Director: **R. J. Maddern Williams**

It was not often that the authors of one of the Society's productions had the opportunity to see it. It must have been something of an event that both the composer Montague Phillips and librettist Gerald Dodson attended one of the performances. Norwich-born Dodson became Recorder of London from 1937 to 1959, having been in the Royal Naval Volunteer Reserve during World War I. As he explained:

Montague Phillips ought to have joined the R. A. F. in the Great War instead of the Navy. As a composer he was an 'air' force all by himself. However, he became a blue-jacket. It also happened that 'Monty' Phillips was sent to my station.

Of course, we were very busy winning the war. But now and then there wasn't *much* fighting. So to break the silence and cheer up Monty, I suggested we should write an opera.

The whole thing took us six months; some days were worse than others. One day we wrote 'The Fishermen of England' – then we felt better. We chose the Monmouth Rebellion because we liked the dresses; also because the Bloody Assize, which followed it, sounded so nautical. And so amateur societies have been playing it for the last twelve years all over the world.

What was our aim? Well, we aimed at capturing the spirit of a happy, vigorous England; we wanted to get away from jazz. And sometimes, when I hear the Chorus joyously singing 'Sunshine and Laughter' or filling the house with the tumult of 'The Fishermen of England' I feel they really embody and reflect the true splendour of England.

In its way, Phillips and Dodson's 'romantic opera in three Acts' harkened back to an earlier age; in its way born fustian, not having the excuse of having been written a few decades earlier. Dodson thought the Norwich production 'magnificent'; it had captured the spirit of England. Over the years, people had encouraged him to have the old Maid renovated, to add a dab of lipstick, but he insisted he and Phillips did not want her to be like other girls. 'We don't want her to grow up'. It seems that its salvation, after the mildly successful run of 114 performances at the Empire Theatre from 12 March 1921, with Phillips' wife the soprano Clara Butterworth as its leading lady, was very much thanks to the army of amateur operatic companies, despite considerable critical praise at its London debut. The *Era* had recognised a score that poured forth melodies 'in an amazing stream, each one more delightful than the last. The finales build up to climaxes of quite ambitious quality'. The *Stage* agreed, with Phillips' music 'of delightful quality, some of it running to grand opera rank, and most of it melodiously and fragrantly English'. *The Times* had no doubt: 'One after another there is a series of charming numbers and it is difficult to recall any English comic opera of recent years that was so well endowed in this respect'. Gervase Hughes appreciated that Phillips had 'made a brave attempt to recapture the mood of *Merrie England*' but 'He only succeeded in emulating the more questionable side of [Edward] German's art, but now and again there was a welcome if rather self-conscious display of harmonic imitative (the occasional inconsequent shiftings of tonality were curiously suggestive of Prokofiev) and his instrumentation was skilful'.[6] Whether anyone in the Norwich audience appreciated these niceties is quite another matter, but many would have left the theatre with the resounding celebration of 'The Fishermen of England' ringing in their ears.

11. A. G. Whittle and Harry G. Cook looking over the script for *The Rebel Maid* (1934). Courtesy of NNOS Archive.

And when the foes of England, set sail in fury blind
The children of the storm arise, and leave their nets behind
With merry oath and laughter, and a smile upon their lips,
The fishermen of England go down to the sea in ships.

Enthusiasm for *The Rebel Maid* seems to have been modest, with a total attendance of 3,382 patrons and a net loss of £110.9.7d. The committee expressed its disappointment. 'This serious decrease is greatly deplored by the Committee as it is felt that the merits of the work chosen and the artistic success of the production deserved support as great as, if not greater than has been accorded to previous productions.'[7] Between the 1925 *Dorothy* and the 1933 *The Yeomen of the Guard* the Norfolk and Norwich Hospital, the Jenny Lind Hospital, Norwich Blind School, and the Deaf and Dumb Centre, had benefited by the Society's gifting of £877.

Cast
Derek Lanscombe (Robert Brown), Lord Milverton (T. G. Woolley), Sir Stephen Crespigny (A. A. Emmett), Captain Percy Jerome (Clement Smith), Septimus Bunkle (Harry G. Cook), Solomon Hooker (A. G. Whittle), Sam (Brian Wicks), Roger (F. T. Cushing), William Prince of Orange (E. J. Furley), Sergeant (P. E. Thain), Lady Elizabeth Weston (Lottie Hallam), Abigail (Babs Bacon), Dorothy (Ivy Bundey), Maids (E. M. Carter, Marjorie Matthews), Lady Mary Trefusis (Annie Callis)

Gentlemen of the Chorus Herbert Alford, Stanley W. Blofield, William Boatwright, J. H. Brand, S. Bruce, R. S. Cannell, W. Chapman, W. J. Cheshire, Ernest Codling, W. R. English, E. Forster, D. A. Gifford, P. F. Grover, W. P. Harvey, B. C. Hopkins, S. D. Houghton, Donald Miles, Geoffrey Miles, W. J. Newton, L. H. Oxley, R. Potter, D. J. Williams

Ladies of the Chorus M. H. Boatwright, Irene Booth, Lillie Burgess, Bea Chanteri, Joan Clutten, Gwen Coltman, Mary Curson, Grace English, Joyce English, Irene L. Gaze, Doris Gowing, Marjorie Greenacre, Doreen George, Enid Habberfield, M. Willoughby Hall, E. M. Hawkins, Dora Hurst, Dorothy Imrie, Beatrice Miller, Ivy Oxley, Delia Reid, Audrey Sawer, Joan Thain, Peggy Walpole, Dorothy Warden, Ethel C. Wars

1935

IOLANTHE

Norwich Theatre Royal, 2–7 December
Music: Arthur Sullivan
Book and lyrics: W. S. Gilbert
Associate Director: T. G. Woolley
Musical Director: R. J. Maddern Williams

C. L. A. in the *EDP* applauded the return of the Society to the Theatre Royal. When the fire of June 1934 consumed the old Theatre Royal, Norwich, 'it naturally interfered with the operations of the Norfolk and Norwich Amateur Operatic Society, but it did not consume the Society's enthusiasm for amateur theatrical art.'[8]

Musically and dramatically, *Iolanthe* survives as one of Gilbert and Sullivan's most brilliant works. Its first act finale is a gem of construction. As the *EDP* reported, it was appropriate that the N&N's 'first production in the new building should leap several standards higher in all-round excellence of quality to stamp for itself the best show that they have yet given us'. The first night was 'an unqualified success. One thing stands out beyond all others – the perfect balance, at once obvious in every department, from principals to chorus'.

C. L. A.'s review could not have been more encouraging, for 'This production is, frankly, one that all local theatregoers should see. It stands by itself, on its own merits, irrespective of amateur status, or the call of charity'. Indeed, C. L. A. considered that 'the dividing line between amateur and professional standards is a very fine one'. It was well-cast, with Gerry Whittle in the key role of Lord Chancellor, a part he had apparently awaited years to play. Audiences could now look to Whittle as the company's principal comedian whenever Gilbert and Sullivan were the authors.

Matching him in authority, Bea Chanteri was an imposing Queen of Fairies, still imploring Captain Shaw to quench the fires of romantic passion with his water hoses, even though there would have been very few in the 1930s who recalled that Captain Shaw had been a real person, the well-known Captain of the London Fire Brigade no less. His name would almost certainly have raised a laugh at the opera's premiere in 1882. Hopefully, Chanteri knew how to alert the audience to the witticism. C. L. A. was greatly impressed by this 'vocally supreme' contralto in 'a piece of work which demands instant recognition', especially notable in her 'O Foolish Fay', 'queenly in bearing when the regal moment demanded it, atmospherically correct when the subtlety of Gilbertian wit crept into the phantasy, and always dominant in stage personality'. Her

Majesty was supported by her compliant fairy attendants Celia (Annie Callis), Leila (Ivy Oxley) and Fleta (Joyce English).

As the young troubled titular heroine obliged to live with the frogs until her Queen reconstituted her to the fairy troupe, Marjorie Matthews played one of Gilbert and Sullivan's most sympathetic characters flanked by the opera's two young lovers Phyllis (Allie Haworth) and the Arcadian half-fairy Strephon (Clement Smith). The government of the day provided two politically-minded peers Earl Tolloller (Herbert Alford) and Earl Mountararat (T. G. Woolley, also the show's associate director). As might have been expected, the arrival of the House of Peers with their trumpeted 'Tantaras' brought down the house. Robert Brown would have made the most of his act two opening number 'When All Night Long', subsequently seduced by the Queen of the Fairies' invitation to fly with her to Fairyland. Leslie Baily reminds us:

> The pastoral quality of *Iolanthe* appealed to Sullivan, it was a quality he could match to perfection. The fairy element was something he enjoyed, too; it took him back to the first great success of his youth, when he wrote fairy music for *The Tempest*. There is much of the sweet and gentle side of Sullivan's character in the music of *Iolanthe*. The persistent musical call of 'Iolanthe' haunts anyone who has seen this opera.[9]

The Society revived the work in 1947 and 1955.

Cast

Lord Chancellor (A. G. Whittle), Earl of Mountararat (T. G. Woolley), Earl Tolloller (Herbert Alford), Private Willis (Robert Brown), Strephon (Clement Smith), Queen of the Fairies (Bea Chanteri), Iolanthe (Marjorie Matthews), Celia (Annie Callis), Leila (Ivy Oxley), Fleta (Joyce English), Phyllis (Allie M. Haworth)

Gentlemen of the Chorus William Andrews, H. A. Barfield, Stanley W. Blofield, J. H. Brand, G. A. J. Browne, W. Chapman, Harry G. Cook, F. W. Cowling, Stanley J. Cross, Eric Cullingford, F. T. Cushing, W. R. English, E. Forster, P. F. George, F. S. Haworth, B. C. Hopkins, S. D. Houghton, L. H. Oxley, Arthur Ward, H. Weston, Brian Wicks, B. Knyvet Wilson, A. Forbes Wright, J. S. Wyatt

Ladies of the Chorus Ruby Addison, Vera Blofield, Irene Booth, Peggy Brown, Lillie Burgess, Joan Clutten, Gwen Coltman, Grace English, Lorna Gaze, Irene L. Gaze, Marjorie Greenacre, Doreen George, Lottie Hallam, Doria Hurst, Eileen Penny, Sylvia Perkins, Mollie E. Rippier, Audrey Sawer, Bettie Southey, Ethel C. Ward, Dorothy Warden

There was no production by the N&N in 1936.

1937

THE GONDOLIERS

Norwich Theatre Royal, Norwich, 5–10 April
Music: Arthur Sullivan
Book and lyrics: W. S. Gilbert
Director: T. G. Woolley
Musical Director: R. J. Maddern Williams

Ten years after its first production of *The Gondoliers*, the Society revived it in a new production that retained the happy 1927 casting of A. G. Whittle and Bea Chanteri as Duke and Duchess of Plaza-Toro, now accompanied by their new daughter Casilda (Annie Callis) and new attendant Luiz (Roy Thurston). Whittle and Chanteri were shoe-ins for the aristocratic absurdities that beset their lives. Equally imposing, Robert Brown's Don Alhambra brought solidity to one of Gilbert's most memorable characters. Percy Woods' Marco, lanky and appealing, partnered Dennis Batchelor's Giuseppe, originally to be played by the indisposed Clement Smith, with Ivy Oxley as Gianetta and Marjorie Matthews as Tessa. The massing of the 61-strong chorus (34 mesdames and 27 messieurs) made for colourful stage pictures. The Venetian girls twining white and red roses included Allie M. Haworth as Fiametta, Joyce English as Vittoria, and Jenifer (*sic*) Thurston as Giulia. In a cameo speaking role, Lottie Hallam's last-minute entrance as the King of Barataria's foster mother Inez solved the plot's conundrum of who the rightful King of Barataria might be. Some of the 1937 cast members appeared in the Society's third production of *The Gondoliers* in 1950, with Chanteri, Batchelor and Oxley in their original roles. Further encouraging the staging of other Savoy operas, the 1937 *Gondoliers* broke box-office records, with £240 distributed to local charities.

Cast
Duke of Plaza-Toro (A. G. Whittle), Luiz (Roy Thurston), Marco Palmieri (Percy Woods), Guiseppe Palmieri (Clement Smith*), Antonio (H. Weston), Francesco (Leslie W. Nunn), Giorgio (H. R. Barlow), Annibale (W. R. English), Duchess of Plaza-Toro (Bea Chanteri), Casilda (Annie Callis),Gianetta (Ivy Oxley), Tessa (Marjorie Matthews), Fiametta (Allie M. Haworth), Vittoria (Joyce English), Giulia (Jenifer Thurston), Inez (Lottie Hallam)

*Programme note: 'Owing to the indisposition of Clement Smith, "Guiseppe Palmieri" will be played by Dennis Batchelor'

12. A dashing Clement Smith and Percy Woods in *The Gondoliers* (1937)
Courtesy of NNOS Archive.

Gentlemen of the Chorus William Andrews, Peter Ashurst, Alec T. Balls, H. A. Barfield, W. Stanley Blofield, J. H. Brand, J. L. Brighton, W. Chapman, Granville Cleveland, Harry G. Cook, Ronald H. Cook, F. W. Cowling, F. T. Cushing, T. R. M. Dale, David Denny, E. Forster, P. F. George, N. E. Harvey, F. S. Haworth, B. C. Hopkins, S. D. Houghton, L. H. Oxley, A. E. Pye, B. H. Robertson, Arthur Ward, A. Forbes Wright, J. S. Wyatt

Ladies of the Chorus Dorothy Adamson, Ruby Addison, C. M. Barraclough, Hilda Barlow, Vera Blofield, Irene Booth, Peggy Brown, Doreen Browne, Lillie Burgess, Enid Burrow, Rose Canham, E. M. Carter, Mary Curson, Gwen Dewing, Hilda C. Edwards, Grace English, Evelyne Fowler

1938
TRIAL BY JURY / H. M. S. PINAFORE

Norwich Theatre Royal, 25–30 April
Music: **Arthur Sullivan**
Book and lyrics: **W. S. Gilbert**
Director: **T. G. Woolley**
Musical Director: **R. J. Maddern Williams**

Leslie Baily claims that *Trial by Jury* 'marked the re-awakening of English comic opera' when it premiered at the Royalty Theatre in 1875. It was not Gilbert and Sullivan's tyro collaboration. The first example of their partnership was the opera *Thespis or The Gods Grown Old* (1871) written in three weeks and hastily staged. Gilbert thought *Thespis* 'a crude and ineffective work, as might be expected, taking into consideration the circumstances of its rapid composition'.[10] *Trial by Jury* shared its first night with two other works, a curtain-raiser titled *Cryptoconchoidsyphonostomata* by Samuel Coleridge-Taylor, and Offenbach's *La Périchole*. Thomas F. Dunhill claimed that Gilbert and Sullivan's bijou courtroom operetta 'with its continuous musical activity and unflagging humour, is almost the only English classic which can, without irreverence, be fairly matched with Mozart's *Cosi fan tutte* in the playground of music'. Baily recognised that 'This new kind of opera was ridiculous, and yet it was not rubbish. As entertainment it was far more intelligent than any of its rivals. The unique secret of Gilbert and Sullivan is that it can be both ridiculous and intelligent at the same time.' It also gave licence to Sullivan's impersonation and constant pastiche of conventional musical styles, a prime example being the usher's calling the bride-to-be into court.

For the *EDP*, the previous year's *Gondoliers* had set 'a very high standard which, for this season's production, demanded first-class performances in every department and the happiest choices in material'. Now, not only has 'that high standard been maintained, but in the case of one or two performances it is safe to claim that our leading amateur Society has never given us anything better. The choice of material is decidedly refreshing.'

C. L. A. was generous in his praise. In *Trial by Jury* Dennis Batchelor's Judge 'deals with the polished hand of an experienced professional, drawing roars of laughter with his delicious caricature', and after the interval impressing with his sinister Dick Deadeye in *Pinafore*. Roy Thurston appeared only in *Trial*, his singing voice 'a valuable asset to the Society, and he knows how to walk the stage'. Ivy Oxley's coquettish Plaintiff must have been fun: she had 'never given us anything more virile'. The performers for *Pinafore* also impressed when 'the bigger work of the evening brought all the big guns of the Society into action', including Robert Brown as Captain Corcoran, and ever-welcome Percy Woods 'singing with the eloquence of a lyrical tenor, makes a perfect lover'. Our Percy 'brought down the house' with his singing for 'The Nightingale Sighed for the Moon's Bright Ray'. As one of the company's most noted comedians A. G. (Gerry) Whittle's Sir Joseph Porter was 'easily the most subtle thing he has evolved'.

On the distaff side, Winifred Batchelor's Josephine began shakily but relaxed into the role, reaching her best form in 'Refrain Audacious Tar'. The worthy dame known to sailors as Little Buttercup was impersonated by Bea Chanteri, with the assurance of her fine contralto voice to support her vocal work. She 'displays a comprehensive grasp of the dramatic' eventually 'stealing most of the thunder in the penultimate situation of the last act'. The only critical complaint seems to have been that 'there are moments in the last act which demand acceleration'.[11] The Society revived the double-bill in 1951.

Cast

Trial by Jury
Learned Judge (Dennis Batchelor), Plaintiff (Ivy Oxley), Defendant (Roy Thurston), Counsel for Plaintiff (Clement Smith), Usher (Harry Cook), Foreman (L. H. Oxley), Associate (E. J. Furley), First Bridesmaid (Vera Hawer)

Gentlemen of the Chorus Alec T. Balls, W. Stanley Blofield, J. L. Brighton, G. A. J. Browne, W. Chapman, F. T. Cushing, E. Forster, P. F. George, F. S. Haworth, B. C. Hopkins, A. Forbes Wright

Ladies of the Chorus Ruby Addison, C. M. Barraclough, Peggy Brown, Lillie Burgess, Enid Burrow, E. M. Carter, Mary Curson, Hilda C. Edwards, Marjorie Greenacre, Lottie Hallam, Allie M. Haworth, Constance Lumkin, Margaret

"Defendant" (Roy Thurston)   "Plaintiff" (Ivy Oxley)   "Counsel" (Clement Smith)

"See my interesting client, victim of a heartless wile."

13. Roy Thurston and Clement Smith with an ingénue Ivy Oxley at a trial by jury in 1938. Courtesy of NNOS Archive.

Olorenshaw, Audrey Payne, Eileen Penny, Audrey Sawer, Jennifer Thurston, Paddy Weinle, Joan Woodeson

H. M. S. Pinafore
Sir Joseph Porter (A. G. Whittle), Captain Corcoran (Robert Brown), Ralph Rackstraw (Percy Woods), Dick Deadeye (Dennis Batchelor), Bill Bobstay (Harry Cook), Bob Becket (L. H. Oxley), Tom Tucker (Peter Ashurst), Sergeant of Marines (Eric Varnon), Josephine (Winifred Batchelor), Hebe (Marjorie Matthews), Mrs Cripps (Bea Chanteri)

Gentlemen of the Chorus William Andrews, Alec T. Balls, H.A. Barfield, V. Betts, H. Blanchflower, Stanley Blofield, J. H. Brand, J. L. Brighton, G. A. J. Browne, W. Chapman, F. T. Cushing, T. L. Duncan, W. R. English, E. Forster, P. F. George, N. E. Harvey, F. S. Haworth, B. C. Hopkins, C. A. Lumkin, Leslie

W. Nunn, L. H. Oxley, A. E. Pye, Clement Smith, D. Sperrings, Roy Thurston, Arthur Ward, W. Williment, A. Forbes Wright, W. Youngman

Ladies of the Chorus Dorothy Adamson, Ruby Addison, C. M. Barraclough, Vera Blofield, Peggy Brown, Lillie Burgess, Enid Burrow, Rose Canham, E. M. Carter, Mary Curson, Hilda C. Edwards, Grace English, Marjorie Greenacre, Lottie Hallam, Vera Hawer, Allie M. Haworth, Winifred Hingle, Doria Hurst, Constance Lumkin, Margaret Olorenshaw, Ivy Oxley, Audrey Payne, Eileen Penny, Audrey Sawer, Jennifer Thurston, Ethel C. Ward, Paddy Weinle, Joan Woodeson, Adelaide Woods

1939
MERRIE ENGLAND

Norwich Theatre Royal, 17–21 April
Music: **Edward German**
Book and lyrics: **Basil Hood**
Director: **T. G. Woolley**
Musical Director: **R. J. Maddern Williams**

Gilbert and Sullivan's *Utopia Ltd* and Franz Lehár's *Gypsy Love* were considered for the 1939 production but rejected in favour of *Merrie England*. The *EDP* informed its readers that in its choice of show the company had 'temporarily departed' from their recent diet of Gilbert and Sullivan. But a 'merrie' England could only be historical; there was little time for merriment in 1939 Britain, with the growing possibility of war in Europe (it would begin five months later). It was no time for frolicking on the village green, but merry-making was desperately needed to bring a smile to the British face. What better time, then, to look back over history's shoulder at the reign of Good Queen Bess and her romantic feeling for Sir Walter Raleigh, no matter how fanciful a treatment it received.

Hood and German's rose-coloured musical play had its London premiere in 1902, earning its respectable place in Edwardian light opera. It has almost certainly lost some of its potency in well over 100 years as it bathed Elizabeth in a romantic, gallant glow. This was a work that would be beloved of amateur companies, with its offerings of decent roles and stout dances, with generous lashings of fol-de-rolls and derry-down-derries. Mr German's music is always agreeable but, in our humble opinion, merely serviceable; liable at any moment to begin orchestrally gallumping around the maypole. Surely E. F. Benson's splendid Lucia would herself have played England's monarch in her

P. E. DRIVER
President

OSCAR H. CARTER
Hon. Secretary

CHARLES G. LUFKIN
Hon. Stage Manager

R. J. MADDERN-WILLIAMS
F.R.C.O.
Conductor

14. Prominent officers of the Society in 1939. Courtesy of NNOS Archive.

own production of *Merrie England* given half the chance, in a splendid riparian recreation of olde England in her own back garden.

As Traubner writes, the work's popularity has persisted because 'it was a historical pageant, besides being a tuneful operetta in the first place, and in the second it did not pose as many vocal or comic-dramatic obstacles to an untrained company as did some of Sullivan's music'.[12] In no small degree it was amateur operatic companies that kept the opera in front of the public well beyond the work's use-by date, although the coronation of Queen Elizabeth II in 1953 encouraged a revisiting and a handsome London revival, its dialogue and lyrics tweaked and with the starry presence of June Bronhill, at Sadler's Wells in 1960.

The much-appreciated Norwich chorus (33 female, 25 male) supported a strong cast, with the *EDP* singling out three performers. As Queen Elizabeth Bea Chanteri, now well recognised for her elderly-late-middle-aged *grande* contralto roles, provided 'a magnificent central personality' especially impressive in her 'O Peaceful England' that brought the house down. Dennis Batchelor enjoyed 'a personal triumph' as Walter Wilkins, and Harry Cook was praised for his Silas Simkins. These three drew the remark that 'Their part in this production would demand instant recognition based even upon professional standards'. Others remarked on were Percy Woods' elegant Raleigh getting into the spirit of the thing as he informed the audience that 'It Is the Merry Month of May', and Marjorie Matthews as a characterful Jill-All-Alone.

Gervase Hughes reminds us that German's light music 'inclined to a mannered style intended to typify the merriness of England in the days of Henry VIII, Elizabeth I, Charles II, George III or Victoria; this has been described unkindly but not altogether inappropriately as "olde-englyshe -tea-shoppe"'.[13] Writing in 1962, Hughes applauded the amateur revivals of the old piece, for 'After sixty years these songs [among them "Dan Cupid Hath a Garden" and "Who Were the Yeomen?"] when well sung still draw deserved applause, and there must be many members of amateur operatic societies who have enjoyed giving their support to the big tune from the first Act finale'. Certainly, Hood and German combine majestically with Her Majesty's tribute 'O Peaceful England', which still has power to test our patriotism.

> O peaceful England, while I my watch are keeping
> Thou, like Minerva, weary of war, art sleeping!
> Sleep on a little while, and in thy slumber smile,
> While thou art sleeping, I'll be wakeful, ever wakeful!
> Sword and buckler by thy side
> Rest on the shore of battle-tide
> Which, like the ever-hungry sea
> Howls around this isle.
> O sleep, till I awaken thee
> And in thy slumber, smile!

Cast

Earl of Essex (Robert Brown), Sir Walter Raleigh (Percy Woods), Walter Wilkins (Dennis Batchelor), Silas Simkins (Harry G. Cook), Long Tom (L. H. Oxley), Big Ben (P. F. George), Queen's Fool (A. Forbes Wright), Butcher (F. T. Cushing), Baker (A. E. Pye), Tinker (A. G. Whittle), Tailor (W. Chapman), Lord (J. H. Brand), Soldier (B. C. Hopkins), First Royal Page (Peter Ashurst), Second Royal Page (Philip Daniels), Queen Elizabeth (Bea Chanteri), Bessie Throckmorton (Viola Atherton), Jill-all-Alone (Marjorie Matthews), May Queen (Allie M. Haworth), Marjory (Marjorie Greenacre), Kate (C. M. Barraclough), Lady-in-Waiting (Lottie Hallam)

Gentlemen of the Chorus H. Aldrich, R. Attoe, Alec T. Balls, H. A. Barfield, V. Betts, Bernard S. Black, Stanley Blofield, G. A. J. Browne, F. W. Cowling, L. Davies, T. L. Duncan, M. G. English, W. R. English, E. Forster, T. E. Hall, N. E. Harvey, F. S. Haworth, P. G. Hoare, Tom Imrie, C. A. Lumkin, Eric Varnon, Arthur Ward, G. H. Weston, W. A. Wilson

Ladies of the Chorus Dorothy Adamson, Ruby Addison, Winifred Batchelor, Vera Blofield, Dorothy Bowerbank, Peggy Brown, Doreen Browne, Lillie Burgess, Rose Cahham, E. M. Carter, Mary Curson, Gwen Dewing, Hilda C. Edwards, Muriel G. Edwards, Marjorie Hale, Winifred Hingle, Jean Howlett, Doria Hurst, Jean Lee, Elizabeth L. Mallett, Margaret McBratney, Margaret Olorenshaw, Audrey Payne, Eileen Penny, Sylvia Perkins, Betty Phillippo, Betty Sale, Audrey Sawer, Joan Scarles, Stella Thouless, Ethel C. Ward, Paddy Weinle, Joan Woodeson

The 1940s

Having closed down after the 1939 *Merrie England* for the duration of the Second World War, the N&N resurfaced in 1947 seemingly intent on providing its audiences with annual helpings of Gilbert and Sullivan. As performances of Savoy operas by amateurs remained under the gimlet eye of the D'Oyly Carte Opera, it was a body of work that allowed only very limited rethinking and fresh interpretation. This moribund situation endured from 1947 through to 1953, without even recourse to some of the lesser-known Gilbert and Sullivan works, such as the brilliant *Patience*, perhaps overlooked because it might be too aesthetic for East Anglian taste. Faced with the inevitable time lag between the professional production of a musical and its availability to amateur operatic societies, they were to some degree caught in a time trap: the atmosphere and tone of a work only now and again seemed to chime with the time at which it was made available for amateur performance. It was to some degree a matter of currency, or the lack of it. Where, in what was left of the limited period before the end of the decade, was freshness, innovation, immediacy, to be found?

The transplanting of Rodgers and Hammerstein's *Oklahoma!* to London in 1947 was little less than a revelation to domestic audiences, but there was little sense of changing tastes in London entertainments. 1947 saw A. P. Herbert and Vivian Ellis' valentine to the past in his operetta *Bless the Bride*, a work that might as well have come from a much earlier decade. Another operetta-ish effort was Eric Maschwitz's *Carissima*, passing itself off as a sort of new foreign operetta with music by the little more than workmanlike Hans May. One of the most solid London successes of the 1940s was Ivor Novello's *King's Rhapsody*, which would have to wait until 1975 before the N&N's production. Meanwhile, it was only in 1956 that the Society ended its obsession with Mr Gilbert and Mr Sullivan.

1947
IOLANTHE

Norwich Theatre Royal, 10–15 November
Music: **Arthur Sullivan**
Book and lyrics by **W. S. Gilbert**
Director: **T. G. Woolley**
Musical Director: **Heathcote Statham**

The *EDP*'s headline had no doubt; this was an 'Amateur Society's Triumph' marking the resumption of the N&N's productions, the company having closed down in 1939 for the duration of the Second World War.

> Even before the curtain went up at the Theatre Royal last night the Norfolk and Norwich Amateur Operatic Society's revival seemed destined to be a great success. The theatre was crowded, but from the moment the familiar overture began the large audience was all attention - a fitting reward for the pains that the Society had taken to muster an orchestra worthy of Sullivan's lovely music. The overture set a standard which was well sustained throughout the evening, and those on the stage will be the first to admit that the success of this post-war revival is largely owed to splendid playing of the orchestra and the care which Dr. Statham bestowed on the balance of instruments and voices.

The cast was a happy blend of accomplished experience and gifted newcomers. Gerry Whittle's Lord Chancellor, Bea Chanteri's Fairy Queen, and Marjorie Matthews's Iolanthe all bore the guinea-stamp of the Savoy tradition, and a notable Private Willis (E. Booth) made a welcome return after 15 years' absence. The Phyllis (Ivy Oxley) and the Strephon (Clement Smith) were also well known, and the company was greatly strengthened by newcomers to the Society, the two lovesick peers (A. R. Gerrard and R. Birkhead) and the new Celia (Sylvia Hogg).

The *EEN* concurred, recognising that 'This is a production of which the Society can be proud. It has lightness, colour and spontaneity; there are fewer points of detail to polish as the week goes by than is usually the case with even the bigger amateur shows of this kind.' The chorus work was 'admirable' ('one could hear most of the words as well as realise the great amount of rehearsal which had gone to make a successful performance'), as were Booth as a striking Private Willis, and Gerrard and Birkhead's well-matched Peers. In preparation of her reputation as one of the grandest divas of the Society's leading ladies, Ivy Oxley's Phyllis was spectacularly Arcadian, handsomely partnered by Smith's Strephon.

15. An urgent need for crowd control for the 1947 fairies of *Iolanthe*.
Courtesy of Jarrolds Ltd, Norwich.

Established as the Society's favourite veterans in Gilbert and Sullivan, Gerry Whittle as the Lord Chancellor was 'a joyous example of ripe stage-craft', and Bea Chanteri's ample Queen of the Fairies returned to the role 'admirable' and 'commanding'. Her nymph-like attendants could hardly have been better cast, with Sylvia Hogg as Celia, Betty Heptinstall as Leila, and Margaret Johnston as Fleta. At curtain fall, the Society's chairman Oscar Carter told the audience 'This has been the greatest triumph the Society has ever had'. The week's box office takings were £1,361.

Cast

Lord Chancellor (A. G. Whittle), Earl of Mountararat (A. R. Gerrard), Earl Tolloller (R. Birkhead), Private Willis (Ernest Booth), Strephon (Clement Smith), Queen of the Fairies (Bea Chanteri), Iolanthe (Marjorie Matthews), Celia (Sylvia Hogg), Leila (Betty Heptinstall), Fleta (Margaret Johnston), Phyllis (Ivy Oxley), Train-Bearer (W. Elsey)

Gentlemen of the Chorus Harry Balders, R. A. Barker, B. S. Black, W. S. Blofield, W. B. Boatwright, J. H. Brand, C. J. Brown, G. A. J. Browne, W. F. Chapman, C. L. Cheesman, H. G. Cook, Harry Cook, S. J. Cox, F. T. Cushing, W. R. English, E. Forster, E. Hartley, B. C. Hopkins, G. M. Johnson, L. H. Oxley, A. E. Pye, B. H. Robertson, A. D. Ward, F. T. Weyer, H. P. Whiteside

Ladies of the Chorus Ruby Addison, Eileen Ashley, Olive Barnes, Doreen Browne, Pauline Cann, Margaret Frost, Gwenda Gooderham, Mabel Gunton, Lena Heighton, Sheila Horne, Joyce Johnson, Barbara Laws, Barbara Ling,

Amy Mason, Olive Notley, Pauline Rice, Kathleen Rose, Daphne Sandle, Marjorie Seeley, Nancy Thompson, Ethel Ward, Paddy Widowson, Audrey Wilson

1948

THE MIKADO

Norwich Theatre Royal, 1–6 November
Music: **Arthur Sullivan**
Book and lyrics: **W. S. Gilbert**
Director: **Ross Hills**
Musical Director: **Heathcote Statham**

The Theatre Royal programme found space to promote the forthcoming tour of Ivor Novello's *The Dancing Years* with 'Full West End Company and Chorus of 80' and 'Augmented Orchestra of 30', but now it was the N&N's return to the most popular of Gilbert and Sullivan operas, previously produced by the Society in 1932. Refreshed in a new production by Ross Hills and with musical direction by Heathcote Statham, the *EEN* predicted that 'Obviously the week will be an artistic as well as a financial success.'[1] It reported that 'the show has no stamp of amateur-ness', and 'no weak spot and a pleasing level of confidence'.

Practised Gilbert and Sullivan specialist Gerry Whittle made for a nimble Ko-Ko in a cast list that reflected changing personnel in the company. The staunch mature contralto role usually taken by Bea Chanteri now fell to Mabel Gunton as Katisha ('as satisfying as is possible with this decidedly unhumorous role') alongside Eric Hartley as the Mikado who infused into this none too easy role an impressive force and sense of characterisation'. In later years, Hartley's vivid reincarnation of Victorian melodramatic sequences at the Maddermarket Theatre Music Hall were splendidly lurid. Ernest Booth had the right build and swagger for Poo-Bah, while star-crossed lovers Nanki-Poo and Yum-Yum (Robert Birkhead and Nancy Thompson) had the charming support of Pitti-Sing (Pauline Rice, evolving as one of the company's brightest soubrettes) and Peep-Bo (the dependable Margaret Johnston).

Cast
Mikado (Eric Hartley), Nanki-Poo (Robert Birkhead), Ko-Ko (Gerald Whittle), Pooh-Bah (Ernest Booth), Pish-Tush (Bernard Black), Yum-Yum (Nancy Thompson), Pitti-Sing (Pauline Rice), Peep-Bo (Margaret Johnston) Katisha (Mabel F. Gunton), Sword-Bearer (David Heighton)

16.   'Everybody on stage!' for *The Mikado* (1948). Courtesy of NNOS Archive.

Gentlemen of the Chorus Harry Balders, R. A. Barker, William Boatwright, J. H. Brand, C. J. Brown, G. A. J. Browne, W. F. Chapman, Claude L. Cheesman, Harry G. Cook, Derek R. Cook, Fred T. Cushing, William R. English, Ernest Forster, Gerald H. Johnson, Peter L. Lindsey, William E. Heighton, L. H. Oxley, John E. Ransome, Philip H. Richardson, W. R. Stammers, John E. Thaxton, A. D. Ward, Frank T. Weyer, Harold P. Whiteside

Ladies of the Chorus Ruby Addison, Olive Barnes, Doreen Browne, Pauline D. Cann, Muriel A. Cobbold, Eileen Cooper, Grace English, Sandra Fowler, Margaret Frost, Paddy Gladden, Nora E. Gotts, Lena Heighton, Sylvia Hogg, Paddy Horne, Edna Jackson, Joyce Johnson, Barbara Laws, Barbara Ling, Gweneth Lyon, Amy Mason, Olive Notley, Ivy Oxley, Barbara Page, Kathleen Rose, Daphne Sandle, Ethel Ward, Paddy Weinle, Audrey Wilson

1949
RUDDIGORE

Norwich Theatre Royal, 14–19 November
Music: Arthur Sullivan
Book and ***Lyrics***: W. S. Gilbert
Director: Thomas J. Bell
Musical Director: Heathcote Statham

'How can we describe the scene which followed the last note?' asked the *Leeds Mercury*.

> Let the reader imagine an audience rising to its multitudinous feet in thundering approval; a chorus either cheering with heart or soul, or raining down flowers upon the lucky composer; and an orchestra coming out of their habitual calm to wax fervid in demonstration. Never was a more heart-felt ovation.[2]

This was not, alas, the *Leeds Mercury*'s reaction to the N&N's Gilbert and Sullivan's ghostly opera *Ruddygore or The Witch's Curse*, 'a new and original Supernatural Opera in Two Acts', but its review of Sullivan's 1886 oratorio *The Golden Legend*, a setting of Longfellow's poem. Sullivan made his friend the suffragist composer Dame Ethel Smyth a present of the full score of *The Golden Legend*, saying 'I think this is the best thing I've done, don't you?' She told him that in her opinion his masterpiece was *The Mikado* (Ethel was fond of tunes). Sullivan exclaimed 'Oh you wretch!' but, although he laughed, she could tell he was disappointed.

Ruddygore had its London premiere at the Savoy Theatre in January 1887, Sullivan (typically) only completing the score a few days earlier. It was a difficult evening during which some of the audience started whispering that the title of the opera was not quite 'nice'. As the plot unfolded the audience was plunged to-and-fro between the heat of enthusiasm for its frequently brilliant and charming scenes, and the cold bath of disappointment at its lapses into familiar Gilbertianism. The 'galleryrites' shouted their disapproval. As for the original title offending the sensibility of the Victorian audience, Gilbert suggested *Kensington Gore or Robin and Richard were Two Pretty Men*. Gilbert came back with the alternative *Not So Good as The Mikado* before the title was gently adjusted to *Ruddigore*.

In some ways the piece hovers somewhere below some of its fellows in its effectiveness, but its undercurrent of red-blooded melodrama, its salty air that blows in sailor-lad Richard Dauntless to dance a hornpipe, distinguishes it, and there is no shortage of brilliant numbers, not least Mad Margaret and Despard's

17. Ghostly remains of the haunted *Ruddigore* (1949). Courtesy of Jarrolds Ltd, Norwich.

blithely eccentric 'I Once Was a Very Abandoned Person' and a brilliant set piece in 'The Ghost's High Noon', unmistakably mechanical melodrama. It also offers one of the team's most brilliant patter songs 'My Eyes Are Fully Opened'. The *EDP* was impressed, announcing

RUDDIGORE' BY AMATEURS – OPERATIC SOCIETY DRAWS FULL HOUSE.

> When the Norfolk and Norwich Amateur Operatic Society appear in a Gilbert and Sullivan opera the combination is usually much enjoyed, and the Society opened with *Ruddigore* to a full house at the Theatre Royal last night. This opera is one of the most difficult for amateurs to tackle because the material has less fun in it than some of the others. Despite this it is still very entertaining, and the Society handled it well. The smoothness of last night's performance was a credit to the producer, Mr. Thomas J. Bell.
>
> Dr. Heathcote Statham, who directs the augmented orchestra, also contributes largely to the opera's success. The sunny decor of the first act contrasted well with the chilly gloom of the second, and the care taken over costumes and make-up gave quite a professional air. Sylvia Hogg was exactly right as Rose Maybud, singing and acting delightfully and looking every inch the part. Mabel F. Gunton played Dame Hannah with warmth and authority, and her last song with Eric Hartley was especially good. Mad

Margaret was both touching and very funny as performed by Winifred Batchelor. The women, in fact, set the men players quite a task to keep up with them. Harry Balders, as the luckless Sir Ruthven, started nicely, got better as the evening went on and finished handsomely. Ernest Booth showed a nice turn for comedy as Sir Despard, Eric Hartley made a spectacular Sir Roderick and Alexander Ward was a lively Richard.[3]

Cast

Sir Ruthven Murgatroyd (Harry Balders), Richard Dauntless (Alexander Ward), Sir Despard Murgatroyd (Ernest Booth), Old Adam Goodheart (Dennis Batchelor), Rose Maybud (Sylvia Hogg), Mad Margaret (Winifred Batchelor), Dame Hannah (Mabel F. Gunton), Zorah (Doreen Browne), Ruth (Kathleen S. Rose), Sir Roderick Murgatroyd (Eric Hartley)

Gentlemen of the Chorus Russell Barker, Stanley Blofield, William Boatwright, J. H. Brand, W. F. Chapman, Claude L. Cheesman, Harry G. Cook, F. W. Cowling, Harry Dawson, W. R. English, E. Forster, Harold L. Mould, L. H. Oxley, James J. Peel, Michael J. Poulton, R. H. Richardson, Harry Sharp, John E. Thaxton, A. D. Ward, Harold P. Whiteside, A. G. Whittle

Ladies of the Chorus Ruby Addison, Jo Balders, Olive Barnes, Florence Benison, Pauline D. Cann, Muriel A. Cobbold, Eileen M. Cooper, Evelyn M. Curtis, Grace English, Margaret M. Frost, Paddy G. W. Gladden, Gwenda Gooderham, Nora Gotts, Lena Heighton, Paddy Horne, Edna Jackson, Joyce Johnson, Barbara Laws, Gweneth Lyon, Gwendolyn M. Mabbott, Amy Mason, Ivy Oxley, Barbara Page, Pauline Rice, Daphne Sandle, Wilfred R. Stammers, Ethel Ward, Paddy Weinle, Barbara Weyer, Audrey Wilson

The 1950s

We cannot know to what extent the continuing turnover of various directors visiting Norwich affected the company's work. Did the ever-changing personnel in charge of production bring refreshment or impede the character and development of the Society? By the beginning of the decade it was locked into an apparently never-ceasing repertoire of Gilbert and Sullivan; all was set for another decade of wall-to-wall works by that most quarrelsome of duos. If the Society was to flourish and develop change must surely come. It did, but not until halfway through the new decade, with *The Maid of the Mountains*. One last gasp of the 1950s was a third edition of *Iolanthe*. At last the Society had severed its connection to the Savoy operas.

The company briskly went through a number of directors in the 1950s. One of the most enduring was Thomas J. Bell with his six-year tenure from 1949 to 1954, followed by Maurice Dixon (1955), Alison MacClaren (1956 and 1957) and Maisie Griffiths (1958). The theatre programmes of this period pay little attention to their former achievements, as in the case of Ms Griffiths with her 'high reputation for successful amateur productions in many parts of the country'. Equally coy descriptions of other directors make us wonder about their qualifications, as with that accorded to the director of the 1959 *Show Boat*: 'Our Producer, Charles Ross, comes to us as a stranger, but with fifty years experience at home and abroad'. Informative is not the word. Such a dearth of information only accentuated the amateur character of the enterprise, and implied that the director was of little importance. The 1950 *Gondoliers* marked the end of Heathcote Statham's period as musical director. His presence since assuming the responsibility when the company resumed activity after the Second World War undoubtedly lent the company a welcome lustre. He was succeeded by W. H. Walden Mills (1951–53), Richard Butt (1954), George B. Bullen (1955) and Maurice Illiffe (1956–62).

The final years of the decade saw a sudden rash of British musicals in London that included the 'two Peters' (composer Greenwell and librettist Wildeblood) hymn to Soho *The Crooked Mile* (it cries out for revival if only scripts and original orchestrations can be found) and the 'low-life' *Fings Ain't Wot They Used T'Be*. Where is the Society willing to take on John Osborne's only musical *The World of Paul Slickey*, a major theatrical and critical failure (well, not to mince words, unmitigated disaster) when it opened in London in 1959? Does the score still exist or did its composer destroy the evidence? Why should we dally with what has been described as one of the most spectacular disasters in English theatre? Its songs are eminently forgettable but provoking (one recommended being a man all week and a woman at the weekend), its music almost disowned by its composer Christopher Whelen. Perhaps the show's infamous reputation recommends it as ripe for reawakening. This is a musical without a shred of romance, sentiment or sentimentality, dream ballets, emotional tugs, orchestral swells, hummable tunes, believable characters, warmth or charm. It does, however, feature a sex change. Its revival might cause a sensation that would blow through the amateur operatic movement without fear or favour. Your author suggests that 'If *Slickey* altered the British musical in one way it was in its insistence not to send out its audience in a happy glow'. Osborne's inscrutable lyrics include the love duet 'We'll Be in the Desert and Alone'('Our song will be sung when our loins cease to groan'). No wonder the hero announces 'The day is coming when mass diversions of the flesh will be launched like new washing powders by gigantic commercial empires in fierce competition with each other'. That is the stuff to give the troops! What hope for *Oklahoma!*?

1950

THE GONDOLIERS

Norwich Theatre Royal, 13–18 November
Music: **Arthur Sullivan**
Book and lyrics: **W. S. Gilbert**
Director: **Thomas J. Bell**
Musical Director: **Heathcote Statham**

The N&N's third and last outing with *The Gondoliers* can hardly have created a buzz of excited anticipation from many performers or prospective patrons, but the *EDP* reviewed it respectfully, explaining that Bell's

> well-handled production had the advantage of a fresh, gay setting and the excellently welded playing of the orchestra under Dr. Heathcote Statham, even if the noisy, ill-mannered audience almost obliterated the overture by its constant talking. None of the voices could be called powerful but all were well modulated and mellifluous. The chorus was strong and its enthusiasm amply compensated for an occasional lack of precision.

The *EDP* thought the first act slow but 'the company improved to achieve a second Act which realised Gilbert's wit and Sullivan's melodies'.

Compliments to the main principals went along standard lines: Ernest Booth, 'amorous and benevolent as the Inquisitor, quickly mastered the measure of the comedy. Harry Balders as the Duke performed his irascible antics with a light foot.' Gerry Whittle had played the Duke in 1927 and 1937 but now looked on from the chorus. The singing and acting of Sylvia Hogg as Casilda were firm and assured, and Bea Chanteri brought her rich contralto to the Duchess. The gondoliers and their brides were a delightful and competent quartet, the most notable individual success going to Alexander Ward for his melodious singing of the popular 'Take A Pair of Sparkling Eyes'.

Cast

Duke of Plaza-Toro (Harry Balders), Luiz (Frank T. Weyer), Don Alhambra del Bolero (Ernest Booth), Marco Palmieri (Alexander Ward), Guiseppe Palmieri Dennis Batchelor), Antonio (L. H. Oxley), Francesco (W. F. Chapman), Giorgio (F. T. Cushing), Annibale (James H. Peel), Duchess of Plaza-Toro (Bea Chanteri), Casilda (Sylvia Hogg), Gianetta (Ivy Oxley), Tessa (Pauline Rice), Fiametta (Aileen Ainger), Vittoria (Kathleen Rose), Guilia (Margaret Johnston), Inez (Florence Benison), Trumpeters (Gordon Kay, John Ransome), Pages (Jeremy Allen, Jonathan Allen)

Gentlemen of the Chorus Russell Barker, Derek Baverstock, William Boatwright, J. H. Brand, Geoffrey Browne, Claude L. Cheesman, F. W. Cowling, Harry Dawson, W. R. English, E. Forster, Eric Hartley, Harold L. Mould, P. H. Richardson, Harry Sharp, Clement Smith, Wilfred R. Stammers, John E. Thaxton, Raymond Tibbenham, John Underhill, A. D. Ward, Harold Whiteside, A. G. Whittle

Ladies of the Chorus Ruby Addison, Jo Balders, Oliver Barnes, Winifred Batchelor, Doreen Browne, Muriel A. Cobbold, Evelyn M. Curtis, Grace English, Paddy G. W. Gladden, Nora Gotts, Lena Heighton, Paddy Horne, Edna Jackson, Barbara Laws, Amy A. Mason, Una Melia, Barbara Page, Daphne Sandle, Paddy Weinie, Barbara Weyer

1951
TRIAL BY JURY / H. M. S. PINAFORE

Norwich Theatre Royal, 18–23 June
Music: Arthur Sullivan
Book and lyrics: W. S. Gilbert
Director: Thomas J. Bell
Musical Director: W. H. Walden-Mills

This double-bill of Gilbert and Sullivan operas had previously been performed by the Society in 1938. The 1951 production was moved from its usual winter booking in order to be included as an event in the Norwich Festival. Ultimately, this proved to be financially mistaken, and the experiment was not repeated. However, a celebratory atmosphere roused the audience to demand encores in act two of *H. M. S. Pinafore*, and audience and performers joined forces in 'Rule Britannia!' There had been 28 consecutive rehearsals, including Sundays.

Writing the music was a test of endurance for Sullivan. He wrote that he was 'suffering agonies from a cruel illness. I would compose a few bars, and then be almost insensible from pain. Never was music written under such distressing conditions.' Inevitably, Gilbert's libretto included a role for contralto, but not along his usual lines. Mrs Cripps (presumably widowed and more fondly known to sea-farers as 'Little Buttercup') is 'the only one of the Gilbert contralto parts to escape ridicule on account of age, ugliness or unreturned affection' and gets her man too!'[1]

The sea may always have been in Gilbert's blood. One of his forebears was the Elizabethan navigator Sir Humphrey Gilbert who discovered Newfoundland, and Gilbert's father had been a naval surgeon. First seen at London's

Opéra Comique in 1878, *Pinafore* struggled to survive against disparaging reviews, with musical journals supercilious or aloof. Audrey Williamson's brilliant reassessment of the Savoy operas throws new light on the Gilbert and Sullivan phenomenon. She draws attention to Josephine's social comment in 'The hours creep on apace', one of the few moments in the operas that identifies with the squalors that struggling Victorians had to cope with, imagining

> ... a dark and dingy room
> In some back street with stuffy children crying,
> Where organs yell, and clacking housewives fume,
> And clothes are hanging out all day a-drying.
> With one cracked looking-glass to see your face in,
> And dinner served up in a pudding basin![2]

A rare moment when Gilbert seems almost Dickensian!

Cast

Trial by Jury
Learned Judge (A. G. Whittle), Plaintiff (Aileen Ainger), Defendant (Ray Tibbenham), Counsel for the Plaintiff (Harry G. Evans), Usher (L. H. Oxley), Foreman of the Jury (Harry C. Dawson), Associate (Harold Whiteside), Clerk (M. Towers), First Bridesmaid (Kathleen Rose)

Gentlemen of the Chorus Tom Ashcroft, Russell A. Barker, G. A. J. Browne, W. F. Chapman, Claude L. Cheesman, P. H. Richardson, Harry Sharp, John E. Thaxton, F. W. Turvey, Fank T. Weyer

Ladies of the Chorus Ruby Addison, Vivien F. Amond, Jo Balders, Olive Barnes, Doreen Browne, Muriel A. Cobbold, Margaret Dean, Grace English, Paddy G. W. Gladden, Gwenda Gooderham, Lena Heighton, Paddy Horne, Edna Jackson, Margaret Johnston, Amy Mason, Barbara Page, Pauline Rice, Elizabeth Walter-Joseph, Paddy Weinle

H. M. S. Pinafore
Sir Joseph Porter (Harry Balders), Captain Corcoran (Robert Yates), Ralph Rackstraw (Alexander Ward), Dick Deadeye (Eric Hartley), Bill Bobstay (Harold L. Mould), Bob Beckett (Ernest Booth), Tom Tucker (Geoffrey Oxley), Sergeant of Marines (A. Forbes Wright), Josephine (Isabelle Aspin), Hebe (Dorothy M. Oakley), Mrs Cripps (Florence Benison)

Gentlemen of the Chorus T. Ashcroft, Russell A. Barker, F. Bass, Derek Baverstock, J. H. Brand, G. A. Browne, W. F. Chapman, Claude L. Cheesman, Harry C. Dawson, Paul A. England, W. R. English, Harry G. Evans, Ivan Green

Ladies of the Chorus Ruby Addison, Aileen Ainger, Vivien F. Amond, Jo Balders, Olive Barnes, Doreen Browne, Muriel Cobbold, Margaret Dean, Grace English, Paddy W. Gladden, Gwenda Gooderham, Nora Gotts, Lena Heighton, Paddy Horne, Edna Jackson, Joyce Johnson, Margaret Johnston, Amy Mason, Barbara Page, Pauline Rice, Kathleen Rose, Margaret Thompson, Elizabeth Walter-Joseph, Paddy Weinle

1952
THE PIRATES OF PENZANCE/COX AND BOX

Norwich Theatre Royal, 21–26 April
Music: Arthur Sullivan
Book and lyrics: W. S. Gilbert (*The Pirates of Penzance*), F. C. Burnand (*Cox and Box*)
Director: Thomas J. Bell
Musical Director: W. H. Walden Mills

After the curtain fell at the first performance of the N&N's 1952 double bill, the Lord Mayor of Norwich Eric Hinde said the city was under a debt of gratitude to the Society. He pointed out that it had lost considerably last year by agreeing to bring forward its winter production to the Festival fortnight, and hoped therefore that a 'first class show' would now recoup some of that loss.[3]

J. R. D.'s review for the *EDP* referred to this welcome double bill of Gilbert and Sullivan's *The Pirates of Penzance* and Burnand and Sullivan's curtain-rising operetta *Cox and Box* as 'the Norfolk and Norwich Amateur Operatic Society's "annual" Savoy Opera presentation'. Was this how the company was going to grow, prosper, develop, dependent merely on a continuous annual diet of Gilbert and Sullivan (even overlooking those that even supposed devotees of the genre did not easily recognise)? J. R. D. could be forgiven for thinking that this was now the company's unspoken but irrevocable policy, surely a decline for a Society that had never originally intended to confine itself to so inflexible an undertaking. There had, after all, been nothing *but* wall-to-wall Gilbert and Sullivan since 1947, and rather too much of it in earlier years. Even now, it would be three years before the Society cut its bonds with the couple. For some, a continuous supply of the Savoy operas could never be surfeit. In fact, the Society's regular annual supply kept the D'Oyly Carte Company away.

The Pirates of Penzance has always been one of the collaborators' best-loved works, originally performed in 1879, simultaneously in New York and Paignton's Royal Bijou Theatre, in an effort to establish the work's copyright in the United States. It is a masterly work, suffused with Gilbertian wit and some of

18. *The Pirates of Penzance* in 1952 © Eastern Daily Press, Norwich.

the most attractive theatre music from Sullivan, with its terrific succession of winning numbers such as 'The Policeman's Song' and Mabel's 'Poor Wandering One'. In fact, *Pirates* confirms the fact that, having established their reputation with *Pinafore*, the author and composer sat down to polish their template that persisted throughout their works, just as we may see that many years later, Rodgers and Hammerstein polished their own. As Leslie Baily points out:

> Someone has said that *The Pirates of Penzance* is *H. M. S. Pinafore* transferred to dry land. Instead of satire on naval discipline and tradition there's satire on the army, the police, and the Englishman's sense of duty, enough for Mr Gilbert to treat in a thoroughly serious manner. Instead of a dapper little landlubbing First Lord of the Admiralty there's a dapper little out-of-date Major General of the Army.[4]

The *EDP* thought Thomas J. Bell's production for the N&N was 'in the Society's best tradition, though there are reservations' including problems with audibility and poor make-up. Overall, there was commendable 'snap and gaiety [...] good chorus work, particularly on the male side' and 'staging and general technical excellence'. Harry Balders, 'an adornment to any Savoy Opera', was firmly in the Savoy tradition of comedy players from George Grossmith onwards as Major General Stanley. There was solid casting, too, with Harold Mould as Pirate King, Stanley Littlechild as Frederic noted for his 'outstandingly good tenor voice', and Ernest Booth relishing the role of Sergeant of Police. Ivy Oxley as Josephine, and Audrey Yates as the Pirate Maid of All Work Ruth, went unmentioned.

Much more rarely seen, and perhaps unknown to many who attended this week, was the dapper little *Cox and Box, or The Long-Lost Brothers*, first performed in 1867 at a private function and subsequently at the Adelphi Theatre. Not *Gilbert* and Sullivan, but F. C. Burnand and Sullivan, based on J. Maddison Morton's 1847 farce *Box and Cox*. The magazine *Fun* sent W. S. Gilbert to review Sullivan and Burnand's modest entertainment. He wrote that 'Mr Sullivan's music is, in many places, of too high a class for the grotesquely absurd plot to which it is wedded. It is very funny, here and there, and grand or graceful where it is not funny.'

To some degree, the same might be said of the works that Gilbert would write for Sullivan to score. As has been pointed out 'The scoring of *Cox and Box* is rich because mock-operatic: here, as in later operas (*Trial by Jury* most notably) Sullivan tweaks the noses of other composers and proves capable of a full-blooded *Trovatore*-style recitative.'[5] The only work not by Gilbert and Sullivan to remain in the repertoire of the D'Oyly Carte until its later years, Decca recorded the opera in 1961. It is a superlative performance, conducted by Isidore Godfrey with its three performers on spanking form. The N&N's trio seemed perfectly cast in its excellent players, Robert Yates as James John Cox, his unbeknown-to-him sharing tenant John James Box (Tom Ashcroft) and military-mannered landlord Sergeant Bouncer (Eric Hartley) with his distracting repetition of 'Rat-a-Plan'. A few days later, at the Society's annual dinner and dance at Norwich's Regent Ballroom, chairman A. S. H. Dicker told members he did not think he had ever experienced such a happy spirit as had persisted throughout the week of the performance.

Cast

The Pirates of Penzance Major General Stanley (Harry Balders), Pirate King (Harold Mould), Samuel (P. H. Richardson), Frederic (Stanley Littlechild), Sergeant of Police (Ernest Booth), Mabel (Ivy Oxley), Ethel (Enid Hebley), Kate (Margaret Johnston), Isabel (Pauline Rice), Ruth (Audrey Yates)

Gentlemen of the Chorus F. Bass, Derek Baverstock, Claude L. Cheesman, F. T. Cushing, Harry Dawson, Paul England, William English, Eric Hartley, M. Hilling, Ivor Hook, Sidney Lisseter, Harry Sharp, Philip Smith, Wilfred Stammers, John Thaxton, Michael Towers, Frank Turvey, A. J. Wakely, A. D. Ward, Frank T. Weyer, J. Wheeler, A. G. Whittle

Ladies of the Chorus Ruby Addison, Vivian F. Amond, Olive Barnes, Florence Benison (*sic*), Doreen Browne, Muriel Cobbold, Mollie Davidson, Margaret

Dean, Peggy Dunham, Grace English, Nora Gotts, Joan Haynes, Lena Heighton, Paddy Horne, Edina Jackson, Joyce Johnson, Una Melia, Dorothy M. Oakley, Lilian Prince, Betty Read, Judith Reynolds, Margaret Thompson

Cox and Box James John Cox (Robert Yates), John James Box (Tom Ashcroft), Sergeant Boxer (Eric Hartley)

1953
THE YEOMEN OF THE GUARD

Norwich Theatre Royal, 2–7 March
Music: **Arthur Sullivan**
Book and lyrics: **W. S. Gilbert**
Director: **Thomas J. Bell**
Musical Director: **W. H. Walden Mills**

Twenty years after its first production of the Gilbert and Sullivan work that most resembled 'serious' opera, the beefeaters returned to the N&N, awaiting the arrival of Harry Balders as the tragic travelling jester Jack Point, in the trail of Gerry Whittle's 1933 characterisation. Balders was accompanied by Geraldine Rash as his strolling singer companion Elsie Maynard.

Recent recruits husband and wife Robert and Audrey Yates brought assurance to the company as Sergeant Meryll and housekeeper to the Tower Dame Carruthers. Perhaps this is the one Gilbert and Sullivan work that needs more natural actors than any others. Gilbert himself pointed out the difficulties involved in finding singers of the required grand opera standard who would also be capable of acting the parts he wished to write.

Of its 1888 premiere, the *Daily Telegraph* suggested: 'The composer understands perfectly well the special need for this when he has to deal with voices of limited compass and, exceptions apart, of imperfect training.' The strict style of presentation at the backbone of the D'Oyly Carte Opera Company remained strictly in place throughout that company's long history, with Gilbert's original stage instructions followed to the letter. One step to the right or left, one alteration of a line of dialogue, created a rebuke to D'Oyly Carte performers. We would be interested to see whether the N&N treated the Savoy operas with such rigidity. Of course, amateur performances of the works were constantly in play throughout the time when D'Oyly Carte was presenting the 'genuine' article. As Ian Bradley explains:

19. *The Yeomen of the Guard* in 1953 © Eastern Daily Press, Norwich.

Amateur performances are the backbone and bedrock of G&S's enduring popularity. They have been around a long time – the first took place on 30 April 1879 when the Harmonists Choral Society performed *H. M. S. Pinafore* in the Drill Hall, Kingston-Upon-Thames. Since then church halls and schoolrooms across the English-speaking world have resounded on winter evenings to the strains of would-be pirates, policemen, fairies and bridesmaids.[6]

Alternative entertainments were of course available. The Norwich audience's insatiable appetite for musicals was well satisfied by the professional attractions that immediately followed the N&N's *Yeomen* at the Royal, 'Johann Strauss's Loveliest Musical' *Gay Rosalinda* and more Strauss (this time Oscar) with *The Chocolate Soldier* involving 'Full London Company and Corps de Ballet'.

Cast

Sir Richard Cholmondeley (Frank W. Turvey), Colonel Fairfax (Stanley Littlechild), Sergeant Meryll (Robert Yates), Leonard Meryll (Sidney Lessiter), Jack Point (Harry Balders), Wilfred Shadbolt (Harold L. Mould), Headsman (F. G. Tinsley), First Yeoman (Harry Sharp), Second Yeoman (Paul England), First Citizen (Christopher A. Peal), Second Citizen (Geoffrey A. Browne), Elise Maynard (Geraldine Rash), Phoebe Meryll (Ivy Oxley), Dame Carruthers (Audrey Yates), Kate (Charlotte Pank)

Gentlemen of the Chorus A. J. Allison, George Allison, Russell Barker, Fred Bass, Derek Baverstock, Ernest E. Booth, Claude L. Cheesman, Arthur C. Cooper, F. T. Cushing, Harry C. Dawson, William R. English, M. Hilling, Michael Hull, Peter Lindsey, Brian Pymer, P. H. Richardson, Philip G. Smith, Rodney Stone, Michael Towers, A. D. Ward, Frank T. Weyer, A. G. Whittle

Ladies of the Chorus Ruby Addison, Vivian Amond, Oliver Barnes, Joan Blamire, Doreen Browne, Mollie Davidson, Margaret Dean, Peggy Dunham, Grace English, Gertrude Freeman, Elizabeth Garner, Nora Gotts, Lena Heighton, Enid Jackson, Joyce Johnson, Margaret Johnston, Amy Mason, Una Melia, Dora Mould, Dorothy Oakley, Barbara Page, Pauline Rice, Margaret Thompson, Paddy Weinle

1954
THE MAID OF THE MOUNTAINS

Norwich Theatre Royal, 26 April–1 May

Music: **Harold Fraser-Simson**

Book: **Frederick Lonsdale, revised by Emile Littler**

Lyrics: **Harry Graham**

Additional music: **James W. Tate**

Additional lyrics: **Harry Graham, F. Clifford Harris, 'Valentine'**

Director: **Thomas J. Bell**

Associate Director: **John Lewis**

Musical Director: **Richard Butt**

Breaking free from Gilbert and Sullivan after seven post-war productions of Savoy operas, *The Maid of the Mountains* represented a hopeful advance by the Society, although *Iolanthe* would return for its third outing in 1955.

A 1972 London revival of this Grand Old Man (or Maid) of British musical theatre attracted mixed reviews form the critics. John Barber for the *Daily Telegraph* was ecstatic: 'I wouldn't have missed it for worlds'; for Barber 'good pop is indestructible'. Welcoming a 'musty relic' back on stage, Milton Shulman admitted that 'Perhaps for audiences of a very advanced age, catching faint echoes of tired jokes through their ear trumpets, *Maid of the Mountains* may still be a nostalgic change from the telly.'[7] The *Tatler*'s critic was shocked that the poor old thing had been dug up at all:

20. *The Maid of the Mountains* in 1954 © Eastern Daily Press, Norwich.

To think that here and now, in the middle of 1972, a production of this nature is actually occupying the stage of a major London theatre is frankly chilling … it is in fact hard to think of anyone short of God who could possibly have helped the show rise above its own kitsch awfulness: when a musical is as old as this one, so old in fact that anyone with happy memories of it can reasonably be accused of senility, there is a lot to be said for letting sleeping doggerel lie.[8]

That fastidious and waspish chronicler of foolish operettas Gervase Hughes thought Fraser-Simson's melodies 'though tiresomely conventional in patter, were often very pretty, he rarely descended to vulgarity or cheap sentimentality and never fell prey to jazz'.[9] Writing as late as 2020, Thomas Hischak considered the piece 'one of the most complicated of British operettas but the libretto plays beautifully on stage and still thrills audiences in revival'.[10] This is a behemoth of a musical, apparently compiled by a Frankenstein-like committee of contributors. Frederick Lonsdale had written the play nine years before the completed musical version opened in London in 1917, achieving 1,352 performances. Its star, José Collins, remained in place throughout the production, which was eventually obliged to close because she was vocally exhausted. On its very last night, she had completely lost her voice. What an occasion that must have been! The show seemed indestructible. At one time, there were no less than 14 companies performing it on tour. Fraser-Simson had already written much of the score for a proposed musical about Nell Gwyn. At a late stage in the show's development he agreed that the show needed a big melody. Something, someone suggested, like Lehár's waltz for *The Merry Widow*. By adapting Lehár's opening notes, Fraser-Simson discovered 'Love Will Find a Way', one of the most sumptuous melodies from any British musical, period.

The famed music-hall performer-writer-composer James W. Tate wrote four numbers with lyricists Clifford Harris and 'Valentine' (the pseudonym of the domineering television chef Fanny Cradock's father). Tate, often masquerading on the halls as a monocled silly-ass type, married the singer Clarice Mayne, wrote hugely popular songs for her and accompanied her on piano as she sang his still-remembered compositions. Their music hall act was called 'Clarice Mayne and "That"'. Between them, Tate, Harris, and Valentine (when he was not writing one of his more than 80 novels) wrote four of the best songs that proved invaluable to the work's success: Teresa's ardent declaration that 'My Life is Love', 'A Bachelor Gay' for Beppo, Beppo's delightful duet with Teresa 'A Paradise for Two' and the musical-comedy-like duet for Teresa and Malona 'When You're In Love'.

There were London revivals in 1921 (it brought back the by now legendary Collins), 1930 and 1942. There was less welcome for the 1972 revival at the Palace Theatre, although Lynn Kennington was a muscular and vocally swooping presence. The *EDP* could hardly have been more enthusiastic about the N&N's production. After all 'This great musical romance has lost none of its charm through the years. There is a timeless heart-appealing quality about those Fraser-Simson songs that make them captivating numbers to delight any generation.' In fact

> voices at times did not get through the orchestration and some of the lines were rushed [but here was] an entirely new departure for the Society after the Gilbert and Sullivan series since its post-war revival, and it made possible some interesting changes of roles for older members and the infusion of new blood. No one could resist 'The Maid' of Barbara Whitehouse, who was making her debut with the Society. She was so charming and attractive that it added to the poignancy of the rejection of her love by the brigand chief Baldasarre, played by John Thompson who is well known to Maddermarket audiences. Not only had Barbara the voice to infuse that old favourite 'Love Will Find a Way' with all its direct emotional appeal, but her acting of the love-sick passionate girl was fully convincing, as was her duet 'A Paradise for Two' with Val Allister, a fine singer who is also in his first principal role with the Society.[11]

Whitehouse's Teresa and Allister's flirtatious Beppo had excellent support from established favourite Ernest Booth as Malona, teamed for comedy with Harry Balders as Crumpet. We should remember that this is a charmingly amusing piece, much of the comedy in the hands of Tonio and Vittorio. We may only imagine the partnership of Tom Ashcroft and Ivy Oxley dealing with such gems as 'Husbands and Wives', 'I Understood' and the delightfully lugubrious 'Over Here and Over There'.

A magnificent 2000 recording of the entire score, with its original orchestrations, is testament to the splendour of this survivor. Why have 70-odd years whistled by without the Society turning back and reinventing it for a present-day audience? The wit of its lyrics, notably in the glorious 'Over Here and Over There', a brilliant devastation of a love duet, is superbly crafted as Tonio (threatened with imprisonment) and Vittorio express their regrets at the prospect of being parted:

> She: I shall feel quite broken-hearted when my loved one's far away
> He: When my darling has departed then the outlook will be grey
> She: Though your path with heartaches bristles
> And your life's a bed of thistles
> You must write me long epistles
> He: I shall cable every day
> She: Think of me all lonely sitting in a flat that's meant for two
> He: You must start a bit of knitting, it's the only thing to do.
> She: Work they say's a great consoler
> I shall buy a pianola
> He: When I push the prison roller I shall always think of you!

What a gem! And who could resist that final curtain as Teresa realises she will live life with her beloved brigand Baldassare? Preparing the way for Rodgers and Hammerstein's Maria von Trapp, she declares her intention to live without love, without Baldassare: 'I'm going back to where I was happiest. I'm going back to the mountains. They understand me.' He tells her 'You and I are all that matters to me. Teresa, my Maid of the Mountains!' The final orchestral reprise of 'Love Will Find a Way' brings the curtain down with a thrilling endorsement of one of the longest surviving gems of British musical theatre. Here are writers who knew how to bring a curtain down! We await a radical revival from the N&N. That maid has been too long lost in the mountains.

Cast

Baldasarre (John Thompson), Tonto (Tom Ashcroft), General Malona (Ernest E. Booth), Beppo (Val Allister), Carlo (Eric Hartley), Andrea (F. T. Cushing), Pietro (Harold L. Mould), Zacchi (Paul England), Lieutenant Rugini (Christopher A. Peal), Crumpet (Harry Balders), Mayor of Santo (Geoffrey Browne), Corporal (P. H. Richardson), Teresa (Barbara Whitehouse), Vittorio (Ivy Oxley), Angela (Joan Blamire), Gianetta (Dorothy Oakley).

Gentlemen of the Chorus Harry Balders*, Russell Barker, F. Bass, Geoffrey Browne*, Milton Chapman*, Claude L. Cheesman, F. T. Cushing, Harry C. Dawson, Paul England, William R. English, Harold L. Mould, Christopher Peal,

P. H. Richardson, Harry Sharp, Philip Smith, Arthur D. Ward, Frank D. Weyer, A. G. Whittle*

Ladies of the Chorus Ruby Addison, Vivien Amond, Susan Apsey, Olive Barnes, Florence Benison, Doreen Browne*, Vera Bucknell*, Mollie Davidson*, Margaret Dean, Grace English, Gertrude Freeman, Elizabeth Garner, Nora Gotts, Lena Heighton, Joyce Johnson, Margaret Johnston, Dorothy J. Kemp, Constance M. Mathieson, Amy Mason, Una Melia, Dora Mould, Barbara Page, Pauline Rice*

*Understudies

1955
IOLANTHE

Norwich Theatre Royal, 21–26 March
Music: Arthur Sullivan
Book and lyrics: W. S. Gilbert
Director: Maurice Dixon
Musical Director: George B. Bullen

Not again, surely? Did the Society and its audience really need yet another production of *Iolanthe*? They had already done justice to it in 1935 and 1947. The box office seemed unexcited by the prospect of this £1,000 production. Gross receipts for the week were £903, the lowest since the Society began, with a loss of £122, leaving the Society in a precarious financial position. The circus was in town, but was it performing animals that drew the crowds away from the Theatre Royal or the show on offer?

George Usher's review in the *EDP* was measured but reserved. In general, he felt 'the local company had the right feeling for the piece', but was not always audible. Alexander Ward (Tolloller) and Robert Yates (Mountararat) 'are both finished with polish and sung with gusto and quality', while Geraldine Rash's Arcadian Dresden-china-like shepherdess Phyllis brought 'a nice vivacity' and 'an attractive mixture of guile and innocence, with an expressive voice', well partnered by Frank Weyer's Strephon. Geraldine Barber's sturdily constructed Fairy Queen also impressed. Other established names within the company could be relied on to give good accounts as with Harry Balders' Chancellor. Although his character 'could be enlarged a little', here was 'a very distinct performer', while Ivy Oxley's Iolanthe and Ernest Booth's statuesque Private Willis won praise.

21. 'I am generally admired!' Private Willis meets the fairies in the 1955 *Iolanthe*
© Eastern Daily Press, Norwich.

Usher reported that 'Tempo provided some difficulties occasionally but, considered as a whole, it was a pleasing performance'. This was not the stuff to get the box office ringing. The performance was 'too slow in its earlier scenes, and there was a lack of attack' notably in the famous chorus of Peers in the first act. The house was far from full. Usher thought it deserved a larger audience: 'I can only assume that many of the younger generation are out of touch with the delights of the Savoy comic operas. Yet in the main these works share the same traits and atmospheres of the nation's present humour.'

At this point of the mid-1950s it seemed unlikely that Gilbert and Sullivan, no matter how witty and tuneful and nicely performed, would electrify interest among the younger generation. After all, the teenager was about to be invented. This new classification of a young person was fascinated by American influences in music and, a year or so later, Tommy Steele struck new chords that soon reached deafening volumes in coffee bars with hissing Gaggias and twanging guitars. Through it all, the reputation of the D'Oyly Carte Opera Company and of Gilbert and Sullivan remained embedded in British cultural life, acceptable and agreeable entertainment for the middle classes if not always the choice of the musical *cognoscenti*. There was no place for hand-jiving here.

Happily, business bucked up at the box office as the week progressed, and a crowded auditorium gave the company a rousing reception on its last night. Various encores held things up, and the act two trio 'Faint Heart Never Won Fair Lady' for the Lord Chancellor, Mountararat and Tolloller was called back on stage several times. The audience was further delayed as numerous bouquets were handed to the leading ladies. Aware that such a tradition might irritate those on stage who had *not* been selected to receive a floral tribute, and the fact that audiences might be worried about missing the last bus home, this procedure was eventually abandoned, along with committee members coming on stage at curtain fall to say often more than enough valedictory words. It has to be said that, worthy as such after-show speeches were, they were anti-climactic. Some of those delivering them might have heeded Usher's observation that the 1955 *Iolanthe* 'cannot be fully enjoyed unless you can hear the words'. It was the Society's farewell to Gilbert and Sullivan. Or was it?

Cast

Lord Chancellor (Harry Balders), Earl of Mountararat (Robert Yates), Earl Tolloller (Alexander Ward), Private Willis (Ernest Booth), Strephon (Frank Weyer), Queen of the Fairies (Geraldine Barber), Iolanthe (Ivy Oxley), Celia (Mollie Davidson), Lelia (Pauline Rice), Fleta (Margaret Johnston, Phyllis (Geraldine Rash), Trainbearer (Muriel Archer)

Gentlemen of the Chorus Tom Ashcroft, Russell Barker, F. Bass, Derek Baverstock, Geoffrey Browne, Claude L. Cheesman, F. T. Cushing*, Geoffrey Debenham, Paul England, Len Greenacre, Eric Hartley*, Ivor Hook, A. Jones, Robin Peck, P. H. Richardson, Ron Say, Harry Sharp, Frank Turvey, Arthur Ward, A. G. Whittle*

Ladies of the Chorus Ruby Addison, Susan Apsey, Olive Barnes, Florence Benison, Joan Blamire. Doreen Browne, Vera Buckell, Margaret Dean, Barbara English, Grace English, Pauline Findlow, Gertrude Freeman, Elizabeth Garner*, Nora Gotts, Lena Heighton, Joyce Johnson, Amy Mason, Constance M. Mathieson, Dora Mould, Marjorie Robertson

1956

THE QUAKER GIRL

Norwich Theatre Royal, 16–21 April
Music: Lionel Monckton
Lyrics: Adrian Ross, Percy Greenbank
Book: James T. Tanner
Director: Alison MacClaren

Director Alison MacClaren's intention was to preserve the original atmosphere of this delightful British musical play, the only work by Edwardian composer Lionel Monckton to be performed by the Society. Monckton's music has a charm, lightness of touch and robustness evident from his many scores for such as *The Arcadians* with its piping 'Pipes of Pan' and haunting 'Arcady is Ever Young', and his sublimely touching 'Under the Deodar' from *A Country Girl*. The critic Andrew Lamb has an obvious affection for Monckton's music,

> much played in Britain until after the Second World War. Then it increasingly became obscured by the taste for American musicals and pop music. His wonderful melodies, though, are surely timeless, and their lyrics remain enjoyable for their period naivety and innocence. A world brightened by Monckton's music is surely an altogether happier place.[12]

The Quaker Girl had successful runs in London (1910) and New York (1911) and was produced in Paris as *La Petit Quaker*, with West End revivals in 1934, 1944 and 1945. In a quietly respectable English village, pretty young Quaker girl Prudence Pym is caught drinking a glass of champagne. Her strict elders are appalled. Prudence escapes to Paris where she joins Madame Blum's 'Maison Blum' as a mannequin.

Following in the Edwardian footsteps of the original Quaker Girl, the legendary Gertie Millar (Monckton's wife), the Society's Prudence was Margaret Dean 'a delightful unsophisticated study in her first leading role', with Prudence's admirer Tony Chute played by Harry Balders, noticed for his 'light and lively performance which has polish and verve'. Others prominent included Pauline Rice as Phoebe, one of her several soubrettish roles, 'outstanding' in her duet with A. Forbes Wright. As Madame Blum, Ivy Oxley was congratulated on superbly capturing all the mannerisms of speech and gesture. Memorable melodies flood this score, not least the irresistible call to enjoyment in 'Come to the Ball', the jaunty 'Tony, from America', and the brilliantly suggestive 'The Little Grey Bonnet'.

S. J. A. in the *EDP* had no doubt. Here was a production with 'life and liveliness, comedy and kick'. The chorus sang excellently but 'was not always

22. *The Quaker Girl* (1956) © Eastern Daily Press, Norwich.

movement-perfect in the intricate manoeuvres' but this was the members' 'best effort of recent years'.[13] Box office receipts were £1,505 compared with Iolanthe's £813. The production cost £1,330.00, 50% more than the previous year's *Iolanthe*. The company now had 108 vice presidents, 45 non-acting members and 67 acting members, and was attracting younger performers.

After *The Quaker Girl* the Society seemed to lose sight of the (admittedly ailing and frequently disappointing) British musical, only returning to it in 1975 with Ivor Novello's *King's Rhapsody*. *Oliver!* (a rare standout from 1960) had to wait until 1994. In 2000 there was Cockney cheeriness in *Me and My Girl*. Andrew Lloyd Webber and Tim Rice's *Jesus Christ Superstar* was chosen for 2005, and the team returned in 2016 with *Sunset Boulevard*. Two other British musicals followed: *Made in Dagenham* (2020) and *Betty Blue Eyes* (2024).

Cast

Jarge (Russell Barker), Mrs Lukyn (Margaret C. Thomas), William (Geoffrey Debenham), Nathaniel Pym (Ernest Booth), Rachel (Elizabeth Garner), Phoebe (Pauline Rice), Captain Charteris (Tom Ashcroft), Princess Mathilde (Marie Hayward), Madame Blum (Ivy Oxley), Tony Chute (Harry Balders), Jeremiah (A. Forbes Wright), Prudence Pym (Margaret Dean), Toinette (Barbara Page), Monsieur Larose (Donald Burton), Diane (Joan Blamire), Prince Carlo (Harold L. Mould), Monsieur Duhamel (Ernest Booth)

Gentlemen of the Chorus Derek Baverstock, Maurice Bridgeman, Claude Cheesman, Frederick Cushing, Harry Dawson, Paul England, Len Greenacre, Peter Hudson, Robert Lunn, Ronald Say, Harry Sharpe, Arthur Ward, Frank Weyer*, James Wheeler

Ladies of the Chorus Ruby Addison, Gillian Ashford*, Kathleen Bailey, Olive Barnes, Florence Benison*, Doreen Browne*, Merrilyn Browne, Betty Carver, Audrey Cockaday, Mary Cook, Grace English, Pauline Findlow, Gertrude Freeman, Norma Gotts, Lena Heighton, Marie Jenkins, Margaret Johnston, Dorothy Kemp, Brenda Kett, Joan Loveday, Mabel Lowne, Amy Mason, Constance Mathieson, Dora Mould, Valerie Ramm, Marjorie Richardson, Norma Scarll, Bridget Sullivan, Margaret Wallage

*Understudies

1957

THE BELLE OF NEW YORK

Norwich Theatre Royal, 29 April–4 May
Music: **Gustave Kerker**
Book and lyrics: **Hugh Morton**
Director: **Alison MacClaren**
Musical Director: **Maurice Iliffe**

One of the legion of now almost forgotten composers of continental operetta, Gustave Kerker is mostly remembered for his *The Belle of New York*, not much of a hit on Broadway in 1897. When it closed, the entire production, cast, lock, stock and barrel, was shipped to London where it ran for 674 performances at the Shaftesbury Theatre. It remains a work of considerable charm. In London it had the advantage of its original American star Edna May as one of the Salvation Army's most delightful officers Violet Gray. There were six revivals between 1914 and 1942. Perhaps Frank Loesser remembered Violet Gray when writing *Guys and Dolls*; perhaps Kurt Weill knew about Violet when he wrote *Happy End*: both have Salvation Army lassies as their leading ladies. The *EDP* suggested that many would think Alison MacClaren's production 'the best offering by the Society since the war', further removing itself from the stranglehold Gilbert and Sullivan had on the company since 1932. Steve James identified another possible problem:

> It's said of some operatic societies that the 'fat' parts go to the fat members – because it seems that the only ones who get chances are those who have

23. *The Belle of New York* (1957) © Eastern Daily Press, Norwich.

belonged for years, and are consequently suffering from middle-aged spread! That sort of accusation certainly can't be levelled against the Norfolk and Norwich Amateur Operatic Society. The leading lady for their forthcoming production of *The Belle of New York* is a girl who joined them only this year – Norma Wick, of Poringland. New also to a leading part is Pat Lake, playing Mamie. Also taking her first role with the Society is the well-known Norwich dancer Peggy Carr who's training the dance team, too. Handling the earlier rehearsals of the show is stage director John Lewis. Professional producer Alison MacClaren – whose guiding hand had no small part in making last year's production a real success – will be taking over shortly.

Wick's career had begun as a chorus girl at the Norwich Hippodrome, and graduated to professional engagements. George Usher recognised that good as the company was, 'Wick stands above the rest. Her singing has more power and experience, her attack is sharper, her whole performance has more polish.' He saw 'an outstanding leading lady with a presence which is magical'. Wick's warm personality and generosity of spirit struck a direct line of communication with her audience. This was a talent that over the years would prove invaluable to the company.

There was strong support from a resourceful cast. Pat Lake 'showed terrific zest for her work', especially teamed with Lynn Wardle as the Bowery comedians of the piece. Ivy Oxley, surely one of the grandest and most imperious of the Society's several grande dames, was Cora Angelique ('The Queen of Comic Operas'). Oxley was gifted with one of Kerker and Morton's most enjoyable numbers 'When I Was Born the Stars Stood Still'. Pauline Rice seemed a natural soubrette choice as Fifi Fricot, describing 'La Belle Parisienne', and duetting with Tom Ashcroft in one of the show's most memorable songs 'When We Are Married'. Over 60 years after its premiere, MacClaren's reworking showed what appeal the piece still had for audiences. Among her other work, she had co-produced the Frankie Howerd variety show *Laughing Thru* at Britannia Pier Pavilion in 1950.

Kerker's score is captivating, capriciously gentle and touching, and the whole piece remains worthy of revival. MacClaren's reworking, 60 years on, showed what appeal the old piece still had for audiences. The collaboration between Kerker and Morton was prolific. But we are unlikely ever to hear the music from, or see productions of, the many shows they wrote from 1896, among them *Yankee Doodle Dandy*, *The Girl From Up There*, *The Telephone Girl*, *Gay New York* and *All American Beauty*, although there is a tantalising recording of one of their oddest works, the 'Very Grand Opera' *Die Oberen Zehntausend (Burning to Sing or Singing to Burn)* complete with clanging fire engine bells. Need such works for ever be consigned to sitting on dusty shelves of an unvisited archive? Is it not time, too, that some of these much earlier works from British and foreign composers are revived by amateur operatic societies? Who else, after all, would consider reviving them? Have we abandoned them to history, which is almost certain to ignore them?

Cast

Ichabod Bronson (Harry Balders), Harry Bronson (Tom Ashcroft), Karl von Pumpernick (A. Forbes Wright), Doc Snifkins (Ernest Booth), Blinkie Bill McQuirk (Lynn Wardle), Kenneth Mugg (Cecil Clabburn), Mr Twiddles and Mr Snooper (Geoffrey Debenham), Mr Peeper (Robert Lunn), Violet Gray (Norma Wick), Fifi Fricot (Pauline Rice), Kissie Fitzgarter (Peggy Carr), Mamie Clancy (Pat Lake), Pansy Pinns (Margaret Johnston)

Gentlemen of the Chorus Russell Barker, Maurice Bridgeman, Paul England, Len Greenacre, Desmond McMakin, Alan Moore, Ronald Say, Arthur Ward, Fank Weyer

Ladies of the Chorus Ruby Addison, Kathleen Bailey, Audrey Barker, Oliver Barnes, Florence Bennison, Doreen Browne, Vera Buckle, Betty Carver, Mary Cook, Isabel Copeman, Margaret Dean, Dorothy Elven, Pauline Findlow, Gertrude Freeman, Elizabeth Garner, Nora Gotts, Winifred Harper, Lena Heighton, Marie Jenkins, Joyce Johnson, Mabel Lowne, Amy Mason, Dora Mould, Peggy Parker, Betty Read, Margaret Rix, Norma Scarll, Bridget Sullivan, Rosalind Tubby, Annie Woods

Dancers Peggy Carr and Jean Dixon with a troupe from the Peggy Carr School of Dancing

1958
WHITE HORSE INN

Hippodrome, 24 February–1 March 1958
Music: Ralph Benatzky, Robert Stolz and others
English book and lyrics: Harry Graham
Director: Maisie Griffiths
Musical Director: Maurice Iliffe

The continental musical play-cum-operetta renowned for its extravagant spectacle reached London in 1931, when its stupendous success probably saved the Coliseum from closure. Audiences flocked to the twice-daily performances to witness 'one hundred and sixty actors, not counting three orchestras, extra native yodellers and dancers, horses, dogs, goats' and a real rainstorm. Many such luxuriant embellishments were not available for the Norwich Hippodrome production, although the archive includes a photograph of one goat. The *News Chronicle* warned: 'You have not time to breathe in watching this wonderful spectacle.' For Gervase Hughes, *White Horse Inn* proved that:

> Artistic unity might count for little (slapstick jostled 'romance') the tunes might be trivial and the intellectual appeal negligible, but none could deny that the décor was sumptuous. In an age of frustration, unease and much living-near-the-bone, *Im Weissen Rössl* was adjudged *kolossal*. The spectacular 'musical' had arrived; genuine Viennese operetta was now a thing of the past.

Except, of course, for amateur operatic societies.

The parentage of *White Horse Inn* is a tangled affair, based on an adaptation of Oscar Blumenthal and Gustav Kadelburg's 1897 stage comedy. The operetta was the work not only of Benatzky and Stolz (who wrote the outstanding hit of the show 'Goodbye' especially for London) but Edward Künneke and lyricist Robert Gilbert. The *EEN*'s critic S. J. A. recognised the piece for what it was, 'largely a chorus show, with spectacular production numbers overshadowing individual performances … on the whole this is a "look" rather than a "listen" show'. Marshalling the almost 80-strong company was director Maisie Griffiths with her 'high reputation for successful Amateur productions, including Musical Comedy, Revue, Pantomime and Ballet in many parts of the country'.[14] S. J. A. decided she had 'done a tough job resoundingly well', dealing with a gargantuan enterprise that had 'become a legend even if here and there the old white horse ain't what it used to be'.[15] The production was a sell-out, with only 300 unreserved places available at each performance. The somewhat primitive seating arrangements at the Hippodrome were supplemented by 300 cushions loaned for the occasion by Norwich Football Club.

S. J. A.'s review confirmed that the show was principally 'a visual treat' with 'not much intellectual content'. He complained that the first night performance

24. *White Horse Inn* (1958) © Eastern Daily Press, Norwich.

only began to warm up halfway through act two. The audience was badly behaved, happily chattering throughout the overture and entr'acte. He saw the piece as 'largely a chorus show, with spectacular production numbers overshadowing individual performances'. According to Gervase Hughes, it had been left to Austrian Stolz and German Benatzky 'two purveyors of Weimer Republic musical comedy – a morbid growth, which combined nostalgia with affected sophistication – to deal Viennese operetta its most crippling blow'.[16]

Griffiths had the advantage of two impressive leads in Norma Wick as the inn's owner Josepha and Nick Jeffries as her head waiter Leopold. Jeffries may have been less audible in his songs 'but his study of unreturned love was pathetic, funny and immensely human'. Ernest Booth was particularly praised ('the comic hit of the evening') as the manufacturer John Grinkle ('He enjoys himself hugely'). The attractive young lovers were played by Margaret Dean ('sings charmingly') and Frank Weyer, lumbered as they were with the 'thankless task of providing romantic interest'. A. S. Goddard made an impressive Emperor, while Lynn Wardle and Mollie Smith ('who has real personality') brought light relief.

The Society returned to the White Horse Inn in 1970.

25. Joyce Johnson, keeper of the Society's archive, waiting to board the 1959 *Show Boat* © A. R. Miller Photography, Bungay.

Cast
Kathi (Vera Buckle), Karl (Max Whitby), Forester (Harry Dawson), Courier (Maurice Bridgeman), Leopold (Nick Jeffries), Josepha Vogelhuber (Norma Wick), Steamer Captain (Michael Batson), Bridegroom (Brian Smith), Bride (Pat Lake), John Ebenezer Grinkle (Ernest Booth), Ottoline (Margaret Dean), Valentine Sutton (Frank Weyer), Sigismund Smith (Lynn Wardle), Professor Hinzelman (A. Forbes Wright), Gretel (Mollie Smith), Mayor (Harold Mould), Lady Secretary (Betty Carver), Emperor (Alfred S. Goddard), Ketterl (Geoffrey Debenham), Landlord (Russell Barker), Sailors (Peter Lindsay, Eric Campling)

Gentlemen of the Chorus Tom Ashcroft, D. A. Baillie, R. A. Barker, Maurice Bridgeman, C. Cheeseman, F. Cushing, Harry Dawson, Paul England, Percy Garrett, Alan Goose, R. W. Lunn, A. G. Moore, T. J. Neale, P. H. Richardson, Ronald Say, A. D. Ward, T. H. Wild

Ladies of the Chorus Ruby Addison, Kathleen Bailey, Audrey Barker, Olive Barnes, Florence Bennison, Joan Blamire, Doreen Browne, Molly Cook, Isabel Copeman, Gertrude Freeman, Norah Gotts, Winifred Harper, Lena Heighton, Joyce Johnson, Ivy Oxley, Betty Read, Pauline Rice, Marjorie Richardson, Norma Scarle, Elizabeth Spalding, Bridget Sullivan, Rosalind Tubby, Ann Woods

Dancers P. Atkinson, M. Bond, J. Couzens, Wendy Farrell, C. Little, P. Wright, S. Wyatt

1959

SHOW BOAT

Norfolk Playhouse 6–11 April
Music: **Jerome Kern**
Book and lyrics: **Oscar Hammerstein II, based on Edna Ferber's novel**
Director: **Charles Ross**
Musical Director: **Maurice Iliffe**
Stage Director: **John Lewis**

A change of venue for the N&N, potential audiences may have been confused by the fact that the newly named Norfolk Playhouse was no more than the renamed Hippodrome, imminently about to relaunch itself as host to a

26. A melodramatic moment in *Show Boat* (1959) © Eastern Daily Press, Norwich.

permanent repertory company. Alas, that venture would all too quickly fail, and *Show Boat* unknowingly was one of the valiant old theatre's last gasps.

Reviews for the N&N's version of one of American musical theatre's greatest works were encouraging, not least in their welcome to Coral Newell and James Aldous, both making their debuts with the Society as Magnolia and Gaylord Ravenal. The *EDP*'s G. W. U. appreciated Newell's 'sustained line, full of feeling' and, although Aldous as her feckless lover was 'not quite her equal – except perhaps in his *mezza voce* number near the end [presumably his reprise of Kern's stunning little aria 'You Are Love'] – but he wears an attractive romantic air, and their duets are very effective'. It seemed that 'No great heights of vocal art are reached in this Norwich production, but the heart appeal of the numbers is achieved', with Newell and Aldous giving 'extremely confident and well-sung performances. Mr Aldous has a nicely-polished nonchalance, Mrs Newell an appealing charm though her emotional moments could do with a little more sincerity of feeling.'[17]

S. J. A. was especially impressed by Ivy Oxley's Julie in 'a sincere and well-delineated performance and one marked, too, by some very good singing'. In the sublime 'Can't Help Loving That Man of Mine' and her tragic torch song 'Bill' with its disarming P. G. Wodehouse lyric, Oxley had two of the finest numbers of the evening. For S. J. A., on board the paddle-wheel steamer, Cap'n Andy (Ernest Booth) and his sharp-tongued but soft-hearted wife Parthy (Betty Carver) oversaw the melodrama scenes with 'great spirit and vigour' and there were crisp performances from the Cotton Blossom's song and dance juveniles Frank (Lynn Wardle) and Ellie (Pat Lake) in which Lake's 'bubbling vivacity beats Mr Wardle's less-exuberant vitality by several big bubbles'.[18] In the crucial role of Joe, entrusted with one of the greatest of Kern's songs 'Ol' Man River', G. W. U. heard 'a rich chocolatey bass' from a blacked-up Robert Richardson, coupled with his devoted Queenie (Kathleen Bailey).

This was the only N&N production directed by Charles Ross. 'Our producer', the programme explained 'comes to us as a stranger, but with fifty years experience at home and abroad'. He 'obtained from his cast a great deal of energy and drive. They do what they have to do with vigour and confidence.' The company's new musical director, Maurice Iliffe, had been musical director for the Great Yarmouth Amateur Operatic Society for ten years.

One of the production's major problems was in the casting of the several black roles. The obvious lack of black performers available to many amateur companies was still a problem in 2023 when casting the N&N's *Kinky Boots*. The Norwich *Show Boat* company of 70 players was dwarfed in comparison with the original 1927 Broadway production's numbers, with its chorus of 96 including 36 white chorus girls, 16 white chorus boys, 16 black chorus girls and 12 black girl dancers.

The shortage of black artistes made 'blacking-up' necessary. It had long been a feature of musical entertainment in Britain, well-established in the United States before thriving in Victorian England. Gilbert and Sullivan guyed such 'minstrel show' diversions in their *Utopia Limited,* and several substantial music-hall careers depended on white performers blacking up (and even black performers blacking up). Eugene Stratton's deliciously lazy representation of Leslie Stuart's evergreen 'Lily of Laguna' was a typical example of this habit in British culture, a tradition that reappeared with G. H. Elliott, affectionately (then) billed as 'The Chocolate Coloured Coon'; all his numbers were performed in blackface. The most eerie blacked-up music-hall act was undoubtedly G. H. Chirgwin's act as the 'White-Eyed Kaffir', whose repellent make-up accompanied the singing of his most popular item 'My Fiddle is My Sweetheart'. In his remarkable survey of British music hall *Sweet Saturday Night* Colin MacInnes describes Chirgwin as 'a complete mystery, for everything about his act seems revolting'.[19]

The phenomenon continued in Britain long after many deemed it inappropriate, not least in the BBC's hugely popular television variety series *The Black and White Minstrel Show* that ran from 1958 to 1978 'when it became obvious, if not offensive, that the Minstrel's black face performance was becoming increasingly outmoded in a multiracial culture'.[20]

Cast

Windy (Maurice Bridgeman), Steve (Keith Reynolds), Pete (Bob Lunn), Queenie (Kathleen Bailey), Parthy Ann Hawks (Betty Carver), Cap'n Andy (Ernest E. Booth), Ellis (Pat Lake), Frank (J. Lynn Wardle), Rubber-Face (Geoffrey Oxley), Julie (Ivy Oxley), Gaylord Ravenal (James Aldous), Vallon (Anthony Took), Magnolia (Coral Newell), Fatima (Sally Pearl), Joe (Robert Richardson), Backwoodsman (Stanley Gibson), Jeb (Paul England), Barkers (Harry Dawson, Paul England, Philip Richardson), Landlady (Florence Bennison), Ethel (Audrey Shingler), Jake (Geoffrey Oxley), Max (Keith Reynolds), Guitar Man (Graham Powell), Charlie (Michael Batson), Announcer at Trocadero (Brian Smith), Lottie (Betty Cole), Kim (Coral Newell)

Gentlemens White Chorus T. Ashcroft, H. Dawson, E. Dunnell, P. England, C. Linton, P. Richardson, F. Weyer

Gentlemens Coloured Chorus M. Batson, F. Cushing, G. Debenham, P. Garrett, A. Goose, L. Greenacre, R. Lunn, A. Moore, R. Say, N. Thrower, A. Ward

Ladies White Chorus Doreen Browne, Betty Cole, Pauline Findlow, Gertrude Freeman, Lena Heighton, Joyce Johnson, Barbara Lewis, Pauline Rice, Bridget Sullivan, Pat Till

Ladies Coloured Chorus Mary Ruby Addison, Olive Barnes, Molly Cook, Isabel Copeman, Margaret Dean, Norah Gotts, Norma Scarle, Elizabeth Spalding, Ann Woods

Dancers Mary Bond, Pat Brandish, Jacqueline Couzens, Valerie Cracknell, Margaret Fawcett, Pat Wright

The 1960s

So far as audiences at the N&N were concerned, the productions' producers (what we would now call directors) remained almost anonymous as the decade began with a burst of shows that might almost have been regarded as pastiches of themselves. The theatre programme for the 1960 *Rose Marie* introduced producer Frank Rydon who 'comes from a well-known theatrical family and has performed in many renowned musicals, visiting Norwich on a number of occasions. Was Stage Director at Her Majesty's and Palace Theatres, London, for many years, and is now devoting his talent to Amateur Production.' Mr Rydon returned the following year with his wife Frances Davis as co-director for *The Gypsy Princess*. Pip Jenkinson remembered Miss Davis as a bit of a slave-driver, keeping the girls rehearsing until well after midnight. Audiences were informed that she 'has had wide experience of Amateur Societies, having produced for our neighbouring Society, Colchester, for fourteen years with great success. This combination of husband and wife is, to us, unique' exclaimed the excited programme note.

Mrs Rydon stayed home for 1962's *The Student Prince* but was perhaps buoyed up by the *EEN*'s comment that her husband 'has again brought a touch of originality to many of the numbers'. In 1963 the Rydons were replaced by R. D'Arcy Richards. Poor Mr Richards had to wait until *The Merry Widow* of 1965 before he was biographed and photographed for the theatre programme.

Patrons were advised that 'Our Producer needs no introduction this being his third successive production for the Society. He has a national reputation both as a producer for Amateur Societies and as a Festival adjudicator.'

Beginning the 1960s, the Society again found itself in the grip of operetta with two prime examples *The Desert Song* and *The Student Prince* rudely interrupted by *The Gypsy Princess*. It finally got round to *Oklahoma!* in 1963, before reverting to operetta with the ersatz *Pink Champagne* and perhaps inevitably the rather more welcome *The Merry Widow*. The N&N's decade ended with more American musical theatre in the timeless *Brigadoon, Song of Norway, Rose Marie* and *Kismet.* Throughout the 1960s, the company underwent several changes of director; the Rydons between 1960 and 1962, D'Arcy Richards in his three-year stint, followed by Willie Martin's two-year tenure, and Frances Davis from 1968 through to 1971.

We momentarily bring into focus the distinguished musical actress Patricia Michael who had a long professional career in British musical theatre, establishing herself through a series of leading roles in the 1960s. Her many West End successes include playing Melanie in *Gone with the Wind* (Theatre Royal, Drury Lane), Anna in *The King and I* (Adelphi Theatre), Polly in *Divorce Me, Darling!* (Globe Theatre), Margot Bonvalet in *The Desert Song* with John

Hanson (Palace Theatre) and Rosemary in *How to Succeed in Business Without Really Trying* (Shaftesbury Theatre). After her final West End appearance in *Peg* (Phoenix Theatre) she emigrated to America, married professional musician Josh Siegel, and began producing amateur societies in pantomimes in Connecticut. She writes:

> This last was a somewhat risky endeavour since, to Americans, 'Pantomime' is Marcel Marceau and the rich British history and traditions of 'Panto' are completely unknown. The first production got off to a rocky start. After a First Night full of family and friends, the second night had only two patrons booked and one of them was the local critic! The whole cast got on their mobile phones and summoned their families and friends back to the theatre to see the Panto a second time for free! It worked and gradually word spread that, far from being a Marcel Marceau Mime (or puppets as some people thought), British Pantomime was FUN! And from then on the Sherman Players British Pantomimes became a much anticipated annual event.
>
> As is often the case with Amateur Theatre (or Community Theatre as it is known in the USA) the majority of the casts are either retirees or teenagers since working folk often don't have the time to devote to this form of recreation. It was a delight to see the response to the project from the community.
>
> The joyous experience made me reflect that I have long been saddened by the negative connotation that the word 'amateur' conjures up. 'Amateur' comes from 'amatore', Latin for love. It means 'someone who does something for love rather than money' and has nothing to do with having less talent or technical expertise. Some of the finest performers that Josh and I have come across have chosen this path. The pure unadulterated love and the exultant and jubilant joy projected by the actors at Connecticut's Sherman Playhouse came winging across the footlights, and always brought a very special magic to every performance.

The Society's future was threatened when Essoldo took over the ownership of Norwich Theatre Royal in 1956. The old theatre was dilapidated and worn-out. Essoldo withdrew from the battle in the mid 1960s. Meanwhile, the Hippodrome became the Norfolk Playhouse, housing a professional repertory company, but it was not financially viable. As Michael and Carole Blackwell's brilliantly researched *Norwich Theatre Royal: The First 250 Years* tells us, 'The city had earned itself a reputation as a theatrical graveyard'. There was one more attempt to promote professional repertory at the renamed Hippodrome but the game was up, and the old theatre closed in June 1959; 'That same week six other resident companies in Britain had to disband as well'. The Playhouse reopened shortly after as a cinema but closed for good in April 1960. Its takings on the last day amounted to £3. The building was eventually purchased by Norwich council in 1966, pulled down and replaced by St Giles' Car Park. What followed was a protracted delay as to how to proceed with the Theatre Royal, with much argument and controversy.

27. Patricia Michael as Polly in *Divorce Me Darling!* (1964) Courtesy of Josh Siegel.

1960

THE DESERT SONG

Norwich Theatre Royal, 22–27 February
Music: Sigmund Romberg
Lyrics: Otto Harbach, Oscar Hammerstein II and Edward Smith
Book: Harbach, Hammerstein and Frank Mandel
Director: Frank Rydon
Musical Director: Maurice Iliffe

As it moved into the 1960s, the Society seemed intent on reviving well-matured operettas of a bygone Golden Age: now *The Desert Song*, Kálmán's *The Gypsy Princess* (1961) and a return to Romberg with *The Student Prince* (1962). The task of recreating Romberg's romance of the sands fell to director Frank Rydon, according to the theatre programme 'now devoting his talent to Amateur Productions', and musical director Maurice Iliffe.

At least 50 of Romberg's shows are no longer in the repertoire, but *The Desert Song* has always nestled in the public's consciousness, beginning with its London premiere in 1927 and West End revivals in 1931, 1936, 1939, 1943 and a 1967 touring version with John Hanson and Patricia Michael that was hurriedly shuffled into the Palace Theatre when another American musical unexpectedly flopped. To everyone's astonishment (almost certainly to its performers) Hanson and co. stayed at the Palace for a year, suggesting that this sort of old pleaser could still pull in the public in a London that prided itself on being swinging. It even won some rave reviews. Our personal memory of having seen Mr Hanson perform this piece is not of his somewhat throaty singing of 'One Alone' whose last piercing high note was marked by a highly dramatic flourish of his hands that had to be seen to be believed. Much more fascinating was seeing him dashing upstairs as one character (Pierre Birabeau) and almost immediately coming downstairs as another (the Red Shadow) before he had time to take off the face-mask that the Shadow wore to protect his true identity. The possibility of severe costume malfunction when quick-changing his breeches added even more spice to the occasion.

The *EDP*'s reaction to the Norwich production was appreciative but muted. Newcomer William John Prescott travelled from Gorleston to play the dual role, one that might even have promised the allure that Rudolph Valentino had brazenly displayed to the public in his 1921 silent film *The Sheik*. The image of Valentino wearing only several strings of pearls may have heightened expectation at the Theatre Royal. The *EDP*'s George Usher could see that the Red

28. Norma Wick (centre) with girlfriends in *The Desert Song* of 1960, Courtesy of NNOS Archive.

Shadow was 'by no means an easy role with its quick changes from milksop to mysterious rebel, but the impression he creates would be heightened if he 'cut a more commanding figure in his bandit guise'. The *EEN* agreed, praising Prescott's stage presence and singing but 'I feel he is capable of an even better showing if he will think of an even more rousing performance'. Much the same advice was offered to his co-star Valerie Rushworth as Margot, with some of the show's finest numbers including 'Romance' and the stirring 'French Marching Song'. They were 'well sung'. Here was 'a most appealing voice which she uses stylishly and effectively' but 'Here again a bit more liveliness and spirit would not come amiss'.

As columnist turned war reporter Benny (Brian Patridge) and his secretary Susan (Pauline Rice) 'successfully give the uninhibited kind of performances this show demands in all its roles', with Ernest Booth as a sheikh and Tom Ashcroft, Robert Lunn and John Thaxton as some of the Red Shadow's 'Riffs', even if occasionally there was a 'sloppy showing of some of the troops'. There was quality in Norma Wick's portrait of the Spanish harem girl Clementina, fine in her sultry number 'There is a Golden Gateway' for which Wick had 'the right kind of dark voice; she is expert, too, in the way she projects the image of the passionate creature'. Betty Cole's Azuri 'wreaking her jealous spite with snakey movements and realistic accent', also impressed. This was the first production in which the company had cast its own dancing troupe, 'but, like some of the rest of the show, it could do with a little more zip in places'.

Romberg's lovely old score may still stir romantic notions in the tired breast. There is a wealth of melody in the deathless title song ('Only stars above you to say I love you'), and 'Romance'. Most surprising of all is 'It', a quasi-Freudian glimpse into the extraordinary literary world of Elinor Glyn. The question was widely asked in the mid-1920s

> Would you like to sin with Elinor Glyn on a tiger skin?
> Or would you prefer to err with her on some other fur?

Mrs Glyn wrote the sort of books that parlourmaids were said to read beneath the bedsheets. Edward Smith's lyric wastes no time in defining what Mrs Glyn meant by 'It'. As Lorenz Hart wrote in 'My Heart Stood Still' 'I read my Plato, Love I thought a sin, but since your kiss I'm reading Mrs Glyn.' 'It' was already the title of a volume of stories by Glyn and a 1927 silent film in which she appeared. Now the number was delivered by the N&N's Benny (Brian Partridge), possibly accompanied by Benny's colleague Susan (Pauline Rice).

> There was a time when sex
> Seemed something so complex
> Mr Freud then employed
> Words we never had heard of
> He kept us on a string
> We kept on wondering
> But the seed of sin
> Now at last has been
> Found by Elinor Glyn
> She calls it 'It'.

What nobody seemed too bothered about is the fact that the old piece could hardly be taken seriously. The welcome outbursts of Rombergian melody, showing their age as they may, remain welcome interruptions in a sandstorm of otherwise romantic tosh. Unsuspecting damsels being swept off their feet and being transported by camels persisted, featuring in such diverse places as a Cliff Richard film *Wonderful Life*, and Julian Slade's musical *Wildest Dreams*, in which the innocent heroine fantasises about just such a fate.

Cast

Sid El Kar (Tom Ashcroft), Hadji (Russell Barker), Neri (Lena Heighton), Benjamin Kidd (Brian Partridge), Capt. Paul Fontaine (Michael Richardson), Margot Fontaine (Valerie Rushworth), General Birabeau (Eric Hartley), Pierre Birabeau (William John Prescott), Susan (Pauline Rice), Edith (Margaret Elliott), Azuri (Betty Cole), Ali Ben Ali (Ernest Booth), Clementina (Norma

Wick), Mindar (Robert Lunn), Hassi (John Thaxton), Lieut. La Vergne (Alan Moore), Sergeant De Boussac (Harry Dawson) Servants (Peter Garrett, Arthur Ward)

Gentlemen of the Chorus R. Barker, R. Bridgeman, W. Bridgeman, F. Cushing, A. Dalby, R. Davies, Geoffrey Debenham, E. Dunnell, Paul England, J. Garrett, Alan Goose, L. Greenacre, A. Minter, B. Richardson, Ron Say, R. Scales, A. Spelman, Frank Weyer

Ladies of the Chorus Ruby Addison, Olive Barnes, Doreen Browne, Betty Carver, Molly Cook, Isabel Copeman, Lesley Cox, Ruth Dawson, Pauline Findlow, Gertrude Freeman, Norah Gotts, Joyce Johnson, Pat Lake, Coral Newell, Norma Scarle, Thelma Smith, Alison Spencer, Bridget Sullivan, Patricia Till, Rachel Tomlinson, Kathleen Wright

Dancers Sonja Barnes, Jean Bell, Pauline Bonny, Pat Cannell, Rita Gibbons, Maureen Mitchell, Jean Roe, Pamela Waterson

1961
THE GYPSY PRINCESS

Norwich Theatre Royal, 20–25 February
Music: **Emmerich Kálmán**
Original book and lyrics: **Leo Stein and Bela Jenbach**
Book: **Conrad Carter**
Lyrics: **Phil Park**
Directors: **Frank Rydon and Frances Davis**
Musical Director: **Maurice Iliffe**

A return to continental operetta, earlier represented by *The Marriage Market* (1930) and *Sybil* (1931), this flamboyant extravaganza of Romany life came fast on the heels of the sand-blown *Desert Song*. *The Gypsy Princess* began its theatrical life in London in1921 as *Die Csárdásfürstin*. The *EDP's* review of *Kálmán's* flamboyant Romany romance decided that although this 'Musical of Monocled Aristocrats' could not be wholly classed as vintage champagne, 'it sparkles with vivacity and colour':

> Clichés may abound in the waltz-dominated score, but the show adds up to a piece of romantic escapism which, synthetic although it is, has a certain charm and a good deal of amusement. It lacks the power to make you

29. Lynn Wardle depending on the ladies in *The Gypsy Princess* (1961), another operetta from a bygone age © Eastern Daily Press, Norwich.

surrender to the stage fiction, but those many people who have no time for modern 'pop' music will find it light-heartedly entertaining.[1]

Gervase Hughes laconically remarks that the composer was prone to exploit 'wild gipsy rhythms to the full', and that when they ran riot 'audiences gladly surrendered to their magic'.[2] As for a plot, Traubner considered *The Gypsy Princess* 'in spite of general high spirits and a particularly varied score' had a book 'no more contrived or silly than others'. Those in search of profundity withdrew disappointed as the unlikely tale of romantic love between glamorous café singer Sylva Varescu (Norma Wick) and Prince Peter Von Leydersheim (Alan Temple) wound itself into knots before unravelling to their mutual satisfaction. It was Temple's first major role on stage. George Usher thought him 'inclined to stiffness' but with 'a good quality of voice for the love songs'.

Of course, one could say much the same sort of thing about John Hanson or Nelson Eddy. Much of the praise centred on Wick's portrayal of the titular royal. For Usher, 'She looks the part, acts expressively, sings with great artistry and power and all the time convinces with her theatrical know-how'. However, Usher's main laurels went to Lynn Wardle, bringing his 'comic gift' to Count

Boni, Sylva's manager. 'He overdoes it occasionally, but he is the life and soul of the party.'[3] S. J. A. in the *EEN* agreed that Wardle was 'quite outstanding' in a show that 'will possibly go down in the annals of the Society as one of its most successful efforts.'[4]

In support, Ivy Oxley and Ernest Booth injected wit into their number 'Noblesse Oblige'. There were valuable contributions from Elizabeth Moore as Countess Anastasia ('Stasi'), and an aristocratic trio comprising Terry Mobbs, John Garrett and Alan Moore. The public response was not overwhelming. Perhaps the Society's patrons were growing a little tired of flimsy Ruritanian romances that were not much like operas and sometimes were something that might be called operetta or sometimes musicals dressed up to the nines set in lands where likely as not the tankards from which the men's chorus quaffed were patently empty. Reckoning came with the fact that the show had cost £350 more to stage than the 1959 *Show Boat* and that 1,200 fewer customers had sat through the exploits of the gypsy princess.

Cast

Sylva Varescu (Norma Wick), Count Ferencz (Terry Mobbs), Andrey (Alan Moore), Count Bonifaska (Lynn Wardle), Miska (Jim Farnworth) Aranka (Elizabeth Garner), Rizzi (Pauline Rice), Juliska (Pat Lake), Flunkey (Harry Dawson), Prince Peter Von Leydersheim (Alan Temple), Captain Eugen Von Rohnsdorff (John Garrett), Kisch (Russell Barker), Prince Leopold Von Leydersheim (Ernest Booth), Princess Karen Von Leydersheim (Ivy Oxley), Countess Anastasia (Elizabeth Moore), Senator Bland (Michael Richardson), Mrs Bland (Alison Spencer), Waiter (Geoffrey Debenham)

Gentlemen of the Chorus Russell Barker, Maurice Bridgeman, Richard Bridgeman, Roy Claybon, Fred Cushing, Harry Dawson, Paul England, Percy Garrett, Alan Goose, Robert Lunn, Tony Minter, Bruce Robinson, Ron Say, Ralph Scales, Frank Weyer

Ladies of the Chorus Ruby Addison, Olive Barnes, Doreen Browne, Betty Cole, Molly Cook, Isabel Copeman, Ruth Dawson, Margaret Elliott, Gertrude Freeman, Pauline Findlow, Bridget Goose, Norah Gotts, Lena Heighton, Margaret Howard, Joyce Johnson, Norma Scarll, Beryl Shore, Thelma Smith, Alison Spencer, Pat Till, Kathleen Wright, Annie Woods

Dancers Sonja Barnes, Sheila Gosling, Christine Grint, Janet Hall, Maureen Mitchell, Sally Pearl, Elizabeth Roney, Sandra Slaughter, Janet Smith, Bernice Vickers

1962
THE STUDENT PRINCE

Norwich Theatre Royal, 26 February–3 March
Music: Sigmund Romberg
Book and lyrics: Dorothy Donnelly, based on Rudolf Bleichman's play *Old Heidelberg*, itself based on Wilhelm Meyer-Forster's story 'Karl Heinrich'
Director: Frank Rydon
Musical Director: Maurice Iliffe

Not surprisingly, some must have been considering what future the Society could look to if it continued to produce works that were so blatantly vintage. S. J. A. suggested: 'The older musicals are rapidly approaching the stage long ago reached by Victorian melodramas, which even when played straight, now seem parodies of themselves.' Perhaps, but John Hanson, with countless performances of such old warhorses of operetta under his belt, was still lifting his tankard of apparently foaming beer in the London revival of *The Student Prince* in 1968. Even in swinging London, this musical adventure of the ageing royal scholar still drew the public. If you saw it you may have seen the 65-year-old twins Violet and Gladys Bennett who every week of its 282 performance run sat through the Saturday matinee and evening performances. As Hanson told the *Sunday Times*: 'It's escapism not realism they want, away from the kitchen sink and all that – romance, melody, colour, the sweeter side of life.' As for the young, 'they come to laugh but stay to cheer'.[5]

Romberg struggled to get his work to Broadway in 1924. His producers thought his score too operatic, held their hands up in horror at the unhappy ending and were mystified as to why he demanded a large male chorus rather that a line-up of feminine cuties. At least the prince 'does nothing to conceal his identity; it seemed less preposterous than the usual Ruritanian romances that figured with numbing regularity in prior operettas'.[6] Perhaps partly because of its German associations, the 1926 London production did not have a long run, the critic James Agate observing that 'though Art has no frontiers there are some frontiers behind which there is apparently precious art'.[7] In New York *The Student Prince* reached old age as the longest running musical of the 1920s, and toured in the United States for 25 years.

In 1962 Norwich, reviews for the N&N production were mild, suggesting that resuscitating this geriatric schoolboy was not altogether wise. The orchestra was thin, and almost certainly lacked the original Broadway orchestrations. George Usher felt that:

30. The male chorus insisting on 'Drink, Drink, Drink' and holding their patently empty tankards aloft for *The Student Prince* of 1962. Courtesy of NNOS Archive.

After modern musicals and especially the post-war invasion from America, this vogue of entertainment wears a rather artificial air. It is to the credit of producer Frank Rydon, however, that he has done a great deal to give it movement, although the stage is overcrowded with a company of about 70.[8]

Vocally, the N&N's Alan Temple was ideally cast as the prince. Usher thought he tended to melodrama but sang well 'with plenty of feeling in a well-sustained line'. This student was no longer youthful, but neither were those who played the role in professional productions down the years (among them Bryan Johnson, struggling through shoddy touring versions). Nevertheless, for S. J. A. in the *EEN*, Temple 'shows improved acting form on last year but is not always convincing in emotional moments' although 'his singing is always a delight to hear'.

Newcomer Joan Edwards ('fresh and unsophisticated' with 'a sweet voice which she employs artistically') played Kathie, the Heidelberg barmaid with whom the student prince falls hopelessly in love. For S. J. A., Edwards was 'appealing rather than striking' with 'a voice not yet able to produce power without strain'. There was praise for Nick Jeffries and for the comedy pairing of Vincent Hadley and John Glyn Jones in their 'Strolling in the Park'; for S. J. A., Hadley gave the outstanding performance, but his main concern was whether the Society should still be reviving elderly operettas. In the case of *The Student Prince* 'the plot is thin even for a musical from the days when plots were the least important ingredient of such shows. The present principals make a brave effort, but it does not entirely come off.' This was a show that 'emphasises that the Society ought to think seriously of "going modern" in its future choices'.[9]

Cast

Von Mark (Alfred Goddard) Dr Engel (Nick Jeffries), Prince Karl Franz (Alan Temple), Ruder (Robert Lunn), Gretchen (Pauline Rice), Toni (Geoffrey Debenham), Detleff (Tom Ashcroft), Lucas (Tony Minter), Von Asterberg (Frank Weyer), Nicolas (Russell Barker), Kathie (Joan Edwards), Lutz (Vincent Hadley), Hubert (John Glyn Jones), Grand Duchess Anastasia (Ivy Oxley), Princess Margaret (Barbara Fielden), Capt. Tarnitz (John Garrett), Countess Leydon (Elizabeth Garner), Baron Arnheim (Michael Richardson), Rudolph Winter (Terry Mobbs).

Dancing Chorus Ann Barber, Sonja Barnes, Mary Bond, Jill Humphrey, Marye Stevenson, Bernice Vickers, Barbara Westwood, Judith Wright

Gentlemen of the Chorus Tom Ashcroft, John Bacon, David Baillie, Russell Barker, Maurice Bridgeman, Fred Cushing, Harry Dawson, Geoffrey Debenham, John Drinkwater, Paul England, Percy Garrett, Alan Goose, Robert Lunn, Tony Minter, Terry Mobbs, Alan Moore, Bruce Robinson, Michael Richardson, Ron Say, Ralph Scales, Stan Turner, Frank Weyer

Ladies of the Chorus Ruby Addison, Doreen Browne, Mary Clabon, Beth Cole, Isabel Copeman, Pauline Findlow, Elizabeth Garner, Bridget Goose, Norma Gowen, Lena Heighton, Maryann Howard, Joyce Johnson, Pat Lake, Amy Mason, Beryl Shore, Tessa Skoyles, Allison Spencer, Thelma Smith, Rosalind Welsh, Ann Whitehead, Annie Woods

1963
OKLAHOMA!

Norwich Theatre Royal, 25 February–2 March
Music: **Richard Rodgers**
Book and lyrics: **Oscar Hammerstein II**
Director: **R. D'Arcy Richards**
Musical Director: **Frederick J. Firth**

Change was in the air. In the *EDP* George Usher, who had already sat through nine N&N productions, celebrated the Society's continued existence:

> This is the first time the Society has chosen so recent a musical, and the switch in repertoire seems to have done a power of good. In audience, too, it should come out tops. Two nights at least are sold out. The escape from the conventions of some of the earlier works of the musical stage has injected

new life, particularly in the acting. The naturalistic style of the Rodgers and Hammerstein show, which can rightly be considered a classic of our times with a poetry of its own, gives the cast of about 70 freer rein for expression.

Freddy Firth's 24-piece amateur orchestra (the first non-professional orchestra in many years) 'draws interpretations which do whole-hearted justice to the well-known Rodgers' tunes. There was fulsome praise for the chorus, 'especially impressive in its visual line-up, synchronised gestures and quality of singing, developing telling crescendos – just one instance of the excellent training this season'. There was regret that in the ballet that closed act one 'the sex element is perhaps a bit reticent', but the company was strongly cast. James Aldous as Curley and Norma Wick as Laurey made an attractive pairing, even if Wick may not have seemed ideal casting for reticent, shy Laurey. Their duet 'People Will Say We're in Love' benefitted from Wick's 'splendidly controlled voice'. Together, 'they make the main love duet tug at the heart strings, so feelingly is it sung'. Usher's only complaint was that the performers could sometimes not be heard. Nick Jeffries as Jud and some others in leading roles were not always audible: 'they do not always project their voices and words clearly'. He reserved his greatest welcome for Angela Hallam's debut with the Society as Ado Annie. She was 'a real discovery for a soubrette role, with a characteristic corncrake voice for the part and a winning way of putting over a wisecrack'.[10]

For the *EEN*, S. J. A. shared Usher's enthusiasm, praising the principals and welcoming Aldous who 'acts with vigour and sings with great polish', and Wick in 'a moving performance which is both sung and characterised extremely well'. He paused only to suggest that 'there are some signs that this is a trip into new territory':

> The acting in places is perhaps inclined to be a little more declamatory than the style of the modern musical demands however suitable such acting might be for the shows written in pre-war days. And the accent of one or two of the players slip a little on occasion. But the great thing is that these performances generate plenty of energy, and the show breezes along like the wind over Oklahoma's prairies. Both the Society and its public have every reason to be delighted with the decision to 'go modern'. You can sense in this production the emergence of a new vitality.[11]

The show was seen by 9,117 patrons.

Cast

Aunt Eller (Ivy Oxley), James Aldous (Curley), Laurey (Norma Wick), Ike Skidmore (Tom Ashcroft), Slim (Terry Mobbs), Will Parker (Lynn Wardle), Jud Fry (Nick Jeffries), Ado Annie Carnes (Angela Hallam), Ali Hakim (Michael Richardson), Gertie Cummins (Pauline Rice), Ellen (Pat Lake), Andrew Carnes (Harold Mould), Cord Elam (Alan Goose), Vivienne (Betty Cole), Virginia (Rosalind Welsh), Faye (Tessa Skoyles), Aggie Pigtails (Linda Moore)

Gentlemen of the Chorus David Baillie, Russell Barker, Maurice Bridgeman, Richard Bridgeman, John Cole, Fred Cushing, Harry Dawson, Geoffrey Debenham, John Drinkwater, Paul England, Percy Garrett, Alex Hewitt, Raymond Light, Robert Lunn, David MacJannett, Tony Minter, Roger Plunkett, Ron Say, Ralph Scales, Andrew Slatter, Frank Weyer

Ladies of the Chorus Ruby Addison, Doreen Browne, Mary Clabon, Isabel Copeman, Gertrude Freeman, Judie Frost, Elizabeth Garner, Christine Garrood, Norma Gowen, Lena Heighton, Joyce Johnson, Ann MacJannett, Thelma Smith, Alison Spencer, Marye Stevenson, Sheila Temple, Ann Whitehead

In the Ballet Laurey (Janet Russon), Curley (David Baillie), Jud (David MacJannett)

Dancing Chorus Ann Barber, Sonya Barnes, Mary Bond, Patricia Brandish, Jean Carter, Wendy Farrell, Jacqueline May, Barbara Peskett, Bernice Vickers, Barbara Westwood

1964
PINK CHAMPAGNE

Norwich Theatre Royal, 24–29 February
Music: Johann Strauss, adapted by Bernard Grun
Book and lyrics: Eric Maschwitz and Bernard Grun
Director: D'Arcy Richards
Musical Director: Frederick J. Firth

Maschwitz is probably best remembered today as the lyricist of 'These Foolish Things' (music by Jack Strachey) and 'A Nightingale Sang in Berkeley Square' (music by Manning Sherwin) but was librettist and lyricist for many London musicals that subsequently proved popular with amateur companies including *Balalaika* (1936), *Paprika* (1938), *Magyar Melody* (1939), *Evangeline* (1946), *Carissima* (1948), *Belinda Fair* (1949), *Love from Judy* (1952), *Zip Goes a Million* (1951), *Romance in Candlelight* (1955), *Summer Song* (1956) adapted from the music of Dvorak, and the disastrous *Happy Holiday* (1952), a misguided attempt to make a musical out of Arnold Ridley's play *The Ghost Train*. Maschwitz remembered:

> I sat in gloomy hotel rooms, writing and rewriting on a diet of sandwiches. By the time the play opened in London I was almost a nervous wreck. I grew angry, then practically went on my knees [to the producer Emile Littler] begging not to be associated with the enterprise.

31. Ersatz operetta? The 1964 *Pink Champagne* © A. R. Miller Photography, Bungay.

During his collaborations with the composer George Posford he wrote a musical version of Tom Robertson's David Garrick play *Masquerade* for the Baltic Operatic Society, and with Bernard Grun wrote bespoke versions for amateur performance including adaptations of *Die Fledermaus, Night in Venice, The Dubarry* and *White Horse Inn*. Maschwitz also holds the record for the shortest West End run, his 1953 play *Thirteen for Dinner* opening and closing on the same night.

First produced in 1958 as an amateur production at London's Scala Theatre, *Pink Champagne* was another theatrical impostor, adapted from Johann Strauss's 1874 *Die Fledermaus*, a work considered by Hughes as 'the apotheosis of Viennese operetta'. For critic Stephen Amyes, Strauss' masterpiece had been adapted 'in a manner calculated to give more appeal to modern popular taste'. He looked on it with a wry eye: 'Whether it is a good thing to present refurbished old operettas when so much worthwhile that is new is there to be done is a matter for some consideration'. Furthermore, 'modern youngsters are going to find it all a trifle "square"'.

In his second production for the Society D'Arcy Richards (according to the theatre programme 'well known throughout the British Isles as a Producer of Amateur Societies and adjudicator at festivals') 'has given it about as much vigour as it will stand'. For Amyes, the show needed a brisker pace for the champagne to sparkle, but he commended the players, not least Norma Wick as Rosalinda ('a commanding bravura and expert mastery of the vocal line').

Tom Ashcroft as Rosalinda's admirer Alfred, Geoffrey Debenham (a teacher at the City of Norwich School) as a lawyer, Harold Mould as the bibulous prison governor and Michael Richardson as his Chief Warder Frosch provided much of the comedy. Bridget Grief was an ideal Adele ('the sort of twinkling performance most in the mood of the piece') and Lynn Wardle dapper as Dr Falke.[12]

The headline for George Usher's review in the *EDP* promised 'An Evening with the King of Waltzes' in a show that allowed for 'far wider vocal scope, especially for choral ensembles' supported by Frederick Firth and his 29-piece orchestra of local musicians that ploughed on as 'the audience kept up a bad-mannered buzz of conversation during the overture'. Never mind: musically, *Pink Champagne* represents an advance'. There was praise, too, for Alan Temple's Gabriel Eisenstein. Although not a natural actor, Temple was a friendly, assured presence on stage, now 'more confident and better-voiced'.[13]

Strauss had to wait until 1982 before the Society got round to the genuine *Die Fledermaus*. Meanwhile, no matter how pink the champagne, this is a choice of show that suggests the Society was marking time and reminds us that, once uncorked, champagne may quickly go flat.

Cast

Mitzi (Tessa Skoyles), Adele (Bridget Grief), Ida (Rosalind Welsh), Lea (Betty Cole), Lilli (Pamela Jackson), Rosalinda (Norma Wick), Gabriel Eisenstein (Alan Temple), Alfred (Tom Ashcroft), Dr Blind (Geoffrey Debenham), Dr Falke (Lynn Wardle), Frau Trauber (Elizabeth Garner), Frank (Harold Mould), Frosch (Michael Richardson), Prince Orlovsky (Peter Winter), Holtzapfel (Alan Moore)

Gentlemen of the Chorus Russell Barker, Maurice Bridgeman, Richard Bridgeman, John Cole, Fred Cushing, Harry Dawson, John Drinkwater, Keith Ellis, Paul England, Percy Garrett, Alan Goose, Michael Hilling, Alex Hewitt, Raymond Laight, David MacJannett, Tony Minter, Ron Say, Andrew Slatter, Frank Weyer

Ladies of the Chorus Ruby Addison, Diana Blasby, Doreen Browne, Mary Clabon, Isabel Copeman, Sheila Dix, Gertrude Freeman, Pauline Findlow, Christine Garrood, Bridget Goose, Norma Gowen, Josephine Gregory, Lena Heighton, Joyce Johnson, Ann MacJannett, Pauline Rice, Alison Spencer, Thelma Smith, Ann Whitehead

Dancing Chorus Solo Dancer (Janet Russon), Ann Barber, Sonya Barnes, Mary Bond, Jean Carter, Sheena Farrell, Wendy Farrell, Margaret Land, Jackie May, Linda Moore, Jacqueline Pond, Bernice Vickers, Barbara Westwood

1965
THE MERRY WIDOW

Norwich Theatre Royal, 22–27 February
Music: Franz Lehár, adapted by Ronald Hanmer
Musical Director: Frederick J. Firth
Original book and lyrics: Victor Léon and Leo Stein
New book and lyrics: Phil Park
Director: D'Arcy Richards
Musical Director: Frederick J. Firth

Having directed 1963's *Oklahoma!* and 1964's *Pink Champagne*, D'Arcy Richards returned for his final N&N assignment with Lehár's *The Merry Widow*, probably the quintessence of Austro-Hungarian operetta. In his brilliant survey of the genre Richard Traubner persuades us that 'There is no better symbol for the *fin-de-siècle*, pre-World Wars era', a work that has come to 'represent a historical age which has in fact been described as one great operetta itself, with its uniforms, its balls, its political intrigue, and its intoxicating glamour'.[14] Its sturdiness even survived being 'adapted' by Ronald Hanmer and Phil Park's libretto based on Léon and Stein's version adapted from Henri Meilhac's play *L'Attaché Ambassade*. *The Merry Widow* first appeared at the Theater an der Wien in December 1905.

The box-office takings suggested a flop but, by the end of 1907, the work was enjoying huge success in almost all cities of the German-speaking world. International productions proliferated. In London it ran through 778 performances and made a star of twenty-one-year-old Lily Elsie in the title role. King Edward VII went four times. The Broadway production began a vogue for associated merchandise such as Merry Widow cigarettes, Merry Widow gowns, hats and (more daringly) Merry Widow corsets. Here was a work that both revived and transformed European operetta, a genre with which the N&N had been closely associated in its early years via *Les Cloches de Corneville* (1926), *The Little Michus* (1929), *The Marriage Market* (1930) and *Sybil* (1931) before returning to domestic product with the Gilbert and Sullivan repertoire, and switching back to operetta through much of the 1960s.

Perhaps the N&N was encouraged to turn to the widow because a Sadler's Wells 1958 revival with June Bronhill had been an outstanding success. A theatrical sensation, the popularity of Lehár's operetta seemed unstoppable and

> crowning the score was a waltz, simple yet haunting both in itself and in the way it functioned in the work. What most people thought of as 'The Merry Widow Waltz' went to the heart of the new operetta genre in its psychological use of music and movement to reveal emotional truths where words failed.

'Anna Glavari' NORMA WICK

'Valencienne' BRIDGET GRIEF

'Count Danilo' CHRISTOPHER SPEAKE

'Baron Zeta' HAROLD MOULD

Photographs by: Montague, St. John Maddermarket, Norwich

32. *The Merry Widow*. Four principals pose for the 1965 theatre programme
© Montague, St. John Maddermarket, Norwich.

In fact, 'The suppressed emotional power in the combination of wordless song and dance overwhelmed audiences'.[15]

Frequently revived on stage, it also found its way into film studios. Erich von Stroheim directed a silent movie version in 1925 (a boon to those who enjoy nothing more than silent operetta), followed by Ernst Lubitsch's 1934 black and white MGM talkie (and 'singie') starring Jeanette MacDonald and Maurice Chevalier, and MGM's 1952 Technicolor remake with Lana Turner as a rather unlikely widow. The *EDP*'s review recognised the show as 'in the Viennese tradition of the N&N' but wondered

> how far it will attract the young is debatable. Certainly its famous tunes live on. Will it be possible to say the same of present-day songs by the end of the century? The style, however, has become elusive. It is hard now to conjure up its combination of elegance and twinkling allure from a period which now seems almost as remote as the mediaeval.

In the circumstances, director D'Arcy Richards 'cannot really be said to recapture it and yet it has other merits which make a revival worthwhile'. These revolved around the playing of the widow to which 'Norma Wick brings her charming stage presence [...] with the vocal resources too. She sings with great conviction and considerable art, very telling in "Vilja". Her Danilo was Christopher Speake, who would play the role again in 1979 opposite Coral Newell, and there was strong casting in support, with the always welcome on any stage Bridget Grief and Tom Ashcroft as the second pair of lovers, with comedy provided by Harold Mould and Michael Richardson.

In the glow of retrospect, the awarding of the title role to Wick seemed inevitable at this point in the Society's history. She was its most resourceful and popular performer at this point of time, perhaps the only one on the Society's books whose entrance raised an audience to applause. She could radiate glamour, but it was never a barrier between her and the stalls or the dress circle (to which she could easily fire off salvos of theatrical effectiveness). Her talent was totally natural. Audiences felt safe with her, knew the sense of adventure she brought on from the wings. Her singing of Lehár's score would have been very different from that of Coral Newell in the N&N's revival of 1979. If there was any opportunity for comedy, Wick would have identified and exploited it, taking the audience into her confidence. She had a close relationship with the people in the dark. On stage, with her brass-playing husband Derek in the pit, she was never less than the complete professional. When she left the stage, something of the audience's warmth walked off with her.

Derek was one of the 24-piece orchestra, many musicians from the Norwich Philharmonic, providing a 'first class contribution with some beautiful waltz playing and plenty of verve'. Meanwhile, the theatre programme's photographs of the N&N's principals suggests that, midway through the 1960s, it may not have been a company where younger performers might thrive.

Cast

Anna, Madama Glawari (Norma Wick), Danilo (Christopher Speake), Baron Zeta (Harold Mould), Valencienne (Bridget Grief), Camille (Tom Ashcroft), Njegus (Michael Richardson), St Brioche (Alan Temple), Cascada (Peter Winter), Kromov (Geoffrey Debenham), Olga (Pamela Jackson), Bogdanovitsch (Alan Goose), Pritsch (Keith Ellis), Sylvia (Josephine Gregory), Praskovia (Betty Cole), Grisettes (Sonya Barnes, Sheena Farrell, Wendy Farrell, Norma Gowen, Elizabeth Hellard, Alison Spencer)

Gentlemen of the Chorus Maurice Bridgeman, Richard Bridgeman, John Cole, Fred Cushing, Harry Dawson, John Drinkwater, Paul England, Percy Garrett, Michael Hilling, Raymond Laight, David MacJannett, Tony Minter, Ron Say, Andrew Slatter, Frank Weyer

Ladies of the Chorus Ruby Addison, Doreen Browne, Mary Cooke, Sheila Dix, Pauline Findlow, Gertrude Freeman, Elizabeth Garner, Christine Garrood, Norma Gowen, Elizabeth Hellard, Joyce Johnson, Ann MacJannett, Diana Newby, Pauline Robinson, Alison Spencer, Rosalind Wade, Rosalind Welsh, Ann Whitehead, Kathleen Wright

Dancers Ann Barber, Sonya Barnes, Mary Bilham, Jean Carter, Sheena Farrell, Wendy Farrell, Margaret Land, Jackie May, Elizabeth Rush, Bernice Vickers

1966
BRIGADOON

Norwich Theatre Royal, 7–12 February
***Music*:** Frederick Loewe
***Book and lyrics*:** Alan Jay Lerner
***Director*:** Willie Martin
***Musical Director*:** Frederick J. Firth

The arrival of director Willie Martin seemed to signal a change of policy in the company. As the *EDP* exclaimed 'Operatic Society Score with Switch to Modern'.[16] Martin brought a wealth of experience, having produced the Moscow State Circus at Wembley (he spoke five languages and knew enough Russian to say 'Let's do it again!'), danced in the 1956 London Palladium panto *The Wonderful Lamp*, and for the Royal Ballet, produced a Jimmy Jewell and Ben Warris variety show at Yarmouth's Britannia Pier, and played Puck at the Old Vic. Steve James detected 'a most lively and mercurial air

33. 'Come to Me, Bend to Me': Margaret Elliott and supporters in *Brigadoon* (1966) © Eastern Daily Press, Norwich.

about him', impressed that Martin was 'meticulous' regarding movement and inflection. He did not tolerate amateurism, telling James that 'Some amateurs are inclined to think they're doing their audience a favour by appearing. That's the wrong attitude. If you're actively interested in the theatre the great thing is not to think what you're going to get out of it but what you're going to give to it.'[17]

The gloriously romantic fantasy that is *Brigadoon*, with its backward glance at the plot of James Hilton's *Lost Horizon*, was one of the most successful and skilfully assembled post-war American musicals, with a London run of 687 performances. A wealth of melody and sentiment swirled around the story of a mythical Scottish settlement that every century comes to life for one day. It is into this mystical world that two young American men step, crossing the bridge that will lead to the final curtain's most thrillingly emotional moment. The quality of the score is unquestionable, at its most fulsome in the sauntering 'The Heather on the Hill' and ebullient 'Almost Like Being in Love'. One of the show's finest achievements is to imbue the piece with numbers that seem exclusively to belong to Brigadoon itself, with moments of high drama. The final scene of the play, before the mist envelops it again for another hundred years, retains the work's potent theatricality as it reunites the real world's Tommy and

Brigadoon's Fiona (Bridget Grief). Mr Lundie, a wise elder of Brigadoon, tells Tommy, 'When you love someone deeply anything is possible. Even miracles.'

G. W. U. thought that audiences 'are likely to vote it the most enjoyable show the Society has done for some years, and it is certainly the best acted'. Stephen Amyes was in no doubt: 'Taken all round, this is the best-acted, best choreographed and best-danced show, best-directed'. The casting approached perfection, with Christopher Speake as Tommy singing one of the finest of Lerner and Loewe's ballads 'There But For You Go I', although Amyes gave the vocal palm to Charlie (George Baker making his debut with the company). Here was a tenor whose every word was crystal clear and reminded G. W. U. of Kenneth McKellar. Equally notable were Margaret Elliott as Jean, Grief's gently light-voiced Fiona, and Norma Wick as Brigadoon's soubrette Meg Brockie tearing up the house in her brilliant comedy numbers 'The Love of My Life' and 'My Mother's Wedding Day'. There were notable appearances from a sword-dancing Lynn Wardle, City of Norwich schoolteacher Geoffrey Debenham as wise Mr Murdoch, Michael Richardson as Tommy's friend Jeff, and Janet Russon as Maggie.[18]

Cast

Tommy Albright (Christopher Speake), Jeff Douglas (Michael Richardson), Angus MacMonies (Maurice Bridgeman), Donald Ritchie (Peter Winter), Sandy (Frank Weyer), Maggie Abernethy (Janet Russon), MacGregor (Jeremy Andrew), Stuart Cameron (Tom Ashcroft), Harry Ritchie (Lynn Wardle), Meg Brockie (Norma Wick), Andrew McKeith (Alan Goose), Fiona (Bridget Grief), Jean (Margaret Elliott), Charlie Cameron (George Baker), Mr Murdoch (Geoffrey Debenham), Frank (Keith Ellis), Jane Ashton (Betty Cole), Piper (Ian Marr)

Gentlemen of the Chorus John Cole, Fred Cushing, Harry Dawson, Paul England, Percy Garrett, Michael Hilling, Raymond Laight, David MacJannett, Tony Minter, Ron Say, Andrew Slatter

Ladies of the Chorus Ruby Addison, Doreen Browne, Ruth Dawson, Pauline Findlow, Gertrude Freeman, Elizabeth Garner, Bridget Goose, Norma Gowen, Josephine Gregory, Margaret Hall, Beryl Halliday, Dorothy Hargreaves, Elizabeth Hellard, Pamela Jackson, Joyce Johnson, Ann MacJannett, Diana Newby, Pauline Robinson, Wendy Scott, Beryl Shore, Alison Spencer, Rosalind Wade, Rosalind Welsh, Ann Whitehead, Kathleen Wright

Dancers Mary Bilham, Jean Carter, Wendy Farrell, Jackie May, Elizabeth Rush, Bernice Vickers, John Cole, Keith Ellis, Raymond Laight, David MacJannett, Roger Plunkett, Frank Weyer

1967
SONG OF NORWAY

Norwich Theatre Royal, 23–28 January
Music and lyrics: **Robert Wright and George Forrest, adapted from the music of Edvard Grieg**
Book: **Milton Lazarus, adapted from the play by Homer Curran**
Director: **Willie Martin**
Musical Director: **Frederick Firth**

The second and final production directed by Willie Martin, the very Norwegian *Song of Norway* (New York 1944, London 1946) was the first of many musical concoctions by the American team of Robert Wright and George Forrest. They collaborated in the manufacture of operettas-cum-musicals that plundered, reused, reorganised and exploited the music of 'classical' composers, the first of their works involving the music of Edvard Grieg. Their collaboration subsequently turned for inspiration and musical motifs to Victor Herbert in *Gypsy Lady*, Villa-Lobos in *Magdelena*, Borodin in *Kismet*, Rachmaninoff in *Anya*, and Strauss in *The Great Waltz*. Now, it was Grieg's turn to be remodelled for the lighter musical stage, exemplified via the dramatic power of Grieg's A-Minor Piano Concerto, its magnificence now accentuated by a fantasy ballet, 'commendably well done'.

At the first night the company was buoyed up by knowing it had a full house and record bookings. For the *EEN* critic Stephen Amyes there was no doubt that, as Louisa Giovanni,

> Norma Wick stands right out. As a singer she has the edge over any of the rest of the cast; as an actress, she knocks spots off most of them. Her fiery and temperamental Italian prima donna in this show is the best thing I have seen her do – a portrayal full of personality and character. It is a superb performance.

George Baker's Grieg was 'another very well-sung role, though the character as such does not quite make the impact it should'. Pip Jenkinson, a newcomer to the Society, played Grieg's fiancée, 'pleasantly sung but a little colourless, due in no small measure to the writing of the role'. Amyes did not think much of the plot (no wonder; as he claimed, it was 'conventional and unconvincing') but thought:

> The music is the outstanding ingredient of this show and here it is on the whole splendidly performed – by the singers, both solo and chorus, by the orchestra under Frederick Firth, the show's musical director, and by

Kathron Sturrock, the solo pianist – in a ballet version of Grieg's concerto. Miss Sturrock is a young player of most promising talent and power.

There were warm words for Jenkinson too, 'her performance of the famous love song one of the best solos of the evening'. Baker was complimented on his 'attractive voice', 'but he could develop the role more romantically.'

The headline for the *EDP* review by G. W. U. happily proclaimed 'Triangle story to Grieg's music sells the tickets', but Mr Usher had warning words, alerting readers that 'One approaches the pastiche of an operetta tongue-in-cheek [but] Whatever the purists might say about those words added to the instrumental tunes, the production at the Theatre Royal this week, directed by Willie Martin, has virtually sold out from the start.' There were warm words for Jenkinson, 'her performance of the famous love song one of the best solos of the evening', and Baker was complimented on his 'attractive voice', 'but he could develop the role more romantically'. In fact, 'The singing varied considerably in quality last night, but the precision in the choruses again showed the influence of Frederick Firth as musical director.' Ultimately, 'Norma Wick, cast as "the other woman" this time, dominated again. As the prima donna Louisa Giovanni, she became the living image of artistic temperament, with just as much fire in her singing, too.'

Cast

Rikard Nordraak (Tom Ashcroft), Sigrid (Jennifer Hill), Einar (Malcolm Shaw), Eric (Kenneth Browning), Gunnar (Jill Harvey), Grimma (Sally-Anne Spruce), Helga (Sally Hudson), Nina Hagerup (Pip Jenkinson), Edvard Grieg (George Baker), Father Nordraak (Geoffrey Debenham), Father Grieg (Stanley Gibson), Mother Grieg (Elizabeth Garner), Freddy (Lynn Wardle), Count Peppi Le Loup (Michael Richardson), Louisa Giovanni (Norma Wick), Professor Helma (Andrew Slatter), Frau Professor Norden (Beryl Halliday), Elvera (Josephine Gregory), Margharetta (Betty Cole), Hedwig (Margaret Elliott), Greta (Pauline Robinson), Miss Anders (Pamela Jackson), Henrik Ibsen (Alan Goose), Tito (Lynn Wardle), Waitresses (Jean Carter, Barbara Peskett), Maestro Pisoni (Christopher Speake), Adelina (Janet Russon). Characters in 'The Concerto Ballet': Spirit of Norway (Janet Russon), Cavalier (William Martin), Spirit of Grieg (Lynn Wardle), Spirit of Nordraak (Keith Ellis)

Gentlemen of the Chorus Maurice Bridgeman, John Cole, Fred Cushing, Harry Dawson, Keith Ellis, Paul England, Percy Garrett, Michael Hilling, John Humphreys, Raymond Laight, David MacJannett, Ron Say, Frank Weyer

Ladies of the Chorus Ruby Addison, Janet Blyth, Doreen Browne, Gertrude Freeman, Pauline Findlow, Bridget Goose, Norma Gowen, Barbara Halliday, Dorothy Hargreaves, Elizabeth Hellard, Faith Humphreys, Joyce Johnson,

Anne MacJannett, Diana Newby, Nora Platt, Beryl Shore, Alison Spencer, Rosalind Wade, Ann Whitehead

Dancers Mary Bilham, Jean Carter, Patsy Citron, Mary Edwards, Margaret Fawcett, Wendy Farrell, Vivian Fleetwood, Glen MacKeith, Sarah Martin, Barbara Peskett, Elizabeth Rush, Bernice Vickers, John Cole

1968
ROSE MARIE

Norwich Theatre Royal, 12–17 February
Music: **Rudolf Friml and Herbert Stothart**
Book and lyrics: **Otto Harbach and Oscar Hammerstein II**
Producer: **Frances Davis**
Musical Director: **Maurice Iliffe**

One of the great survivors from the halcyon days of American operetta, *Rose Marie* had the longest London run of any musical of the 1920s, opening in 1925 and revived in 1942 and again in 1960. In February 1954 Norwich Theatre Royal even offered *Rose Marie on Ice* with a skating chorus of 50 and the special novelty of 'The Mounties in Their Wheel', said to revolve at the potentially dangerous speed of 30 miles an hour. How many of the audience attending the British premiere of the American musical *Little Mary Sunshine* at the Theatre Royal in May 1962 realised this delightful little show by Rick Besoyan was a parody of such shows as *Rose-Marie* – even though we might consider the original *Rose Marie* to be almost parodying itself? Besoyan's happy pastiche had Patricia Routledge and Terence Cooper singing their 'Colorado Love Call', an obvious tilt at *Rose-Marie*'s 'Indian Love Call'.

In Norwich, director Frances Davis ('a film star at eight' according to the programme), and musical director Maurice Iliffe, returning as musical director after a five-year absence, assembled a strong company. As heroic fur trapper Jim Kenyon, Alan Temple was admired more for his singing than his acting, as he wooed Rose-Marie played by Sylvia Dix (late Hogg) in a triumphant return to the company as its leading lady, 'in excellent command of the songs'. Spectacle with the backcloth of the Canadian Rockies was always an essential component of this war-horse of operetta, exemplified by the Totem Dance, staged here as a fluorescent extravaganza. The appearance of girls in miniskirts at least acknowledged that somewhere beyond the theatre's doors the sixties were swinging.

34. Sylvia Dix and her Mounties in the 1968 *Rose Marie*
© Eastern Daily Press, Norwich.

The headline for Stephen Amyes' review was 'Corn and Syrup Never Bettered'. He recognised 'plenty of verve from the whole company, with well-controlled singing and nearly always vivid acting, singling out Christopher Speake's Hard-Hearted Herman as 'first-class in every way'. Speake seems to have overcome the leaden comedy lines. (Question: 'Why do you wear spurs?' Answer: 'Well, you never know when you may meet a horse'.) The eminent critic J. C. Trewin called such material 'the laborious irrelevances of the funny man'. Happily, Speake was surrounded by experienced principals, not least the soubrettish Pauline Rice, George Baker, Tom Ashcroft and Norma Wick. The production seems to have been a sell-out, with the long-loved songs by Rudolf Friml and Herbert Stothart providing a nostalgic link back to the 1920s, interspersed with Harbach and Hammerstein II's libretto. Nevertheless Amyes signed off with 'Next year, I hope we shall see what the Society can do with something more modern.'

Cast

Sergeant Malone (George Baker), Lady Jane (Pauline Robinson), Black Eagle (Roger Fossett), Edward Hawley (Michael Richardson), Emile la Flamme (Tom Ashcroft), Wanda (Norma Wick), Hard-Boiled Herman (Christopher Speake),

Jim Kenyon (Alan Temple), Rose Marie la Flamme (Sylvia Dix), Ethel Brander (Margaret Elliott), Caretaker (Alan Goose)

Gentlemen of the Chorus Maurice Bridgeman, John Cole, Fred Cushing, Harry Dawson, Keith Ellis, Paul England, Percy Garrett, Alan Goose, Michael Hilling, Raymond Laight, David MacJannett, Tony Minter, Peter Mottram, Roger Plunkett, Ron Say, Donald Shankshaft, Andrew Slatter, Frank Weyer

Ladies of the Chorus Ruby Addison, Miriam Batterbee, Doreen Browne, Sheila Dix, Pauline Findlow, Gertrude Freeman, Elizabeth Garner, Bridget Goose, Norma Gowen, Josephine Gregory, Beryl Halliday, Pip Jenkinson, Pat Jermy, Joyce Johnson, Ann MacJannett, Norma Platt, Jenny Pryke, Violet Shaves, Beryl Shore, Alison Spencer, Rosalind Wade, Cynthia Ward, Ann Whitehead, Kathleen Wright

Dancers Lorna Ashworth, Mary Bilham, Jean Carter, Mary Edwards, Wendy Farrell, Margaret Fawcett, Vivian Fleetwood, Sarah Martin, Jacqueline May, Barbara Peskett, Dawn Peters, Bernice Vickers

1969
KISMET

Norwich Theatre Royal, 10–15 February
Music and lyrics: **Robert Wright and George Forrest, based on the themes of Alexander Borodin**
Book: **Charles Lederer and Luther Davis, based on a play by Edward Knoblock**
Director: **Frances Davis**
Musical Director: **David Kett**

Wright and Forrest were two of the greatest Broadway borrowers working in American musical theatre between the mid-1940s until 1970, making musicals from the catalogues of classical composers. They proved more artistically and commercially successful than the British team of Eric Maschwitz and Bernard Grun's attempts at cobbling a show together from the work of dead and gone composers.

Thus, Wright and Forrest's *Song of Norway* (N&N 1967) made ample use of Grieg, *Gypsy Lady* of Victor Herbert, *Magdalena* of Villa-Lobos, *Anya* of Rachmaninoff, and *The Great Waltz* of Johann Strauss. *Kismet* turned over the pages of Alexander Borodin's scores, plundering his String Quartet in D for

35.   *Kismet* (1969). Courtesy of NNOS Archive.

'Baubles, Bangles and Beads' and 'And This Is My Beloved', and his Polovtsian Dances for the beguiling 'Stranger in Paradise'. These joined the writers' effective and often muscular original score.

A Broadway success, the West End production depended in no small measure on the casting of Hajj, and enjoyed the luxury of importing the Broadway production's Alfred Drake, one of the outstanding leading men of his period, virile and theatrically effective. The *Sketch* thought Drake 'Douglas Fairbanks re-born'. *Punch* described 'a personality with voice, poise, dash, huge authority and the most talkative pair of hands in the West End of London'.

Where could the N&N find his equivalent in East Anglia? Advertisements invited contenders for the role, but none materialised. Frances Davis had previously directed *Kismet* with John Collett, a 48-year-old deputy manager at the Atomic Commission in Wessex. The committee decided that he would be invited to play the role. For G. W. U., Collett's Hajj was 'the biggest asset the performance could have, with all the panache for the role, acting which is always alive and the theatrical know-how in the use of his fine baritone voice'.

On the male side there was the added advantage of another newcomer in Wymondham's John Dunsire, 'most promising in vocal quality', now partnering Pip Jenkinson ('a light-voiced heroine') as Hajj's daughter. Stephen Aymes thought the production 'the most lively and colourful show the Society has presented in recent years' with a feast of choreography in which 'many a bare

36. An unjustly unappreciated gem from 1962. Thank heaven for its original London cast recording LP! © PYE Records, Printed and made by Garrod & Lofthouse Ltd.

midriff is sported but the show generally is a little reticent about the appeal which was obviously one of the authors' intentions'. Norma Wick added spice to the mix as Lalume.

G. W. U. complained that the orchestra 'lacked polish', an opinion that too often dogged productions throughout the years. Perhaps it is just as well that the orchestra almost certainly was not confronted by the original luxurious orchestrations by Arthur Kay, to which they almost certainly would not have done justice.

As late as 2007 *Kismet* was revived at the London Coliseum, widely ridiculed and according to *The Times* 'about as alluring as an Arabian night at Woolworths'. At the time of the Iraq War, this merry, all-singing, all-dancing oriental excursion to happy Baghdad seemed somewhat inappropriate.

Cast

Imam of the Mosque (Alan Temple), Muezzins (George Baker, Frank Weyer, Kathleen Wright), Beggars (Christopher Speake, Peter Mottram, Raymond Laight), Omar (Stanley Gibson), Public Poet, later called Hajj (John Collett), Marsinah (Pip Jenkinson), Hassan-Ben (Barry Saull), Jawan (Leonard Vince), Akbar (John Bill), Assiz (David MacJannett), Bangelman (Alan Temple), Chief Policeman (Peter inter), Wazir of Police (Michael Richardson), Lalume (Norma Wick), Three Princesses of Abadu (Janet Russon, Bernice Vickers, Ann McLeod), Caliph (John Dunsire), Servant (Julian High), Princess Zubbediya of Damascus (Anita Burrage), Ayah to Zubbediya (Kathleen Wright), Princess Samaris of Bangalore (Margaret Fawcett), Widow Yussef (Pauline Robinson), Servant (Christopher Speake)

Gentlemen of the Chorus George Baker, John Bill, Maurice Bridgeman, John Cole, Fred Cushing, Keith Ellis, Paul England, Percy Garrett, Alan Goose, Michael Hilling, Raymond Laight, David MacJannett, Tony Minter, Peter Mottram, Ron Say, Donald Shackshaft, Ernest Shaves, Andrew Slatter, Alan Temple, Frank Weyer

Ladies of the Chorus Ruby Addison, Jenny Batch, Joan Blake, Betty Cole, Sheila Dix, Sylvia Dix, June Dunsire, Margaret Elliott, Pauline Findlow, Gertrude Freeman, Elizabeth Garner, Bridget Goose, Norma Gowen, Josephine Gregory, Pat Jermy, Joyce Johnson, Barbara Lewis, Ann MacJannett, Nora Platt, Pauline Robinson, Violet Shaves, Beryl Shore, Alison Spencer, Cynthia Ward, Ann Whitehead, Kathleen Wright

Dancers Anita Burrage, Jean Carter, Margaret Fawcett, Vivian Fleetwood, Kathryn Garrod, Joan Huggins, Sarah Martin, Barbara Peskett

The 1970s

In 1975, the Society's 50th anniversary was marked by a production of *King's Rhapsody*, the last of Ivor Novello's hugely successful British musicals in the manner of operetta. In conversation with Charles Roberts ('C. V. R' of the *Eastern Daily Press*) three of the company's senior committee members who had been stalwarts of the Society since the 1930s reflected on the Society's achievements: Chairman Geoffrey Browne, Vice Chairman H. T. G. Tinkler (a man of great warmth and vivacity known as Tinks), and Ivy Oxley who came out of retirement to play the non-singing role of Queen Mother.

They considered that in the Society's early years being an amateur was taken very seriously, 'Not as today when the serious business is to attract a big box office in order to pay an enormous theatre rental and awesome production costs, but in the way one approached it.'

Browne explained:

> Up to the war years, amateurs looked upon being in a Society like this one as something they had to do strictly to a high standard. It was their first hobby. Now there are so many distractions that there is not – dare I say it? – the same sense of loyalty. Young people just don't take it as seriously as we used to.

We may point to theatrical or personality tourism, when members of the Society no longer feel obliged to stay with one company but roam to other companies, possibly (understandably) in search of plum roles, but this was happening long before the 1970s. It does not take away from the devotion of many of the acting members who make themselves available for the next N&N production without the urge for a leading role. Some have realised the potency of the cameo role, the fleeting appearance that detracts attention away from the leading players. Some have made their reputations in cameo roles, drip-feeding their faithful public. Looking back on Geoffrey Browne's comments there is clear evidence that at the time of writing, young people are still wholeheartedly willing to commit themselves to the N&N. Without them, there would be no future for the Society.

1970

WHITE HORSE INN

Norwich Theatre Royal, 23–28 February
English book and lyrics: Harry Graham, adapted from the original German by Hans Müller and Erik Charell
Director: Frances Davis
Musical Director: David Kett

The Tyrolean spectacular operetta had been a major success for the company in 1958. Its revival 12 years on proved that this old theatrical warhorse, which had already inspired countless productions including many on ice, had by no means had its day. In 1970, it was performed by 73 British amateur operatic societies. George Usher for the *EDP* offered reasons for the show's longevity:

> What a variety of stage pictures it creates in Tyrolean setting and dress. How many other musicals offer quite the same range of parts or the same opportunities for different types of spectacular ensemble? The N&N is able to cast all the principal roles successfully, having a group of members combining the attributes of vocal talent, acting ability and looks.

His comments were helpful. The dialogue needed to be speeded up, the stage was sometimes 'cluttered to bursting point', there was 'cautious restraint at start of the show', and the dance routines 'inclined to be confusing mixtures of tap and straightforward steps', although in general 'everything zipped along with the degree of confidence which is half of the secret of success on the stage'. The central romantic drama between Josepha (Norma Wick expertly repeating her 1958 role) and her head waiter Leopold (George Baker, taking over the role at a month's notice and rousing the house with his 'Goodbye') was a happy pairing, their ultimate reconciliation 'skilfully done for maximum emotional effect'. A. G. W. in the *EEN* recognised that both Wick and John Dunsire 'possess the polish and aplomb of experience'.

Throughout, the casting was strong, with Margaret Elliott as Ottoline and Dunsire as Valentine especially effective, as was the pairing of Trevor Bason (noted for a 'fetching comedy style') and petite Pip Jenkinson as Sigismund and Gretel. Throughout, this was a company on whom the Society could depend, with names that over the years contributed hugely to the company's strength: Barry Saull as the underwear manufacturer Grinkle; Michael Ranson 'credibly regal' as the Emperor; Stanley Gibson as a pompous Mayor; Peter Mottram as exuberant Karl; Michael Richardson as Professor Hinzel, and Joan Payne as Kathi the postwoman.

Most essentially, *White Horse Inn* relied hugely on its chorus, as all the company's productions have. Now, at the beginning of the 1970s, we look to the list of *Ladies* and *Gentlemen of the Chorus* and see the quality on offer, names that

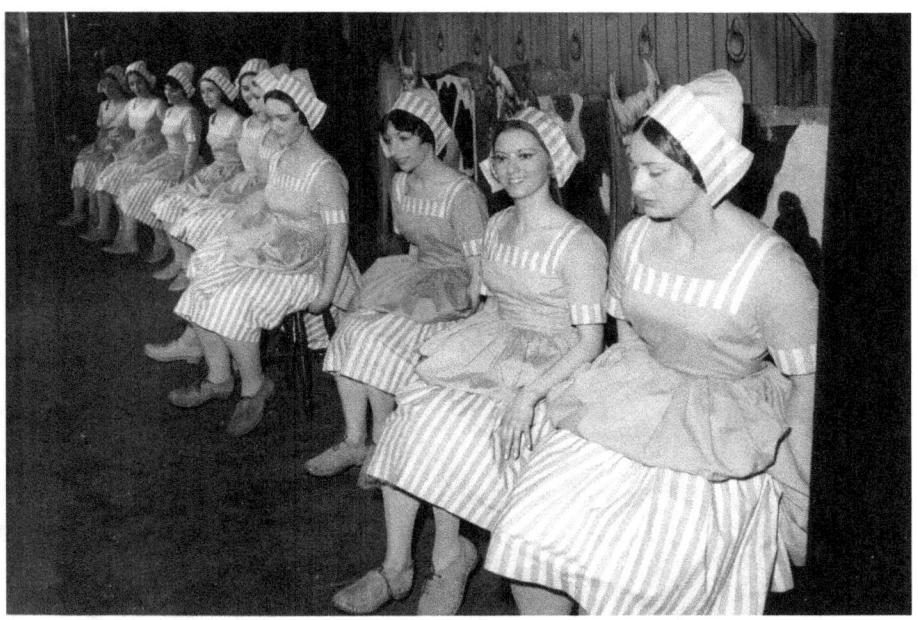

37. Milkmaids await their moment at the White Horse Inn (1970)
Courtesy of NNOS Archive.

38. George Baker and company in the 1970 version of *White Horse Inn*
© Eastern Daily Press, Norwich.

39. Margaret Elliott and John Dunsire book into the White Horse Inn in 1970 © Montague, St. John Maddermarket, Norwich.

40. Margaret Elliott, Pip Jenkinson and Norma Wick (1970). Courtesy of NNOS Archive.

41. A change in the weather: *White Horse Inn* (1970)
© Eastern Daily Press, Norwich.

sometimes remained in the chorus for years with hardly a word spoken or names that had slightly faded from principal assignments to more modest appearances, and names that had yet to make their full impression. All are worthy of warm recollection, but deserve to be remembered for being steadfastly involved in productions, whether their roles be major or minor. Steadfastness was certainly displayed by such as Joyce Johnson, tucked into the chorus list but equally as valued as whoever was playing a major role. A cutting from a local magazine has her photograph below the headline 'Joyce Johnson Opera Singer'. It tells us that she worked in Colman's Transport Department for 25 years and had been in every N&N show since 1946. She was also instrumental in maintaining the Society's archive, although this was never officially recognised. Without her work as unofficial archivist, this book would hardly have been possible.

Credit was due to Frances Davis for organising the vast task of recreating the old inn in Norwich. As always in its history, the company had put its faith in its producer/director and musical director. 'Packed house roars its approval' ran the *EDP*'s headline, reassuring readers that, whatever the production's shortcomings, 'Vivacity and imagination meant technical problems could be overlooked'.

A. G. W. was happy that

> a packed audience provided the roar of final approval which was well merited [but] it is a pity that they failed to hush their hubbub during the overture and the entr'actes. My seat was unfortunately situated next to a continuous chatter of commentary which apparently faded in the third Act solely as the result of exhaustion!

Cast

Kathi (Joan Payne), Karl (Peter Mottram), Forester (Harry Dawson), Zenzi (Jean Welch), Courier (Anthony Rush), Leopold (George Baker), Josepha Vogelhuber (Norma Wick), Steamer Captain (Michael Hilling), Bridegroom (Andrew Slatter), Bride (Bernice Vickers), John Ebenezer Grinkle (Barry Saull), Ottoline (Margaret Elliott), Valentine Sutton (John Dunsire), Sigismund Smith (Trevor Bason), Professor Hinzel (Michael Richardson), Gretel (Pip Jenkinson), Mayor (Stanley Gibson), Mayor's Secretary (Beryl Shore), Emperor (Michael Ranson), Ketterl (Raymond Laight), Landlord (Fred Cushing), Sailor (David Payne), The Village Band (Norwich Lads Club)

Gentlemen of the Chorus Tom Ashcroft, John Bill, John Cole, Fred Cushing, Harry Dawson, Keith Ellis, Paul England, Percy Garrett, Alan Goose, Colin Harris, Michael Hilling, Raymond Laight, David MacJannett, Tony Minter, David Payne, Michael Richardson, Anthony Rush, Ron Say, Donald Shackshaft, Ernest Shaves, Andrew Slatter, Peter Winter

Ladies of the Chorus Ruby Addison, Jenny Batch, Miriam Batterbee, Brenda Baverstock, Sheila Dix, Pauline Findlow, Gertrude Freeman, Elizabeth Garner, Bridget Goose, Norma Gowen, Josephine Gregory, Joyce Johnson, Barbara Lewis, Anne MacJannett, Violet Shaves, Beryl Shore, Alison Spencer, Cynthia Ward, Jean Welch, Ann Whitehead

Dancers Anita Burrage, Jean Carter, Mary Edwards, Margaret Fawcett, Gillian Fisher, Joan Huggins, Barbara Peskett, Georgina Rooney, Hilary Stannard, Bernice Vickers

1971
ANNIE GET YOUR GUN

Norwich Theatre Royal, 22–27 February
Music and lyrics: **Irving Berlin**
Book: **Herbert and Dorothy Fields**
Director: **Frances Davis**
Musical Director: **David Kett**

Yet another showcase role for the N&N's Norma Wick was gun-toting Annie Oakley brought to life in a show (Broadway 1946 with Ethel Merman, London 1947 with Dolores Gray) lavishly filled with great numbers – try 'There's No Business Like Show Business', 'Doin' What Comes Natur'lly', 'The Girl That I Marry', 'You Can't Get a Man with a Gun', 'I Got the Sun in The Morning', 'They

Say it's Wonderful' and the fiercely competitive duet 'Anything You Can Do'. This was American musical theatre at its most vibrant. Originally, the score was to be written by Jerome Kern, but Kern died before embarking on it.

The *EDP*'s C. V. R. celebrated Wick's 'sure-fire entertainment and explosive comedy, with an impact which ricochets with resounding success to the topmost seat in the circle [as she] belts out her songs like a gospel singer at a Billy Graham crusade'. He appreciated 'the Albert Hall organ in Norma Wick's voice-box'. She was ably partnered by John Dunsire who won his own laurels: A. G. W. found him 'an excellent partner and rival ... absolutely right in character, voice and appearance as Frank Butler'. His talent was showcased in 'My Defences Are Down', even if C. V. R. thought him unhelped by an unresponsive male vocal backing: 'from the faces of the chorus-line they might just as well have been intoning the Death March'. 'Dear me', Roberts wrote, 'what expressionless faces, what lack of reaction to situation. Take a look, gentlemen, at the ladies of the chorus around you – and take a tip from their flashing smiles and smiling eyes.'

The orchestra may not have been on top form. For Roberts, it was finding things 'a bit difficult'. Losing its way in some jazzed-up variations it was 'uneven in quality'. There was brightness from Keith Ellis and Bernice Vickers, 'a good-looking and delightful pair' including a 'fair turn in tap-dancing from Miss Vickers'. Sylvia Dix (a very considerable and rather under-appreciated performer) 'delightfully emerges as a comedienne of no mean merit', while Barry Saull's Buffalo Bill and Harry Headden's Chief Sitting Bull had their moments. Ultimately, the show boiled down to Wick, with A. G. W. rightly judging that 'If ever a part was devised to order for Norma Wick, this is it.' The stage may have been cramped by the oversized company, the sounds from the pit sometimes wayward, but as the headline of his review tells us: 'Norwich Annie is Bang on Target'. Wick was walking in the footsteps of Ethel Merman and Dolores Gray, ready to invest the songs with, as C. V. R. described, 'that voice she's found with its spiking of Satchmo gravel'.

Cast

Little Boy (Paul Huddleston / Ian Simcoe), Charlie Davenport (Michael Richardson), Mac (Peter Mottram), Foster Wilson (Stanley Gibson), Dolly Tate (Sylvia Dix), Winnie Tate (Bernice Vickers), Tommy Keeler (Keith Ellis), Frank Buter (John Dunsire), Annie Oakley (Norma Wick), Little Jake (Simon Jary / Peter Elliott), Nellie (Sarah Wilkins / Julie Ward), Jessie (Dawn Pickett / Elizabeth Walpole), Minnie (Susan Lewis / Elizabeth Cole), Buffalo Bill (Barry Saull), Mrs Little Horse (Sheila Dunsire), Guard (Peter Winter), Trainman (Alan Goose), Waiter (Trevor Bason), Riding Mistress (Janet Russon), Major Gordon Lillie (Raymond Laight), Chief Sitting Bull (Harry Headden), Ceremonial Indian (Alan Temple), Wild Horse Dancer (David MacJannett), Pawnie's Messenger (John Bill), Sylvia Potter-Porter (Margaret Elliott), Major Domo (Tony Minter)

Gentlemen of the Chorus Tom Ashcroft, Gordon Brunt, Percy Garrett, Michael Hilling, Gerry Jarvis, Ron Say, Donald Shackshaft, Ernest Shaves, Andrew Slatter, Neil Starr, Frank Weyer

Ladies of the Chorus Miriam Batterbee, Brenda Baverstock, Elizabeth Butt, Frances Dickerson, Penelope Douglas, Sheila Dunsire, Pauline Findlow, Bridget Goose, Norma Gowen, Josephine Gregory, Pip Jenkinson, Joyce Johnson, Barbara Lewis, Ann (*sic*) MacJannett, Coral Newell, Violet Shaves, Beryl Shore, Alison Spencer, Vera Curtis-Troke, Cynthia Ward, Ann Whitehead

Dancers Anita Burrage, Jean Carter, Julia Collins, Rosalind Delf, John Drinkwater, Mary Edwards, Margaret Fawcett, John Fell, Pam Huggins, Roger Plunkett, Ethne Quihampton, Georgina Rooney, Derek Rose, Barbara Simnett, Linda Skillings, Hilary Stannard, Neil Starr

1972

CAROUSEL

Music: **Richard Rodgers**
Book and lyrics: **Oscar Hammerstein II, based on Ferenc Molnar's play *Liliom***
Director: **Ricky Price**
Musical Director: **David Kett**

Watching director Ricky Price rehearsing the N&N company, Charles Roberts saw 'an affably bewhiskered individual with an artist's eye for detail'. His career included a close association with Sadler's Wells. Roberts explained that Price 'enjoys working with amateurs and finds no difficulty in switching back and forth between amateur and professional theatre. On the one hand he finds the keen amateur willing and malleable to the needs and ideas of the producer: 'Your amateur is not so established in his roles; everything is new to him. On the other hand, the pro's attitude is simple: if they trust you to use them to their best advantage in a piece, they will be malleable too.'

Norwich had been visited by the original London production's touring version in 1953 with Edmund Hockridge as Billy Bigelow. Now, critic Jack Gowers sat through the N&N's box-office sell-out's 'draggy first half' with its 'tediously long, scene-setting dialogue between Julie Jordan [Coral Newell] and Billy Bigelow [John Dunsire]', irritated by the stage being stuffed with dancers constricted 'on a pocket handkerchief'. There was, after all, a company of over 80 performers. The chorus was 'very jolly' but 'This company should give much, much more attention to such basics of theatrical training as moving and standing still. Neither is very well done by many of the cast.' Thankfully, Mr Gowers seemed to enjoy the second half.

It was generally agreed that Newell's performance as Rodgers and Hammerstein's tragic heroine was extraordinarily effective. It marked her return to the company having played Magnolia in the 1959 *Show Boat*. Now, Gowers recognised her 'remarkable eye-smarting performance which was quite unexpected in one so gifted as a singer. She is a person upon whom the muses have profusely showered their attentions.' For the *Journal*, the critic C. P. R. M. reported that 'Miss Newell maintains a beautiful sadness throughout, reaching heart-rending peaks of grief, despite the gaiety and frivolousness around her' in a production that was 'a real passionate weepie tempered nicely the right side of sugary sentimentality'. For Charles Roberts, Newell lifted the show 'to a plane of authentic tragedy'.

Dunsire seems to have been a worthy successor to Hockridge, from the same mould as Howard Keel, exuding a confidently warm masculinity. Roberts admired Dunsire's 'consistently fine' singing, notably in 'The Highest Judge of All' and in the demanding 'Soliloquy', although 'the mantle of actor sits thinly on his shoulders, nowhere more evidently than in that Soliloquy'. Margaret Elliott and Tom Ashcroft as Carrie Pipperidge and Enoch Snow were 'masterpieces of casting, resulting in a comedy team which could scarcely have been bettered'. Elliott's portrayal was one of the show's major successes, 'sung with a voice of irresistible chortling tremelo', while 16-year-old Charlotte Corbett was 'most sensitive and moving' as Louise. Roberts went further, on the wings of silver prose. For him, Corbett 'dances like a nymph in the summer afternoon of a faun, and not just with her feet, but with all her heart. In her danced encounter with the Carnival Boy (David MacJannett here as sensitive as she) her pas-de-deux of attraction and rejection is both moving and dramatic'. The irritant to Roberts' appreciation was the audience itself, for it was 'charabanc night, bringing in an audience who were for the most part remarkably unresponsive to the efforts of the performers'. The Society revisited *Carousel* with Ray Jeffery's production in 1999.

Cast

Carrie Pipperidge (Margaret Elliott), Julie Jordan (Coral Newell), Mrs Mullin (Sylvia Dix), Billy Bigelow (John Dunsire), Policeman (Tony Minter), David Bascombe (Michael Richardson), Nettie Fowler (Norma Wick), Enoch Snow (Tom Ashcroft), Jigger Craigin (Barry Saull), Arminy (Beryl Shore), Captain (Raymond Laight), Heavenly Friend (Stanley Gibson), Starkeeper (Leonard Vince), Louise (Charlotte Corbett), Carnival Boy (David MacJannett), Enoch Snow Jnr (John Cranston), Principal (Harry Headden), Dr Seldon (Leonard Vince)

Gentlemen of the Chorus Trevor Bason, Percy Garrett, Alan Goose, Michael Hilling, Gerry Jarvis

Children Monday, Wednesday, Friday, Saturday matinee Urchins (James Conway, Robert Marshall), Lucy Conway, Peter Elliott, Mary Ann Long, Sean Nicholson, Sally Orchard, Elizabeth Walpole, James Wilkins, Sarah Wilkins.

Tuesday, Thursday, Saturday evening Urchins (Michael Gowing, Julian Richardson), Georgina Benison, Nicola Butterfield, Gavin Chaplin, Richard Gowing, Katie Humphries, Carol Jackson, Linda Richardson, Martin Tacon

Dancers John Bill, Jean Carter, John Cole, Keith Ellis, David MacJannett, Barbara Peskett, Margaret Read, Donald Shackshaft, Barbara Simnett, Neil Starr, Bernice Vickers

1973
THE DUBARRY

Norwich Theatre Royal, 26 February–3 March

Music: **Karl Millöcker, arranged by Theo Makeben, adapted and augmented by Bernard Grun**

Book: **Paul Knepler and J. Welleminsky, adapted by Eric Maschwitz**

Lyrics: **Rowland Leigh, Eric Maschwitz**

Director: **Ricky Price**

Musical Director: **David Kett**

Charles Roberts and the recently appointed drama critic of the *EEN* Neville Miller paid close attention to what turned out to be the beginning of the end of the Society's abiding obsession with what some considered light operatic hokum, with shreds of operetta occasionally resurfacing as with the Society's 1979 *The Merry Widow* and 1982 *Die Fledermaus*. There were many of the Society's supporters who preferred to continue down the elderly operetta path. These did not include thankful Mrs. M. S. Dickie from Poringland, who wrote to the *EDP* to thank the Society 'for bringing the charm of spring in Paris to our city of Norwich this week. The delightful costumes, romantic music and gaiety is so refreshing amidst the raggle-taggle-gipsy world of today. Long may the Society contrive to transport us to a dream-world of fantasy and fun.' Ian Geofric wrote in similar vein, grateful for 'a Society which is still willing to include this sort of beautifully-dressed musical show in its repertoire'. Such pleasures were on offer at the Theatre Royal with seats modestly priced at 50p, 60p and 75p.

Of course, this *Dubarry* was some distance away from the genuine article, regurgitated by the not always reliably sensitive Bernard Grun and Eric

Maschwitz, who made modest careers out of reshaping old shows from a lost age, digestible to amateur companies. Long before, Karl Millöcker's operetta premiered in 1879, after which the show underwent considerable tinkering. That most literary of theatre critics James Agate had little respect for the 1932 London production with 'not enough story to engross a child of twelve'.[1] The 1932 British film adaptation named after its hit song *I Give My Heart* captured much of the work's charm, with luxurious décor, beautiful black and white photography in 'a film that is frequently ravishing, with the singing of Gitta Alpár at its heart'. Up to the final frame, she is still matching the nightingale in notes audible only to dogs.[2]

On stage, the N&N's production failed to impress C. V. R., for

> despite the splendour of most of the costumes – and probably in spite of the thinly convincing sets – there is only episodic evidence of the poise and pride and panache for which this period and its dress cries out. The particular demands of this *papier mache* musical suited in the main neither the style nor the strengths of this Society.

C. V. R.'s report commended the supporting cast, but reserved its main barb for Coral Newell. A glowing testimonial of her talents was balanced by his opinion that her singing 'was a trifle worrying last night'. Helpfully, but perhaps ill-advisedly, he suggested that she should 'guard against those "closed" and unlovely vowel sounds. One expects that sort of thing from modern pop groups who know no better. But not from performers of the talent and natural charm of Mrs. Newell'. Mrs Newell's reaction to this public declaration is not known.

The costume department did not escape C. V. R.'s disapproval, highlighting those worn by a newcomer to the Society Bob Arnett as Jeanne's one true love Reneé, for 'Mr Arnett, though he is no model of poise, is badly served by his costume. In particular a set of out gambling house finery which verges on the ridiculous'. In one of his earliest reviews as drama critic of the *EEN*, Neville Miller confessed:

> Experience of the grand old musicals, which have so many good tunes and provide so amply for the talents of the chorus, had led me to expect little cheer from the dialogue and wait confidently to be lifted on the wings of song [but] This production by Ricky Price for the Norfolk and Norwich Amateur Operatic Society changes my view. Here, amid elaborate costumes and the courtly manners, the Dubarry really lives because she is so well acted by Coral Newell. She is an actress with substantial emotional reserves behind a personality of gentle charm [although] Even the Dubarry, giving as much feeling to her singing as to her acting, is far from easy in the top register.

Furthermore, 'The dancing seems mild and occasionally awkward and there is not much humour in the script. But David Kett obtains some good playing from the orchestra, there is allure in the spectacle and to the Dubarry, as the songs says, 'I Give my Heart'.

Cast

Madelon (Audrey Chapman), Fifi (Jean Welch), Lynette (Pip Jenkinson), Suzanne (Frances Dickerson), Gipsy (Miriam Batterbee), Madame Labille (Barbara Lewis), Vicomte de Brissac (Trevor Bason), Lasalle (Tony Welch), Frontignac (Don Shackshaft), Courcelles (Alan Goose), Comte Jean Dubarry (George Baker), Jeanne Bécu (Coral Newell), René Leclerc (Bob Arnett) Madame Sauterelle (Norma Wick), Louis XV (Stanley Gibson), Lammond (Andrew Slatter), Duchess of Luxembourg (Margaret Elliott), Duke of Choiseul (Peter Mottram), Duchess de Grammont (Anne MacJannett), Servants (Laurie Marshall, Peter Winter)

Gentlemen of the Chorus Tom Ashcroft, John Cole, Percy Garrett, Harry Headden, Michael Hilling, Gerry Jarvis, Timothy King, Raymond Laight, Alan Lee, David MacJannett, Tony Minter, Ron Say, Ernest Shaves, Frank Weyer, Alan Willoughby

Ladies of the Chorus Rosalind Arnett, Brenda Baverstock, Merry Crosskill, Penelope Douglas, Pauline Findlow, Elizabeth Garner, Bridget Goose, Norma Gowen, Josephine Gregory, Pamela Jackson, Joyce Johnson, Barbara Lewis, Anne MacJannett, Barrie Marshall, Violet Shaves, Ann Whitehead

Dancers Bill Butterfield, Charlotte Corbett, Pam Huggins, Diana Jones, Susan Mason, Ann McLeod, Margaret Read, Barbara Simnet, Janet Slater, Neil Starr, John Thompson, Bernice Vickers

1974

HELLO, DOLLY!

Norwich Theatre Royal, 18–23 February

Music and lyrics: **Jerry Herman**

Book: **Michael Stewart, based on *The Matchmaker* by Thornton Wilder**

Director: **Ricky Price**

Musical Director: **David Kett**

Jerry Herman's brilliant musical had been a tremendous Broadway success in 1964, with Carol Channing for its essential star, succeeded during its 2,844 performance run by such as Ginger Rogers, Martha Raye, Betty Grable, Phyllis Diller and Ethel Merman. An all-black performers edition headed by Pearl

42. Ready to say 'Hello, Dolly!' in 1974 © Eastern Daily Press, Norwich.

Bailey was included as from November 1967. The British production welcomed Mary Martin back to the Theatre Royal Drury Lane in 1965. It was a personal triumph for Martin, returning to London after leading the company in Noël Coward's 1946 *Pacific 1860* and Rodgers and Hammerstein's *South Pacific* in 1951. In May 1966 Martin was followed by Dora Bryan, whose joyous interpretation of Dolly gave the show a new vigour. Throughout the London run, the ebullient Eleanor Macready stepped into Dolly's shoes when Martin or Bryan were unavailable.

When it came to the N&N, it seemed inevitable that the role would go to Norma Wick. In the *EDP*'s review 'S. E.' recalled her 'great timing and skill', reporting that 'From the moment she enters, until, with a wicked wink, she departs, the audience is captivated'. Neville Miller was as captivated as her audience, noting that her 'warmth and attack of her singing often produce a sound reminiscent of Merman'. In fact, 'every performance is on an extraordinarily high level, easy American accents and all, a sure sign of the producer's strong hand'. This was 'a show that scores in all directions. It is in the best modern American tradition, which means that however simple the fare there is immense variety and wit in the presentation.' The dancing was 'not of the breath-taking athletic kind' as at Drury Lane, where the waiters' routine stopped the show every night. Nevertheless the dancing 'has its charm and a great deal of humour' notably in the antics of the waiters at the Harmonia Gardens.

The N&N's supporting company included some of the most capable performers of that time, with George Baker taking the male lead as Ambrose Vandergelder. Others included newcomer Alan Willoughby, ex-choral scholar and ex-footballer with Leyton Orient and Southend United, as Ambrose Kemper, Bob Arnett, Don Shackshaft, Peter Mottram, Bernice Vickers as Minnie Fay. Coral Newell as Irene Molloy had one of the gentlest numbers of the evening in 'Ribbons Down My Back'.

In a leader, the *EEN* felt that 'We have reached a point where only the best will do, and audiences at the Theatre Royal have come to expect it. The professionals thus act as a spur to the amateurs [...] and the quality of the amateur show is thereby sharpened and improved.' However, 'not all this current upsurge in live shows is to be found in the bigger societies. All over Norwich and Norfolk there are small teams of enthusiasts producing all kinds of entertainment.' Seen by 7,700 patrons, the production's profits acted as a safe buffer at a time when there was doubt about future costs and audience attendances.

Cast

Mrs Dolly Gallagher Levi (Norma Wick), Ernestina (Anne MacJannett), Ambrose Kemper (Alan Willoughby), Horace Vandergelder (George Baker), Ermengarde (Pip Jenkinson), Cornelius Hackl (Bob Arnett), Barnaby Tucker (Don Shackshaft), Irene Molloy (Coral Newell), Minnie Fay (Bernice Vickers), Mrs Rose (Joyce Johnson), Rudolph (Peter Mottram), Judge (Stanley Gibson), Court Clerk (Alan Goose)

Gentlemen of the Chorus Harry Headden, Gerry Jarvis, Tony Minter, Alec Mountain, Barry Saull, Tony Welch

Ladies of the Chorus Brenda Baverstock, Audrey Chapman, Frances Dickerson, Sylvia Dix, Margaret Elliott, Pauline Findlow, Elizabeth Garner, Josephine Gregory, Pamela Jackson, Barbara Lewis, Barrie Marshall, Pamela Warren, Wendy Watts, Jean Welch, Ann Whitehead

Dancers Malcolm Ballard, Deborah Brown, William Butterfield, Roger Cliffe, Keith Ellis, Pam Huggins, Mandy Munday, Barbara Peskett, Roger Plunkett, Margaret Read, Ernest Shaves, Barbara Simnett, Sharon Sinclair, Michael Stamp, Stephen Wilson

1975
KING'S RHAPSODY

Norwich Theatre Royal, 17–22 February
Music and book: Ivor Novello
Lyrics: Christopher Hassall
Producer: Ricky Price
Musical Director: David Kett

I was in my late 20s when I auditioned for the Society's Golden Jubilee production of Ivor Novello's *King's Rhapsody*. My first memory is that Lynn Wardle (already an established favourite in the company) walked out of the audition as I walked in. Having had a serious stammer since boyhood, but being obsessed with theatre and performing, I had up to this time insisted on roles in which I sang rather than spoke. There was no chance of this in *King's Rhapsody*. Novello had written the role of Nikki, the rebellious heir to the throne of Murania, for himself; there was a mountain of words to be spoken. He had only once sung in one of his own spectacularly luscious musical plays (*Careless Rapture*) but wisely decided he was no singer and cut the singing sequence after a few nights. I did not get the chance to show the audience I could sing.

It was fitting that the celebration of the Society's 50 years' entertainment now centred on a British musical. Novello was unquestionably the most successful British composer of musical plays in the first half of the twentieth century, with such improbable musical romances as *Glamorous Night* and *The Dancing Years*. He starred in several of them too, played Henry V at Drury Lane, and was probably the closest British cinemas got to a gay icon in 1932 when he starred in Alfred Hitchcock's classic British silent *The Lodger*. Novello's many light comedies, notably the brilliant *I Lived with You*, with its hilarious tea-party scene (preserved in its film version), have never been revived. He also wrote a defining song for each of the world wars: for World War I 'Till the Boys Come Home', and for World War II 'We'll Gather Lilacs', one of the outstanding numbers from his 1945 *Perchance to Dream*. Novello died at the peak of his career in 1951, having played Nikki in *King's Rhapsody* that evening. Herbert Wilcox cast Hollywood's Errol Flynn as Nikki and Anna Neagle as Marta in the garish 1955 film version.

When Novello played Nikki he was 57 years old; I was a 30-years-younger Nikki, awaiting a baptism of fire with (or was it *opposite*?) five highly skilled leading ladies, all much admired. Coral Newell, resplendently regal as Princess Christiane, was first heard in the ravishing aria 'Someday My Heart Will Awake' shortly after curtain-up. Norma Wick, a natural comedienne and scene-stealer, was supremely in character if slightly corseted by her role as my mistress Marta.

43. Adrian Wright and Coral Newell awaiting *King's Rhapsody* (1975)
Courtesy of NNOS Archive.

44. L-R: Norma Wick, Adrian Wright, Ivy Oxley and Coral Newell in *King's Rhapsody* (1975) © Eastern Daily Press, Norwich.

Despite some of the audience probably thinking she was cradle-snatching me, she radiated glamour and strength as she sang of 'The Mayor of Perpignan'. The contralto role of Countess Vera (written for one of Novello's favourites, Olive Gilbert) can seldom have been sung with such resonance as it now was by Pamela Warren with 'Fly Home, Little Heart', the frisky 'Take Your Girl', and the grandeur of 'The Gates of Paradise' in which she was enjoined with Coral and George Baker as Count Egon. I remember one night when George raced excitedly on stage in the middle of one of my most fervid speeches, realised he had come in at the wrong moment, and stomped off without a word. This may have been the biggest laugh of the night. Ivy Oxley as my mother, otherwise Elena of Murania, made for a distinctive dowager and, for years after, always greeted me as 'My son!' whenever we met. On stage she could be, as C. V. R. realised, 'a magnificent old dragon'. I wish I had got to know Ivy better, but never worked with her again – a lady of great style and warmth. My leading ladies were each in their own way remarkable people, strong women who knew how to behave impeccably on if not always off stage.

Rehearsals were an occasion for considerable hilarity, mostly at the expense of Novello's dialogue, for which our director Ricky Price had little respect. Looking at my battered script 50 years later I see whole pages of dialogue mercilessly deleted. Early on, Ricky decided that the imaginary country in which the show was set, Murania, was the name of a mouthwash. Everyone battled with the dialogue. In one scene, I had to hold Coral in my arms and plead

'Don't melt away, my little snow princess', which seemed a most unlikely fate for someone of Coral's sturdy frame. It was obvious that only one person could ever have got away with saying such lines, and that was Ivor himself. It certainly partly accounts for the fact that, since his death, there have been no successful professional revivals of his musicals. When he died, the world in which he lived effectively died with him. It only recently occurred to me that I am one of a very small number of actors who have played the lead in *King's Rhapsody*, and that indeed is a rare privilege. And what good company surrounded me!

The Society heightened expectations by announcing that for this production it would for the first time construct its own scenery by joining forces with Norfolk Opera Players under the supervision of Alan Temple. Excited at the prospect of the arrival of this impressive décor, we rehearsed for weeks, imagining that we were sweeping down imposing Adam staircases, or draping ourselves in palatial throne rooms, each set being more luxuriantly majestic than the last. At the dress rehearsal with the home-made set still being noisily hammered into position, Ricky called me up to the dress circle. Staring down at the stage, he said 'It looks like a public lavatory.'

The pre-production publicity heightened the excitement around who would play the monster role of the King. Who, indeed, could possibly stand in for Ivor Novello? Who would have the bare-faced cheek, never mind the bravado, to attempt it? Neville Miller seemed in no doubt, introducing prospective patrons to 'a young actor who has shown in performances in local dramatic and musical shows that he has style, intelligence and a gift for polished timing – qualities which aptly fit the Novello role he will be playing.'

Charles Roberts' review for the *EDP* justly heaped praise on the ladies, notably Coral and Norma. Coral sang better than he had ever heard her, singing 'Someday My Heart Will Awake' with 'a sheen which, in its thrilling top notes, particularly, reminded me of those old 78s of Vanessa Lee'. Listening to Warren, he was 'captivated by a most beautiful and lustrous alto-tone'. As for Norma, 'She can simply stand in the centre of a stage – and become the pivot of its action. The throaty voice, the storm-to-sunshine face are but the polished technical attributes of something given and not learned.' For Neville Miller, Coral was 'an unqualified success. Always a sensitive actress, she imbues this part with an extraordinary sense of spontaneity and charm', while Norma gave 'a riveting performance'. 'Musically it is on a very high level ... but the outstanding impression comes from the quality in much of the acting.'

And then Charles fired his icy blast:

> So to the king himself, played by the talented and elegant Adrian Wright, who for reasons I do not understand does his best to convince us that he is neither. Only in the final scenes when that divinity which doth hedge a king becomes clearer to this erring monarch does Mr Wright's playing become credible. Could be I missed the point he was trying to make.

Yes, it could be just that! This taught me something I have always tried to maintain: avoid reading criticisms of your own performance. (Impossible, of course. If they are bad, someone is bound to let you know about them. If they are good, you burn the words into your memory and live on them for as long as life allows.)

When I arrived at the theatre on the second night the stage door keeper informed me that Miss Newell wished to see me in her dressing room. Having sat me down, she said 'Now look here', and proceeded to say things that I am too modest to repeat. She buoyed me up, and said what I think she realised I already knew: I would do exactly as I had done the previous performance. She had faith in me, and sometimes that is all an actor asks. Of course, there was still my semi-hippie hairdo to deal with. I asked one of the backroom girls to cut it there and then.

And so the curtain went up again, and came down a couple of hours later as I knelt, with my back to the audience and holding the rose left by Coral on the altar steps of Murania's Cathedral, as Coral's voice, as if from heaven but from the wings, brought down the slowest of curtains to 'Some Day My Heart Will Awake'. It was one of those rare acting moments, ravishing and supremely theatrical, that actors cherish. I still have a letter from an audience member congratulating me on how brilliantly I acted with my back. Charles Roberts had not noticed that!

Cast

Princess Kirsten (Denise Baxter), Princess Hulda (Fiona Mann), Mr Trontzen (Trevor Bason), Countess Vera Lemainken (Pam Warren), Princess Cristiane (Coral Newell), King Peter of Norseland (Stanley Gibson), Jules (Peter Mottram), Queen Elena of Murania (Ivy Oxley), Vanescu (Jack Wood), Nikki (Adrian Wright), Marta Karillos (Norma Wick), Madame Koska (Margaret Elliott), Count Egon Stanieff (George Baker), Boy Kings (James Conway, Peter Elliott)

Gentlemen of the Chorus Trevor Bason, David Belksey, John Cole, Dominic Conway, Alan Goose, Chris Harkins, Harry Headden, Gerry Jarvis, Robert Kelsey, Raymond Laight, Lawrence Mann, Tony Minter, Peter Mottram, Peter Russ, Don Shackshaft, Tony Welch

Ladies of the Chorus Susan Archer, Miriam Batterbee, Audrey Chapman, Merry Crosskill, Gloria Dyche, Pauline Findlow, Elizabeth Garner, Bridget Goose, Josephine Gregory, Pamela Jackson, Pip Jenkinson, Alvina Johnson, Joyce Johnson, Barbara Lewis, Barrie Marshall, Joan Payne, Wendy Watts, Ann Whitehead

Dancers Brenda Baverstock, Averil Brampton-Gurdon, Pam Huggins, Barbara Peskett, Barbara Simnett, Sharon Sinclair, Malcolm Ballard, William Butterfield, Roger Cliffe, Keith Ellis, Roger Plunkett, Stephen Wilson

1976

SOUTH PACIFIC

Norwich Theatre Royal, 16–21 February
Music: Richard Rodgers
Lyrics: Oscar Hammerstein II
Book: Oscar Hammerstein II and Joshua Logan, based on James A. Michener's *Tales of the South Pacific*
Director: Ricky Price
Musical Director: David Kett

The reviews suggest that this production was not one of the company's finest couple of hours. C. V. R. had few encouraging comments but acclaimed the arrival of newcomer Brian Goodfellow 'a big man with a big voice – a rich, full voice, employed with outstanding warmth, modulation, phrasing and technique'. Beside him, 'no-one else provides anything approaching so rounded a portrayal and technique'. Neville Miller celebrated Goodfellow's voice as 'a baritone that makes a beautiful sound in all its range – a big voice that rides with power and ease – and he shows a wealth of artistry in matters of control and projection'. His 'This Nearly Was Mine' and 'Some Enchanting Evening' were the high-spots of the evening, delivered in a manner 'that strengthens addiction to the theatre-going habit'.

Reviewing the other participants, Roberts recognised 'wooden expressionless interpretation' and 'an awful lot of playing here which is very much in keeping with the sets – flatly one-dimensional cut-outs which fail to convince'. Roberts thought Norma Wick was not ideally cast as Bloody Mary ('this is really not her role, though I loved her velvety singing of "Happy Talk"') and, although leading lady Audrey Chapman as Ensign Nellie Forbush showed 'intelligent, tender acting', it was in the comedy numbers such as 'Honey Bun' that she flourished. She was vocally inconsistent, 'sometimes singing '*à la* Petula Clark or Doris Day but then going into soprano when the music was high'.

Colin Harris was a handsome and engaging Joseph Cable but Miller detected 'vocal difficulty'. 'The fact that his voice will not do all it needs to do is a pity because he sounds and looks right in many ways.' There was more enthusiasm for Irene Parsell in the non-speaking role of Liat. For Roberts, 'Her beautiful, delicately Eastern face and general grace of movement are perfect'. For Miller, she was 'a poem in movement'. The muscularity of the male chorus was much appreciated. Overall, Miller recognised

> a highly efficient production by Ricky Price, but I am not very happy about some of the scenery which is pretty in a pantomime way. Like Nellie, the show has a lot of spunk. Apparently, it also has a tremendous pull. The week's run, including the matinee, is already a sell-out.

Cast

Ngana (Kate Humphries / Jane Jenkinson), Jerome (James Wilkins), Henry (Stephen Wilson), Ensign Nelly Forbush (Audrey Chapman), Emile de Becque (Brian Goodfellow), Bloody Mary (Norma Wick), Stewpot (Don Shackshaft), Luther Bills (Peter Mottram), Professor (Alan Goose), Lt Joseph Cable (Colin Harris), Capt. George Brackett (Stanley Gibson), Commdr. William Harbison (Jack Wood), Yeoman Herbert Quale (Harry Headden), Sgt Kenneth Johnson (Peter Russ), Seabee Richard West (Chris Harkins), Seabee Morton Wise (Tony Welch), Seaman Tom O'Brien (Ray Laight), Radio Operator Bob McCaffrey (Keith Ellis), Marine Cpl Hamilton Steeves (Alan Willoughby), Staff-Sgt Thomas Hassinger (Gerry Jarvis), Pte Victor Jerome (Lawrence Mann), Sgt Jack Waters (Ron Lyon), Lt Genevieve Marshall (Barrie Marshall), Ensign Lisa Manelli (Pip Jenkinson), Ensign Connie Walewska (Alvina Johnson), Ensign Janet McGregor (Pam Jackson), Ensign Bessie Noonan (Brenda Baverstock), Ensign Pamela Whitmore (Jean Welch), Ensign Rita Adams (Susan Wild), Ensign Sue Yaeger (Merrilyn Crosskill), Ensign Cora MacRae (Jacqueline Annis), Ensign Betty Pitt (Lorna Turner), Ensign Dinah Murphy (Wendy Watts), Liat (Irene Parsell), Lt Buzz Adams (Roger Cliffe). Islanders: Elizabeth Garner, Josephine Gregory, Anne MacJannett, Dominic Conway, Robert Kelsey

1977
CAMELOT

Norwich Theatre Royal, 14–19 February

Music: **Frederick Loewe**

Book and lyrics: **Alan Jay Lerner, based on T. H. White's novel** *The Once and Future King*

Director: **Ricky Price**

Musical Director: **David Kett**

Intended as a visual extravaganza rather than an intellectual retelling of Arthurian legend, *Camelot* was weighed down by its opulence. Audiences flocked to see it in New York 1960 and London 1964, without the original Broadway Guenevere Julie Andrews or original Broadway Arthur Richard Burton. At the Theatre Royal Drury Lane theatregoers had to put up with the rather less stellar partnership of Elizabeth Larner and the charmless Laurence Harvey. It seems quite likely that Miss Larner was paid basic Equity rates while Mr Harvey did rather better. The day after opening night he bought an £11,000 Rolls Royce, telling reporters that the show was 'just a lovely fantasy. We all know there aren't any virgins left.' In *My Fair Lady* Lerner had enjoyed the luxury of using

45. The *Camelot* company of 1977 © Eastern Daily Press, Norwich.

dialogue from George Bernard Shaw's *Pygmalion*. No such luck here. Neither did the score compare with the consistent brilliance of Lerner and Loewe's adaptation of Shaw. When it came to bringing Arthurian legend to the musical theatre the strongest numbers belonged to Arthur with two sturdy ballads, 'How to Handle a Woman' and 'If Ever I Would Leave You'.

The London critics did not much care for this follow-up to the stunning *My Fair Lady*. The *Stage*'s veteran critic R. B. Marriott thought it 'very much better than one had learned to expect, worse than one would have thought', lamenting 'a lack of music, or at any rate music that has a striking effect; the book is often stiff and dull; there is some dreadful dialogue. Yet in a curious and surprising way the whole thing works.'[3] Bernard Levin found 'a broken-backed mess', and *The Times* praised its extravagance but 'the rest of the production is an almost total blank'. At over three hours, this was a matter of theatrical endurance.

The *EEN*'s review announced 'Pageantry adds magical touch to land of Camelot'. Neville Miller's subtle comments criticised the piece rather than the gallant company assembled by the N&N. It was strongly cast. As leading lady, Coral Newell had 'vivacity, grace, gentleness and warmth' and was well partnered by Barry Saull's Arthur and Sandy Kennon's Lancelot, but both leading men were 'one dimensional figures in primary colours'. He had thought exactly the same of the London production. Nevertheless, Saull had 'a beautifully clear speaking voice and a gift for speaking poetically so that he creates an imposing figure', and Kennon was 'an intense, handsome Lancelot – slightly overplaying the virtue and the "Mr Universe" bit to good effect'. Newell and Saull 'both gave some inner feeling to their characters – as did most of the principals – and Saull, despite some uncertainty with his lines in one scene, produced some perfect timing in his songs. Elsewhere, John Hawkes brought a satisfyingly sharp edge to Mordred, while Norma Wick's sensuous Morgan le Fey unsurprisingly proved to be 'a gift of a part'.

For Miller 'There is no outstanding vocal quality, although the songs are well "put over", which is not quite the same thing.' What was more,

> The orchestra has its aberrations, and the amplifying system, such a boon to the speaking, becomes uncomfortably obvious in the big choruses. Yes, it's a celebration to look at, all right. Whether it sounds like one or has the feeling of a heart-breaking romance which, as a matter of fact, it is, are matters open to question on first-night evidence.

Cast

Sir Dinadan (Colin Harris), Sir Clarius (Keith Ellis), Sir Lionel (Roger Cliffe), Sir Sagramore (Lawrence Mann), Merlyn (Stanley Gibson), Arthur (Barry Saull), Guenevere (Coral Newell), Lady Anne (Margaret Elliott), Lady Sybil (Audrey Chapman), Nimue (Nicola Butterfield, sung by Susan Wild), Lancelot (Sandy Kennon), Squire Dap (Chris Harkins), Pellinore (Peter Mottram), Mordred (John Hawkes), Morgan le Fey (Norma Wick), Ballad Singer (Alan Goose), Tom of Warwick (Peter Elliott)

Gentlemen of the Chorus William Butterfield, Dominic Conway, John Fiddes, Mike Gibson, Alan Goose, Chris Harkins, Ron Lyons, David MacJannett, Tony Minter, Peter Russ, Don Shackshaft, Tony Welch, Derek Williams

Ladies of the Chorus Jacqueline Annis, Miriam Batterbee, Merrilyn Crosskill, Pauline Findlow, Elizabeth Garner, Bridget Goose, Josephine Gregory, Pam Jackson, Pip Jenkinson, Alvina Johnson, Norma Kennon, Barrie Marshall, Lorna Turner, Wendy Watts, Ann Whitehead

Dancers Nicola Butterfield, Angela Chamberlain, Felicity Fahy, Fiona Mann, Barbara Peskett, Sarah Philip

Tumblers Nicholas Boldero, Paul Davison, Martin Steel, Mark Weeds, James Wilkins

Pages Peter Elliott, James Wilkins

1978
GIGI

Norwich Theatre Royal, 13–18 February
Music: **Frederick Loewe**
Book and lyrics: **Alan Jay Lerner, based on a novel by Colette**
Director: **Ricky Price**
Musical Director: **Frederick J. Firth**

The *Journal*'s Chris Mills could barely disguise his excitement at the prospect that Norwich was presenting the amateur premiere of a major American musical that had only once before been performed professionally in Britain (in Worthing). As 'Whiffler' of the *EEN* explained, the Society 'will have critical eyes upon them from all over the country as other societies take a look to assess their own chances with the show'.

In 1963, the cost of mounting *Oklahoma!* was £2,000; *Gigi* cost £13,000, with a top seat price of only £2.25, although you could get in for a mere £1.25. For Charles Roberts 'It works well, warmly, fluently and tunefully, with the central core of the story delightfully sustained by some lovely acting and characterful flair', although he noted a chorus that now and again lacked motivation and showed signs of strain and uncertainty. His major disappointment was Honoré's duet with Marmita 'I Remember it Well' in which Gordon Canwell and Audrey Chapman's 'sprightly charm and humour' lacked 'the warmth that comes from the fanned embers of nostalgic memory. It takes the edge off one of the show's best cameos.'

This was a production that 'realises the elegance of the piece (barring an overbright colour or two and an ungainly male dancer or two), it realises the charm of the story and, perhaps above all, because the quality is not given to many musicals, its wit'. In his N&N debut, Canwell (well known for his work with the Great Yarmouth Amateur Operatic Society) was perfectly cast. He also played Honoré in their production of *Gigi* with his daughter Julia and with Adrian Wright's Gaston at Yarmouth's Windmill Theatre. Canwell was in many ways the rock around which the company gathered, certainly one of the finest and most gentlemanly leading actors in the Society's long life. C. V. R. described him as 'Bewhiskered and elegant as a plate from a Feydeau first edition, with wickedly flashing eyes, a slow smile and an innate sense of style, he has us instantly in the palm of his hand – and keeps us there'. There was praise, too, for Lynn Wardle as Gaston Lachailles, with Roberts recognising 'all the marks of intelligent consideration and a deal of application, evidenced in his smooth command of dance, character and singing'. C. V. R.'s only reservation was that 'it just lacks heart'.

Bouquets of critical applause rained down on Norma Wick's gift-of- a-part Aunt Alicia, for C. V. R. an 'exhilarating, adorable, shamelessly extrovert performance'. For the *EEN*'s Neville Miller, Wick looked 'marvellous, has total command of everybody, including the audience, and is very funny'. In the *Journal*, Chris Mills concurred, applauding 'another exemplary performance by the outstanding Norma Wick' in 'one of the best amateur productions seen at the Theatre Royal for many years'. All agreed that 17-year-old Lorraine Crotch's Gigi was outstanding, with C. V. R. at his most velvet: 'With her lovely looks and grace and voice, it makes this Gigi a pure, uncomplicated pleasure, a spirit of joyous youth and innocence in a story which is but a hair's breadth away from the destruction of just those very gifts'. For Miller, Crotch was 'an actress of outstanding talent'. By the time she reached *Gigi* she was already acknowledged as a player of great promise.

Originally written as the 1958 film musical with Leslie Caron as Gigi and Maurice Chevalier as Honoré, *Gigi* did not reach the stage until Lerner and Loewe refashioned it for Broadway in 1973. A London production followed in 1985. Loewe's music was plainly in the tradition of Austro-Hungarian operetta, with its catalogue of such memorable numbers as its title song, 'The Night They Invented Champagne', 'I Remember it Well', 'Thank Heaven for Little Girls', and 'I'm Glad I'm Not Young Anymore'.

C. V. R. thanked heaven for a producer 'with the imagination to be an individual', for here was 'an original creation as seen by Ricky Price and his company'.

Cast

Honoré Lachailles (Gordon Canwell), Gaston Lachailles (Lynn Wardle), Liane D'Exelmans (Margaret Elliott), Gigi (Lorraine Crotch), Inez Alvarez (Audrey Chapman), Aunt Alicia (Norma Wick), Charles (Tony Welch), Receptionist (Barry Saull), Telephone Installer (Colin Harris), Manuel (Peter Mottram), Maitre Dufresne (Mike Gibson), Maitre Duclos (John Fiddes, Dancing Instructor (Bill Butterfield), Sandomir (John MacMillan), Jacqueline (Lorna Turner), Juliette (Pam Jackson)

Gentlemen of the Chorus John Bill, Roger Cliffe, Dominic Conway, Chris Harkins, Ray Laight, David MacJannett, Lawrence Mann, Tony Middis, Tony Minter, Peter Russ, Don Shackshaft

Ladies of the Chorus Jacqueline Annis, Miriam Batterbee, Frances Dickerson, Pauline Findlow, Elizabeth Garner, Bridget Goose, Josephine Gregory, Alvina Johnson, Anne MacJannett, Coral Newell, Wendy Watts, Jean Welch, Ann Whitehead, Susan Wild (Children: Sarah-Louise Newell, Paula Watts)

Dancers Ian Boggan, Bill Butterfield, Nicola Butterfield, Angela Chamberlain, Patsy Garland, Geraldine Lambe, Terence McDonald, John McMillan, Jacqueline Sandland, David Todd, Victor Tuck

1979

THE MERRY WIDOW

Norwich Theatre Royal, 12–17 February
Music: Franz Lehár, adapted by Ronald Hanmer
Original book and lyrics: Victor Leon and Leo Stein
New book and lyrics: Phil Park
Director: Ricky Price
Musical Director: Colin Goodchild

Artistically, visually, musically and dramatically, this was one of the company's most distinguished presentations with which to sign off the 1970s. These were testing times with rehearsals in ice-cold school halls during what came to be known as the 'Winter of Discontent', with grave-diggers, rail workers and lorry drivers on strike, and the British public, faced with a shortage of bread, turning into panic-buyers. The very fabric of British life seemed endangered, with the BBC closing down transmission of BBC One and Two, schools closing because of the shortage of heating oil, and *The Times* temporarily shutting down publication.

The opportunity to escape into the timeless milieu of *The Merry Widow* was, if all too briefly, a welcome relief. 'Another Smash Hit With Merry Widow' ran the headline of Chris Mills' review for the *EDP*, a smash hit for a company that 'deserves to be dancing all the way to the bank'. It was an opinion shared by Neville Miller's *EEN* notice: 'In these parlous times operatic societies need a smash-hit at the box office and I have seldom seen a production that deserved one more than this.' There was 'a warmth of spirit that is really a requirement of Viennese operetta but – and I am thinking of professional productions too – eludes the performance of it'.

For Miller it was 'the sort of occasion which makes me glad we still have the Operatic Society movement'. Making his auspicious debut with the Society, Colin Goodchild's musical direction was 'a marvel of judgement in matters of pacing and emphasis – he has an accomplished orchestra' and 'the chorus sound is gorgeous'. Roberts was equally effusive, welcoming the event in the 'drear and troubled today' in which Lehár's work revealed 'a romantic, balmy, wonderfully tuneful world of escapism' which on opening night 'was in essence and spirit consistently at its best. In name it was an amateur performance ... but "amateurism", one may report with undiluted joy, was a million miles away.'

The reviews for Coral Newell's widow and Christopher Speake's Danilo (he had played the role in the N&N's 1965 production) were glowing. For Miller, the pair 'sing outstandingly'. Newell's 'Vilia' was 'a triumph. Her soft-textured

46. Gordon Canwell, Christopher Speake and Coral Newell looking over *The Merry Widow* in 1979 © Alan Howard Photography, Norwich.

soprano is exquisitely controlled and the house is obviously spell-bound.' Roberts considered Speake the perfect 'matinee figure. Good looks, good voice and good acting but infrequently come together in tenor leads. Mr Speake has all three.'

There was warm recognition of the supporting cast, including Martyn Rolfe ('warmly promising' according to Roberts), the ever-dependable Margaret Elliott (a fastidious and technically refined player, with 'immaculate poise in every part of the role' according to Miller) and Gordon Canwell. Proving what a sympathetic and observant observer of theatre work he was, Roberts reserved a special tribute for Peter Mottram (his name so often hidden away in a theatre programme) who was 'always giving colour and vitality and real human credibility to his creations as in this instance'. 'Where,' Roberts asked, 'would principals be without supporting players of this calibre?'

Because of heavy snowfall on Thursday 15 February, Newell was unable to reach Norwich from Beccles for the evening performance. Audrey Chapman took over that evening, with book in hand and helpful on-stage instructions from the cast as they helped her waltz through it. Martyn Rolfe was cut off in Dereham and Lynn Wardle stepped in. Canwell made it for act two, Price having stood in for him in act one. Norma Wick (the 1965 widow), not in the show but credited with Props, could not get out of Poringland. Only 300 valiant enthusiasts made it to the theatre, including Mrs Betty Beales who battled through a four-hour train journey from Cambridge to be there. She had not missed an N&N production in 30 years.

We can only hope her journey (and that of the other 299) was worth it. If Miller's description of Price's stage pictures is anything to go by, it was, for the scenery was 'handsome and the costumes spectacular in a disciplined way – blue and green dominate the opening Act, flame shades the second and red and black the third'.

Cast
Anna Glavari (Coral Newell), Danilo (Christopher Speake), Baron Zeta (Gordon Canwell), Valencienne (Margaret Elliott), Camille (Martyn Rolfe), Njegus (Peter Mottram), St Brioche (Colin Harris), Cascada (Tim Gibson), Kromov (Victor Tuck), Olga (Audrey Chapman), Bogdanovitsch (John Fiddes), Pritsch (Roger Cliffe), Sylvia (Jean Welch), Praskovia (Greta Carver), Lolo (Miriam Batterbee), Dodo (Audrey Foster), Jou-Jou (Josephine Gregory), Frou-Frou (Pam Jackson), Clo-Clo (Beverley Baker), Margot (Pip Jenkinson)

Gentlemen of the Chorus John Bill, Bob Birkhead, Mike Gibson, Ray Laight, Ron Lyons, David MacJannett, Tony Middis, Tony Minter, Peter Russ, Tony Welch, Peter Wilson

Ladies of the Chorus Jacqueline Annis, Beverley Baker, Miriam Batterbee, Pauline Findlow. Audrey Foster, Elizabeth Garner, Sue Gilbert, Josephine Gregory, Pam Jackson, Pip Jenkinson, Alvina Johnson, Barbara Peskett, Violet Shaves, Zelda Smith, Lorna Turner

Dancers Paul Atherton, Jan Boggan, Alex Boyd, Michelle Caston, Kenny Goff, Amanda Hillman, Michelle Hutchinson, Bunny Larkin, Karen Struthers, Jane Young

The 1980s

Having made a brief detour to British musical theatre in the 1970s with *King's Rhapsody*, the new decade concentrated on mainstream American product. By now, the British musical was in an increasingly parlous state. To many, it seemed that Andrew Lloyd Webber might be the only answer to the genre's *dégringolade*. The N&N began the decade with one of the genre's greatest and most moving works, *Fiddler on the Roof*, a piece that tragically has never lost its currency in a world of refugees suffering persecution. It was, and remains, a noble example of musical theatre at its best. However, this was a decade in which Rodgers and Hammerstein remained supreme, with the Society's second production of *Oklahoma!*, *The King and I*, and *The Sound of Music*, to which it returned in 2022. One of the last wisps of the Society's fascination with operetta, *Die Fledermaus*, may have reminded audiences that the work had already been presented in diluted form as the Society's 1964 *Pink Champagne*, but now the genuine (if still a little watered down) article may be seen as bringing the curtain down on the Society's long flirtation with operetta. In fact, the high-water mark of that genre probably happened at the end of the 1970s with *The Merry Widow*. Lerner and Loewe's glorious *My Fair Lady* was inevitably an audience favourite in 1986, and returned in 2003. That team's Scottish fantasy *Brigadoon* enjoyed glowing reviews when the Society produced it in 1966, but there was general disappointment with the 1988 revival. One of the most versatile of American composers Frank Loesser was represented by *Guys and Dolls* (much better when the Society revived it in Chris Cuming's 2019 production) and by the less known to the general public *The Most Happy Fella*, a work that wrestled with many musical forms. In fact the outcome and casting were far from happy. Audiences would probably have responded more warmly to the kindly satire of Loesser's 1961 Broadway hit *How to Succeed in Business Without Really Trying*, with its witty score about climbing the greasy ladder of achievement. As it is, the Society has never shown much propensity for satire. Also, *How to Succeed* at least belonged to the modern world rather than the romantic past that glowed faintly through so many of the Society's offerings.

1980

FIDDLER ON THE ROOF

Norwich Theatre Royal, 18–23 February
Music: Jerry Bock
Lyrics: Sheldon Harnick
Book: Joseph Stein
Director: Ricky Price
Musical Director: David Kett

In ensemble work and at principal level Charles Roberts found 'many musical rough edges' but nevertheless Ricky Price's production was one of 'unfailing taste and infallible sympathy' in which the company realised 'a prime and triumphant objective – a desperately poignant and deeply credible stoicism in face of grief and heart-break'. It could hardly have been a stronger cast, with Gordon Canwell as the dairyman Tevye. For Miller, 'Here, the part and the actor are one. Gordon Canwell simply is Tevye and I cannot pay a higher tribute than that.' Norma Wick had one of her most memorable roles as Golde. For Miller she displayed 'priceless subtleties of inflection, timing and emotional "give". Strength and generosity are inherent in the performance.' In total, this was an occasion 'so full of warmth, music and poetry' with 'a remarkable degree of commitment in the playing', as for example Audrey Chapman's match-maker. Miller recognised an actress 'whose versatility in each show becomes more and more impressive'. The Society's 2011 return to *Fiddler on the Roof* was justified, this being an enduringly significant example of American musical theatre.

Cast

Tevye (Gordon Canwell), Golde (Norma Wick), Tzeitel (Beverley Baker), Hodel (Lorraine Crotch), Chava (Zelda Smith), Shprintze (Belinda Harper), Bielke (Tina Olley), Yente (Audrey Chapman), Motel (Peter Calf), Perchik (Martyn Rolfe), Lazar Wolf (Sandy Kennon), Mordcha (Peter Mottram), Rabbi (Jack Wood), Mandel (Paul Freeman), Avram (Colin Harris), Nachum (Roy Forder), Grandma Tzeitel (Pip Jenkinson), Fruma-Sarah (Coral Newell), Constable (Roger Fossett), Fyedka (Roger Cliffe), Shandel (Margaret Elliott), Priest (Stanley Gibson), Fiddler (Keith Dempsey)

Papas John Fiddes, Colin Harris, Sandy Kennon, Ron Lyons, Tony Minter, Peter Mottram, Peter Russ, Barry Saull, Jack Wood

Sons Timothy Allison, John Bill, Peter Callf, Gordon Carter, Roy Forder, Paul Freeman, Alan Goose, Laurie Mann, Tony Welch

Mamas Audrey Chapman, Margaret Elliott, Betty Garner, Josephine Gregory, Alvina Johnson, Norma Kennon, Coral Newell, Wendy Watts, Norma Wick

Daughters Jacqueline Annis, Beverley Baker, Miriam Batterbee, Lorraine Crotch, Belinda Harper, Pip Jenkinson, Tina Olley, Barbara Peskett, Zelda Smith

Bottle Dancers and Russians Paul Artherton, Kenny Goff, Andrew K. Harrison, Michael Larkin

1981
KISS ME, KATE

Norwich Theatre Royal, 16–21 February
Music and lyrics: **Cole Porter**
Book: **Sam and Bella Spewack, based on William Shakespeare's** *The Taming of the Shrew*
Director: **Ricky Price**
Musical Director: **Colin Goodchild**

Ricky Price's tenth consecutive musical for the N&N was one of the most sophisticated of its time in American musical theatre history, with its generous handful of numbers that remain standards. Price was not new to this piece, having worked on three previous versions, including the 1970 Sadler's Wells Opera West End production, but there was a mixed critical reaction to his fourth. For Neville Miller one of the main problems was that 'the talented leading couple are not ideally cast … Coral Newell ("that lovely no-hardness-round-the-edges-soprano") is not what I would expect of the Lilli's of this world.' He praised 'the sheer musicality of her singing' and enjoyed the confrontations between Lilli and her ex-actor-husband Fred, played by newcomer to the company John Millward, a 42-year-old engineer for Eastern Electricity, who had spent eight years with the Lowestoft Operatic Society and was about to play Billy in Lowestoft's *Carousel*. Miller appreciated an actor who 'who sings very beautifully, with plenty of humour in his acting, and he looks fine'. But it was the secondary roles that Miller preferred, such as Zelda Smith's Lois ('a glittering little soubrette') delighting in one of the best numbers 'Always True to You in My Fashion', and Norma

Wick's 'Too Darn Hot'. Nevertheless, here was 'a very well-turned assemblage of wit, melody and spectacle, if not exactly the hard Broadway panache the show seems born to celebrate'.

For Charles Roberts, 'The Price magic was missing'. As for Newell, 'This is not a role to which she has found the sympathetic key' in 'the general atmosphere of contrivance and – I say it with real regret as a long-time admirer of Mr Price's work – of stereotyped production'. Here was 'a tired vehicle of a show ... a straightforward assemblage of components plucked from the theatrical tack box of well-worn ideas and stagey clichés'. Millward was criticised for his 'tiresome, mid-Atlantic Radio One accent', although it is difficult to imagine that Roberts ever tuned into that station!

He conceded that 'the whole thing has a fair pace and good continuity' and that Newell and Millward threw themselves into 'the hearty spirit of a pub crawl', but the audience had a long wait before Peter Mottram ('ever a reliable man for a character cameo') and Ron Lyons brushed up their Shakespeare, 'pitching it delightfully somewhere between Abbot and Costello and Morecambe and Wise'.

Cast

Fred Graham / Petruchio (John Millward), Harry Trevor (Jack Wood), Lois Lane / Bianca (Zelda Smith), Ralph (Roger Cliffe), Lilli Vanessi / Katharine (Coral Newell), Hattie (Norma Wick), Stage Doorman (Bunny Mann), Paul (John Bill), Bill Calhoun / Lucentio (Martyn Rolfe), First Gangster (Peter Mottram), Second Gangster (Ron Lyons), Harrison Howell (Mike Gibson), Peter Callf (Hortensio), Gremio (Colin Harris)

Gentlemen of the Chorus John Bill, Peter Callf, Roger Cliffe, John Fiddes, Bill Goff, Andrew Harper, Colin Harris, Alan Lee, Bunny Man, Tony Minter, Richard Phillips, Peter Russ, Tony Welch, Peter Wilson

Ladies of the Chorus Jacqueline Annis, Jill Atkin, Beverley Baker, Miriam Batterbee, Audrey Chapman, Elizabeth Garner, Josephine Gregory, Caroline Hopkins, Pip Jenkinson, Alvina Johnson, Christina Pougher, Patricia Rix, Lorna Turner, Wendy Watts

Dancers Julie Aldred, Rebecca Bartrum, Bernadette Boggan, Marisole Campos, Jane Howard, Andrea Jay

1982
DIE FLEDERMAUS

Norwich Theatre Royal, 22–27 February
Music: **Johann Strauss, adapted by Ronald Hanmer**
Book and lyrics: **Phil Park**
Original libretto: **Henri Meilhac and Ludovic Halévy**
Director: **Ricky Price**
Musical Director: **Colin Goodchild**

Whatever the qualities of the N&N's Johann Strauss opera (and they were many), both Charles Roberts and John Aplin recognised it as not quite the genuine article. Roberts understood the character of Hanmer and Park's adaptation intended for the amateur market, signified by 'various changes in the music to make it more accessible, in the plot to introduce chorus scenes where none was before, and a translation in this instance which frequently makes the eyebrows rise in more than mild surprise'. In effect, this was the Society's second attempt at *Fledermaus*, the first being the 1964 *Pink Champagne*, one of many adaptations intended for amateur performance by the too frequently workaday Eric Maschwitz and Bernard Grun. Nevertheless, almost three decades on, Aplin recognised that now the company had to be content with 'the economy model of Strauss's lavish score, which omits the most demanding vocal exigencies in favour of more extensive use of chorus and spoken dialogue'. It seems that the company had 'gone just a little up-market in their choice'. The ever-discerning Gervase Hughes recommended another version: 'I am waiting for some enterprising director to use Reginald Arkell and A. P. Herbert's version entitled *Come to the Ball*, which in some respects flouts convention but retains all the essential ingredients and is far better constructed than the original.'[1] Along the way, Hughes calculated that around 40 persons had at some time contributed to the piece.

In these circumstances Aplin's review was glowing, despite his complaint (a complaint that remains just as appropriate in more recent years) that the amplification of voices at times produced a 'canned result depersonalising individual vocal colours'. There was no doubting the quality of performances, with Roberts' salute to Coral Newell's Rosalinda with her 'lovely chest notes and a wicked sense of fun', although he regretted that her spoken lines were not given as much range as her sung ones. According to Aplin, Frances Dickerson (always a lovely voice capable of producing beautifully effective sounds) 'throws herself at Adele's 'Laughing Song' with abandon', although Roberts thought she could do with a little more 'oomph', and suggested a glass of bubbly before curtain-up.

Aplin consistently praised the performances: Martyn Rolfe ('delightfully overplayed'), and the 'rich mezzo' of Pamela Warren (a 'creamy contralto' according to Roberts) in the trouser role.

Scanning the company, Roberts drew attention to Peter Mottram's Prison Governor and Lynn Wardle as 'a thoroughly stylish Dr Falke'. The role of Frosch demands an actor with great comic skills; no less than Frankie Howerd played the role at the Coliseum for English National Opera. For Roberts, Gordon Canwell's Frosch was 'farcically funny' and 'his step climbing is an education', and he appreciated 'some splendidly robust sound' from the chorus. His one criticism was that Colin Goodchild's tempi throughout was 'at times so slow that practical waltzing would bring into question Mr. Newton's theories on gravity'.

Cast
Rosalinda Eisenstein (Coral Newell), Gabriel Eisenstein (Christopher Speake), Adele (Frances Dickerson), Dr Falke (Lynn Wardle), Alfred (Martyn Rolfe), Frank (Peter Mottram), Prince Orlofsky (Pam Warren), Ida (Zelda Rolfe), Dr Blint (John McInnes), Frosch (Gordon Canwell), Mitzi (Audrey Chapman), Ivan (Mike Gibson)

Gentlemen of the Chorus Andrew Bainham, John Bill, William Butterfield, Roger Cliffe, John Fiddes, William Goff, Colin Harris, Alan Lee, Ron Lyons, John McInnes, Tony Middis, Peter Russ, Jonathan Syder, Keith Wincote, Tony Welch

Ladies of the Chorus Beverley Baker, Miriam Batterbee, Heidi Blyth, Audrey Chapman, Elizabeth Garner, Josephine Gregory, Caroline Hopkins, Caroline Jarrold, Pip Jenkinson, Alvina Johnson, Brenda Milford, Christina Pougher, Pat Rix, Wendy Watts

Dancers Esther Baldock, Alison Barrett, Sandra Davey, Donna Gallo, Alison Hancy, Maxine Tubby

1983
OKLAHOMA!

Norwich Theatre Royal, 14–19 February
Music: Richard Rodgers
Book and lyrics: Oscar Hammerstein II, based on *Green Grow the Lilacs* by Lynn Riggs
Director: Ricky Price
Musical Director: Colin Goodchild

There was no doubting the success of the N&N's *Oklahoma!*, 20 years after the company's first staging of this public favourite. At the time of writing in 2023, the West End has a radically altered production of this Rodgers and Hammerstein masterpiece. Ricky Price's concept met with almost unmitigated acclaim, with Neville Miller's review headline 'Exhilarating Stuff, This Outstanding Oklahoma!'. Miller told readers that this 'exceptionally well cast' presentation 'renews my gratitude to Rodgers and Hammerstein and the amateur operatic society movement in general', his principal complaint concerning the stiffness of the danced dream sequence, a view shared by Derek James, who thought the ballet the only low point of the evening, a 'ponderous, almost painfully slow sequence [that] seemed hopelessly out of place'. Miller's review was perceptive as he recalled a show in which 'Words and music go together with the songs so well' in which 'the songs seem like natural phenomenon rather than anything that has had to be invented'.

The near-perfect casting reflected the strong state of the company at this time, emphasised by the casting of John Millward as Curly and Stephanie Beare as his sweetheart Laurey. Miller was impressed by both. Regarding Millward, 'I don't think he sang a note last night that was not true and beautiful. He looks good and his acting, like his singing, has natural ease'. As for Beare, she sang 'with great accuracy and sweetness and is a persuasive actress too ... a lovely heroine'. There was an outstanding Ado Annie from Pat Tabor (one of the finest soubrettes in the N&N's history), a beguiling Aunt Eller from Norma Wick (as if the part had been written expressly for her), and strong support from Alan Lee as surly Jud Fry, and John Newell as Ali Hakim getting some of the biggest laughs of the night.

Cast

Curly (John Millward), Aunt Eller (Norma Wick), Laurey (Stephanie Beare), Ike Skidmore (John Fiddes), Slim (William Goff), Will Parker (Colin Harris), Jud Fry (Alan Lee), Ado Annie Carnes (Pat Tabor), Ali Hakim (John Newell),

Gertie Cummins (Erica Ogborn), Andrew Carnes (Peter Mottram), Cord Elam (Mike Gibson)

Gentlemen of the Chorus John Bill, Bill Butterfield, Roger Cliffe, Christopher Davies, Richard Davison, John Fiddes, Mike Gibson, William Goff, Ron Lyons, Peter Mottram, Simon Phillips, Peter Russ, Jonathan Syder, Jack Thompson, Tony Welch

Ladies of the Chorus Jacqueline Annis, Miriam Batterbee, Katherine Cook, Frances Dickerson, Audrey Fiddes, Elizabeth Garner, Nona Gray, Josephine Gregory, Helen Hipper, Brenda Milford, Christina Pougher, Pat Rix, Catherine Spencer, Lorna Turner, Wendy Watts

Dancers Alison Barrett, Marisol Campos, Heather Collins, Amanda Foster, Donna Gallo, Belinda Harper, Andrea Jay, Justine Kerry

1984
THE MOST HAPPY FELLA

Norwich Theatre Royal 13–18 February
Music, book and lyrics: **Frank Loesser**
Producer and Choreographer: **Ricky Price**
Musical Director: **Colin Goodchild**

Following his music and lyrics for *Where's Charley?*, his beguiling musical adaptation of Brandon Thomas' classic British farce *Charley's Aunt*, Frank Loesser's songs for *Guys and Dolls* inhabited one of the most vibrant scores of its period. He was sole author for *The Most Happy Fella* (New York 1956, London 1960), based on Sidney Howard's play *They Knew What They Wanted*. Loesser's ground-breaking attempt to make a Broadway musical by melding elements of opera with recitative and musical comedy made for an authoritative, often intensely moving work that told its simple story of the dignity of ordinary folk.

This is a masterwork. Evoking the era of mail-order brides, the drama concentrated on Rosabella (Frances Dickerson), a lonely waitress in New York, who moves to California's Napa Valley to marry ageing wine-maker Tony (John Barnett) without ever having met him. Rosabella yearns for an unseen 'Somebody, Somewhere'. All she knows of him is the photograph of himself he left on her table, but it is a photograph of Tony's handsome right-hand man Joe (Alan Lee). Tony's jealous sister Marie (Coral Newell) undermines Tony's

47. Robin Baines, David Ivins, John Bill and Adrian Wright 'Standing on the Corner' in *The Most Happy Fella* of 1984 © The Cameo Photographic Studio and Frame Boutique, Norwich.

relationship with Rosabella. On the wedding night, Joe seduces Rosabella. She falls pregnant and Tony, now in love with his mail-order wife, rejects her. They are emotionally reconciled in one of the show's most passionate outbursts 'My Heart is So Full of You', but this score is truly an embarrassment of riches, ranging from Tony's soaring operatic arias 'Rosabella' and 'Mamma Mamma' to Joe's cry of despair in the haunting 'Joey, Joey, Joey'. Tony's kindly smiling friend Herman (Adrian Wright) and Rosabella's sunny soulmate Cleo (Pat Tabor) get the musical comedy material with Cleo's opening waitress complaint 'Ooh! My Feet!' and the trio 'Happy to Make Your Acquaintance'. Herman gets some of the brightest moments, not least his little anthem 'I Like Everybody', and his final declaration of defiance 'I Made a Fist'. He also nabs the show's standout number that enjoyed currency beyond the show, 'Standing on the Corner'. *The Most Happy Fella*, with its brilliant original Broadway orchestrations by the legendary Don Walker, is unquestionably a masterpiece of American musical theatre.

The editor of the *EDP* for 14 February 1984 had a brilliant headline for Charles Roberts' review: 'MOST UNHAPPY FELLA BY N&N'. It is a classic example of a title inviting a stinging riposte made possible merely by the prefix

'Un'. Shunning no detail, Roberts began his review by suggesting that 'one could not but be aware that production, performance and orchestral contribution left much to be desired'. A keen sense of disappointment shrouded the enterprise:

> This is the thirteenth production for the N&N by Ricky Price, a man normally full of inspirational ideas, imagination and gusto. Curiously, these qualities here seem to have deserted him: much of what we see is copy-book stuff and visual cliché, with even the choreography, an area in which Mr Price usually excels, being faintly ill-at-ease. If detailed production was given to the show's three principal characters, it is not too apparent, which is a great pity, for each one of them exhibits real vocal quality.
>
> It is left to the 'second leads' to dominate this show: in particular two gorgeous comedy creations from Adrian Wright and Pat Tabor as Herman and Cleo: their zest, style, attention to detail and evident delight in what they are doing, exuberantly reach out from the stage to carry us happily along with them.

The headline for the *EEN*'s review, 'Magic Melodies save this prosaic production', summed up the discerning reaction of Neville Miller. He did not think Tabor or Wright 'missed anything', and 'had not Mr Loesser been so generous in the chance he gives to the leading pair, they would have stolen the show'. There was praise, too, for the chorus and dancers 'raising the roof at one moment and charming you, pianissimo, the next' although for the orchestra 'last night was not so much First Night as an off night' with the orchestra 'patently under-rehearsed'. He understood that 'There are great difficulties in getting musicians together for shows, but as the going gets tougher in the theatre and high standards become imperative, the difficulties must be overcome.'[2] Miller's parting comment was that 'As a production, it often looks prosaic, and in terms of measuring up to all the opportunities it is among the Society's also-rans'. Its unconquerable problem was that the two leading players sang well (Dickerson beautifully) but the temperature fell when acting took over.

Cast

Cashier (Keith Brown), Cleo (Pat Tabor), Rosabella (Frances Dickerson), Postman (John Fiddes), Tony (John Barnett), Marie (Coral Newell), Herman (Adrian Wright), Al (John Bill), Clem (David Ivins), Jake (Robin Baines), Joe (Alan Lee), Pasquale (Peter Mottram), Guiseppe (Martyn Rolfe), Ciccio (Colin Harris), Country Girl (Zelda Rolfe), Country Boy (Johnathan Syder), Doc (Tom Ashcroft), Priest (Tony Welch)

Gentlemen of the Chorus Justin Barnard, Bill Butterfield, Roger Cliffe, Richard Davison, Tony Middis, Jack Thompson

Ladies of the Chorus Jacqueline Annis, Hilary Baines, Brenda Binns, Katherine Cook, Audrey Fiddes, Nona Gray, Josephine Gregory, Colleen Harris, Brenda Milford, Christina Pougher, Hilary Shepherd, Catherine Spencer, Liz Stevens, Wendy Watts, Rita Wright

Dancers Angela Allcock, Sally Dormer, Belinda Harper, Clare Roberts, Rachael Scott, Nicola Stanage

1985
THE KING AND I

Norwich Theatre Royal, 11–16 February
Music: **Richard Rodgers**
Book and lyrics: **Oscar Hammerstein II, based on the novel *Anna and the King of Siam* by Margaret Landon**
Director: **Ricky Price**
Musical Director: **David Kett**

Reviewing the achievements of Rodgers and Hammerstein, Gervase Hughes thought that 'there was plenty to enjoy in *Oklahoma!* (1943), not quite so much in *South Pacific* (1949), less still in *The King and I* (1951)'. Hughes also raised the spectre of Albert Sirmay who 'edited' Rodgers' work, suggesting that 'The Rodgers-Sirmay share has been inconsistent in taste and quality'.[3] This does not negate the fact that Rodgers .and Hammerstein's Siamese musical has a remarkable score, especially effective in the most reflective numbers 'I Have Dreamed', 'Hello, Young Lovers' and 'We Kiss in a Shadow'. In some ways this is a show that foreshadows their 1959 *The Sound of Music*, the story of a woman who takes on the responsibility of a stranger's children and begins to win them over with 'Getting to Know You' (compared to Maria Rainer's 'Do Re Mi') and strengthens their resolve with 'I Whistle a Happy Tune' (compared to Maria's 'The Lonely Goatherd').

The N&N's Golden Anniversary presentation was the 14th directed by Ricky Price, winning high praise from Charles Roberts, who recognised 'an especially strong team of principals, including some new faces who acquit themselves with credit'. Christopher Speake as the King and Coral Newell as Anna showed 'total involvement with the characters, being two of the most experienced and reliable actor-singers in local amateur music theatre'. Speake, computer manager at Start Rite Shoes, saw the King as 'a jolly nice bloke doing his best'. Helpfully, he had never seen the 1956 film with Yul Brynner, who originated the role on Broadway as the King. Neville Miller considered Speake 'remarkable for balancing so convincingly the child-like autocracy and the warm, eager man anxious to do his best', and that Newell's Anna was 'a supreme example of the essentially feminine but certainly not passive woman' that Newell excelled in portraying.

The supporting roles were strongly cast, with Norma Wick's singing of 'Something Wonderful' described by Roberts as 'a resonance of meaning as much as of sound to make it a high point of the whole evening'. He was impressed by Lee Ingham as Louis and Zane Rambaran as Chululongkorn giving 'outstandingly good performances' alongside such stalwarts as Peter Mottram as Prime Minister. Miller reported that the orchestra 'left things to be desired' but 'Visually, emotionally and in some of the voices, the show is a beauty'. Roberts had no complaint in a review that applauded 'a spirit that rings true', finding no fault with the 'brisk and sustained tempi which ensure that the show is never allowed to flag'.

Cast

Captain Orton (John Fiddes), Louis (Lee Ingham), Anna (Coral Newell), Interpreter (John Bill), Kralahome (Peter Mottram), King (Christopher Speake), Phra Alack (David Ivins), Lun Tha (David Rees), Tuptim (Pip Jenkinson), Lady Thiang (Norma Wick), Chulalongkorn (Zane Rambaran), Sir Edward Ramsey (Bob Brister), Ying Yaowalac (Clare Whiley)

Gentlemen of the Chorus John Bencze, Bill Butterfield, Bob Calvert, Roger Cliffe, Richard Davidson, John Fiddes, William Goff, Todd Vision, Tony Welch

Ladies of the Chorus Susan Alport, Fiona Arnold, Katherine Cook, Frances Dickerson, Audrey Fiddes, Josephine Gregory, Brenda Milford, Melanie Russell, Suki Smith, Catherine Spencer, Pat Tabor, Lorna Turner, Joyce Watts, Wendy Watts, Rita Wright

Children Laila Choat, Joanna Dye, Hannah Munden, Tony Olson, Elizabeth Platt, Lee Plummer, Anna Rosbotham, Corinne Saunders, Charlie Webster, Kim Webster, Rachel Welsh

Dancers Prime Dancer: Gine Chant, Susan Bailey, Veronica Bates, Lucy Conway, Sally Dormer, Joanna Lyon, Susan Websdale

1986

MY FAIR LADY

Norwich Theatre Royal, 10–15 February
Music: **Frederick Loewe**
Book and lyrics: **Alan Jay Lerner, based on George Bernard Shaw's** *Pygmalion*
Director: **Ricky Price**
Musical Director: **David Kett**

The distinguished theatre critic Caryl Brahms (obviously also something of a gardener) insisted that 'the evening is Shaw's. His words wing home. His situations hold. His wit is keen and shows no sign of blunting. His play lives on in the songs of Lerner and Loewe and perhaps more particularly in the music of Loewe.' She noted 'the magic of the songs. Never have numbers been more skilfully used to light up and lift a scene, so that the old text, like Spring, comes round again, and flowers, like the prunus, in the most natural, disarming and refreshing way.'[4]

J. W. Lambert, one of Brahms' male colleagues, looked back on Lerner and Loewe's masterpiece as

> the most bruited entertainment of all. Once more we are back in company with a living legend. Once more before we scrutinise it we must respect it, must bow to the power which has set the Western world in a ferment, caused a lively trade in semi-smuggled gramophone records, and, even in London, a brisk black-market in tickets. Somehow the whole thing has become a sort of middle-brow Mecca; those who have been should surely be allowed to dye their beards, or wear a specially designed beauty-spot.[5]

We wonder how many of the N&N's audience was seeing Eliza Doolittle's adventures for the first time? I was completely captivated when, following the closing of the original London production after 2,281 performances, H. M. Tennant sent out a tour that included the Theatre Royal Norwich on its itinerary. I lost count of the number of times I saw that production, turning up for it night after night: Wendy Bowman as Eliza, Tony Britton as Professor Higgins, Gwynne Whitby as Mrs Higgins, Patrick Waddington as Pickering and Bert Brownbill (luckily a Stanley Holloway lookalike) as Alfred Doolittle.

The N&N's Eliza was newcomer to the Society Eileen Love. As one reporter somewhat tactlessly put it, Coral Newell was 'handing over her crown of many years as the Society's leading lady' and acting as assistant to the director. The pressure on Miss Love must have been considerable. She won over Neville Miller with her 'luverly' voice, but her cockney accent and emotional components of the role were lacking', which 'turns the piece into Professor Higgins' show'. Christopher Speake's interpretation of the arrogant Higgins was 'accomplished in all departments, making the arrogance and the human need of the character equally telling'. Colin Thackeray's Colonel Pickering was 'anonymous', but Miller drew attention to the stylish Mrs Higgins (perfectly cast Ivy Oxley) and to Nona Gray's Mrs Hopkins, 'a tiny role memorable for its authenticity'. Trevor Thurston was possibly born to play Alfred Doolittle, easily getting the measure of his numbers 'With a Little Bit of Luck' and 'Get Me to the Church on Time'. Old habits dying hard, it was no surprise that the Norwich audience gossiped and mardled throughout Mr Loewe's overture. Perhaps it showed more respect when the N&N revisited the show in 2003.

Cast

Mrs Eynsford-Hill (Margaret Elliott), Eliza Doolittle (Eileen Love), Freddy Eynsford-Hill (John McInnes), Colonel Pickering (Colin Thackery), Henry Higgins (Christopher Speake), Cockney Quartet (Robin Baines, Colin Harris, Alan Lee, James Suckling), Harry (Roger Cliffe), Jamie (John Fiddes), Bartender (Peter Mottram), Alfred P. Doolittle (Trevor Thurston), Mrs Pearce (Audrey Fiddes), Mrs Hopkins (Nona Gray), Servants (Pip Jenkinson, Teresa Maddison, Catherine Spencer, Liz Stevens, Roger Keen, Peter Mottram, Tony Welch), Mrs Higgins (Ivy Oxley), Lord Boxington (Colin Harris), Lady Boxington (Colleen Harris), Zoltan Karpathy (John Newell), Queen of Transylvania (Jacqueline Annis), Maid (Erica Ogborn)

Gentlemen of the Chorus Robin Baines, John Bill, Richard Boaste, Bill Butterfield, Roger Cliffe, Richard Davison, John Fiddes, Colin Harris, Roger Keen, Alan Lee, Peter Mottram, Tony Parkins, James Suckling, Tony Welch

Ladies of the Chorus Susan Allport, Jacqueline Annis, Brenda Binns, Susan Boone, Nona Gray, Colleen Harris, Pip Jenkinson, Teresa Maddison, Erica Ogborn, Christina Pougher, Melaine Russell, Catherine Spencer, Liz Stevens, Rosemary Stringer, Susan Turner, Wendy Watts

Dancers Susan Bailey, Lynne Beaumont, Marina Bill, Paula Elliott, Leanne Harvey, Tara Stolworthy

1987
GUYS AND DOLLS

Music and lyrics: Frank Loesser
Book: Jo Swerling and Abe Burrows, based on a story and characters by Damon Runyan
Director: Ricky Price
Musical Director: David Kett

The headline for Neville Miller's review 'Bronx Style – Little Spark' suggested overall disappointment in a show where 'most of the guys and dolls of this show go through their paces rather than live, although the amusing and consistent Nathan Detroit of David Rees is one of the happy exceptions'. Ricky Price's direction was 'some distance short of the required vitality and panache; in fact 'Scene follows scene with commendable smoothness but somehow without accumulative effect'. John Millward's Sky Masterson was hampered by laryngitis: 'his poise in these circumstances was remarkable'. Miller expressed disappointment with Stephanie Timewell's Sarah Brown ('not vocally happy') and Pat Tabor's Miss Adelaide, but John McInnes was applauded for his 'very accomplished' 'Luck be a Lady'.

For the *EDP*, Roberts had similar reactions, his review headline 'Guys a little short of zap' painting the picture, for 'Luck will have to be a lady indeed if the Norfolk and Norwich Amateur Operatic Society's *Guys and Dolls* is to get the zap and zest it needs overall to justify this smash-hit musical's reputation'. Here was a spectacle 'notably short on projection, with drive-power energy in even shorter supply' with the exception of 'Luck be a Lady' with the men's chorus 'brightly choreographed and directed'. This scene was 'the first tangible wave of full sound and real "giving" to us out front'. McInnes as Nicely-Nicely Johnson provided one of the highlights with the gospel-rousing 'Sit Down You're Rocking the Boat'. For Roberts, Timewell was 'very sweet, but very under-projected', while Tabor represented 'a classical chip off the musical comedy block'. With Arvide's 'More I Cannot Wish You' Colin Thackery delivered 'the most endearing, beautifully shaped and warmly resonant cameo of the evening'.

Cast

Nicely-Nicely Johnson (John McInnes), Benny Southstreet (Christopher Speake), Rusty Charlie (Stash Kirkbride), Sarah Brown (Stephanie Timewell), Arvide Abernathy (Colin Thackery), Agatha (Margaret Elliott), Harry the Horse (Michael Hudson), Lt Brannigan (Bob Brister), Nathan Detroit (David

Rees), Angie the Ox (Peter Mottram), Brandybottle Bates (Duncan Moore), Scranton Slim (Andrew Lynn), Liverlips Louie (Colin Harris), Society Max (John Bill), The Greek (Roger Cliffe), Miss Adelaide (Pat Tabor), Sky Masterson (John Millward), Joey Biltmore (Peter Mottram), Mimi (Louise Lynn), General Matilda B. Cartwright (Audrey Fiddes), Big Jule (Alan Lee)

Mission Band Margaret Elliott, Eileen Love, Tony Welch

Hot Box Girls Kathryn Gregory, Mo Lancaster, Louise Lynn, Jane Mack, Lesley Rix, Joan Syrett, Susan Turner, Wendy Watts

Guys John Fiddes, Roger Keen, Sammy Leon

Dolls Brenda Binns, Pip Jenkinson, Melanie Russell, Liz Stevens

1988
BRIGADOON

Norwich Theatre Royal, 8–13 February
Music: **Frederick Loewe**
Book and lyrics: **Alan Jay Lerner**
Director: **Ray Jeffery**
Musical Director: **Adrian Connell**

Chairman Desmond Elliott's programme note drew attention to the fact that '*Brigadoon* has been chosen for a repeat presentation after 22 years, but we hope you feel that the passage of time has not in any way detracted from the delight which unfolds when, magically, the village wakes up for one day after its 100 years slumber'. This reprise of the much-admired Scots fantasy marked the debuts within the Society for director Ray Jeffery and musical director Adrian Connell, Head of Music at Broadland High School.

Essentially, Lerner and Loewe's brilliant piece is an illusion. Out of nowhere, Brigadoon thrives again for a day, and then it is gone. It had assuredly been a critical success for the Society in 1966, but critical opinion of the new production emphasised disillusion. In a commendably concise assessment, Neville Miller reported that 'The task of coping with both Scottish and American accents imposes a strain and there was not enough emotional conviction to override the difficulty', while the leading players John McInnes and Della Stone 'seemed unhappy with the vocal demands'. Elsewhere, David Rees was 'a bright but unvaried presence' and Penny Drew in the comedy soubrette role was

48. Della Stone and John McInnes in the 1998 *Brigadoon*
© Peter King Photography.

'garishly overdrawn'. Miller regretted 'if only the heart and confidence of the work had got into individual performances', but it is highly probable that many of the audience found little to complain of. Mr Bert Priest of Norwich wrote to the *EEN*, suggesting that Miller 'must have gone to the wrong place'.

Ted Bell's review did not make for happy reading. 'Sadly, somewhere along the 240-year-old-trail from New York to Norwich, it has lost, in this production, much of the magic, the charisma, so essential to its well-being'. He praised a memorable 'Almost Like Being in Love', sung by McInnes and Jenny Bugg, but 'such moments were far between'. The tinsel was tarnished and it needed more than a hard-working chorus and delightful choreography to polish it to brightness'. There were attractive contributions from Bugg, Alan Willoughby and Pat Tabor, but 'For too long, however, it seemed as if the players were struggling to believe in themselves and to combat the theatre's acoustics. Where, oh where, was the magic?'

Cast

Tommy Albright (John McInnes), Jeff Douglas (David Rees), Angus Macmonies (Colin Harris), Donald Ritchie (Peter Mottram), Sandy (Peter Callf), Maggie Abernethy (Pat Tabor), Macgregor (Ron Lyons), Stuart Cameron (David Ivins), Harry Ritchie (Matthew Hadley), Meg Brockie (Penny Drew), Andrew Mackeith (John Fiddes), Fiona Mackeith (Della Stone), Jean Mackeith (Jenny Bugg), Charlie Cameron (Alan Willoughby), Mr Murdoch (Colin Thackery), Frank (Dougal Smith), Jane Ashton (Jacqueline Annis)

Gentlemen of the Chorus John Bill, Bill Butterfield, Peter Callf, Jim Clayton, Roger Cliffe, John Fiddes, John Grimble, Matthew Hadley, Colin Harris, David Ivins, Ron Lyons, Peter Mottram, Michael Porter, Tony Welch

Ladies of the Chorus Jacqueline Annis, Brenda Binns, Linda Cockaday, Margaret Elliott, Audrey Fiddes, Caroline Fox, Nona Gray, Josephine Gregory, Colleen Harris, Lesley Roberts, Melanie Russell, Jean Sherlock, Liz Stevens, Joan Syrett, Susan Turner, Wendy Watts, Kim Wright

Dancers Susan Bailey, Nikki Bleach, Yvonne Broady, Veronica Edwards, Erica Fawcett, Ruth Hannant, Louis Lynn, Lesley Rix, Frances Rowell, Jill Sullivan

Piper Peter McMillan

1989

THE SOUND OF MUSIC

Norwich Theatre Royal, February 6–12
Music: Richard Rodgers
Lyrics: Oscar Hammerstein II
Book: Howard Lindsay and Russel Crouse, based on *The Trapp Family Singers* by Maria Augusta Trapp
Director: Robert Marlowe
Musical Director: David Kett

The hazards of *any* amateur company presenting Rodgers and Hammerstein's last musical are many. On Broadway, this 1959 account of the von Trapp Family's run-in with the Nazis originally starred Mary Martin as the yodelling nun-to-be Maria Rainer for 1,443 performances. That achievement was eclipsed by the 1961 London production's astonishing 2,385 performances, in its time becoming the longest running Broadway import. The West End casting avoided having to pay a star to play Maria, choosing the little-known Jean Bayless, probably working herself into the ground (in the first act Maria has a string of demanding numbers) for a salary for which Miss Martin would probably not have got out of bed. The London critics seemed a little uneasy with its happy sequences rubbing shoulders with Nazi derring-dos. 'For some critics the main sticking-point was that the whole thing assumed that audiences had a very sweet tooth, an assumption that was proved correct when its huge commercial success made critical objection obsolete.'[6]

One of the most wonderful things about the British version was that it cast veterans Constance Shacklock as Mother Abbess and Olive Gilbert as Sister Margaretta. Both their careers (Shacklock as a classical singer most known for regularly exciting the Proms audience with her last night 'Rule, Britannia', and Gilbert as a great favourite of Ivor Novello, in whose shows she boomed his melodies) seemed about to draw into the shadows, but not a bit of it. Both stayed with the London production for its entire run, after which Shacklock retired but Gilbert, gallant trouper that she was, bravely carried on. There is something wonderful in imagining these two grand ladies turning up at the stage door of the Palace Theatre for this epic engagement for eight performances a week. We can only hope their five-year stay resulted in their enduring friendship, and helped top up their old age pensions.

The London run would probably have been even longer if it had not been for Hollywood's hugely successful 1964 film, with Julie Andrews and Christopher Plummer. It seemed that attendance at the film became almost a rite.

People returned to it again and again. The film reached Norwich's Gaumont Theatre in July 1966, playing continuously up to February 1967. One elderly lady went 21 times, not having seen a film for 35 years, when it had been silent. In September 1966 the Gaumont's manager Ray Cossey presented the understandably bewildered six-year-old Mark Newstead (the 100,000th patron) with a transistor radio.

By 1989, dust had settled on the old piece, now recreated on stage by Robert Marlowe (already well known in the area for directing variety shows on Cromer Pier), assisted by 'immensely enjoyable choreography' by Michelle Neve in what was a sell-out. Critical praise was in short supply, except for Coral Newell's Mother Abbess. Miller reported that she 'sends the show into orbit' with her act one closer 'Climb Every Mountain'. For Roberts this was 'an interlude to savour, a marriage of technique and emotion and richly mellow sound'. The eyes of both Miller and Roberts were drawn to the lesser characters on stage. Miller thought Margaret Elliott's housekeeper was 'impeccable' and Andrew Stone's performance as Rolf offered 'superb dancing'.

The show brightened when the Trapp Family children were on stage, but the leading players must have been disappointed at the critical responses. Miller had no doubt that Julia Canwell had 'charm and stage know-how, but she produced her voice in the modern pop way. To me, it takes the shine off Maria's numbers.' One of the difficulties was that Julie Andrews' performances were so embedded in the public's consciousness. Miller described how David Rees had 'a strut and a smile to signal the two sides of Von Trapp's character but not much substance in between. The traumas of both seem less than skin-deep.' It could be, of course, that the role is anyway underwritten. Roberts agreed that neither Maria nor the captain 'seems to have thought into the role, or felt outwards. And it shows.'

One question remains – when Maria and the Mother Abbess exchange their lists of favourite things, with the Mother Abbess repeating Maria's list word for word. If Hammerstein had allowed the Mother Abbess her own list of favourites, it would have widened the choice available for those attending sing-a-long showings of the film in appropriate costume, forcing fewer people to go dressed as a brown paper parcel tied up with string.

Cast

Sister Berthe (Audrey Fiddes), Sister Margaretta (Greta Carver), Sister Sophia (Susan Horton), Coral Newell (Mother Abbess), Maria Rainer (Julia Canwell), Captain Georg von Trapp (David Rees), Franz (John Fiddes), Frau Schmidt (Margaret Elliott), Liesl (Philippa Lee), Friedrich (Neil Freeman / Jonathan Collen), Louisa (Sadie McMahon / Rebecca Smith), Kurt (Andrew Cohen / Mark Reid), Brigitta (Lucy Middleton / Nicola Middleton), Marta (Lucy Skitmore / Claire Simmons), Gretl (Kerrie Hudson / Emma Kemp), Rolf Gruber (Andrew Stone), Elsa Schraeder (Jacqueline Annis), Max Detweiler

49. Dancing mistress Michelle Neave with Norma Wick during *The Sound of Music* (1989). Courtesy of NNOS Archive.

(Peter Mottram), Herr Zeller (Mike Mills), Baron Elberfeld (Tony Welch), Baroness Elberfeld (Christine Jermy)

Gentlemen of the Chorus John Bill, Bill Butterfield, Roger Cliff (*sic*), Colin Harris, Alan Lee, John Newell, Tony Welch

Ladies of the Chorus Samantha Callaghan, Vanessa Drew, Caroline Fox, Dawn Hall, Debbie Oliver, Frances Rowell, Katherine Spencer, Della Stone

Nuns Brenda Binns, Linda Cockaday, Penny Drew, Josephine Gregory, Christine Robertson, Jean Sherlock, Wendy Watts, Bronwen Woodcock, Kim Wright

The 1990s

Desmond Elliott, the current chairman, welcomed the audience in the programme for the Society's return of *Annie Get Your Gun* to the Theatre Royal after 19 years:

> Many of you will know that in the near future this theatre will close for major improvements and refurbishment. For many years, the Society has been fortunate in being able to present its shows here – even in the lean years when our show was the only live show to be seen on this stage. Happily for all of us, the theatre has been brought back to life again, and we feel privileged to have been able to retain our slot in the theatre's full calendar. When we present our next show in 1991, I sincerely hope it will be the same slot in the refurbished theatre.

The day after *Annie Get Your Gun*'s last performance, the Society featured in a Royal Gala Variety Show in the presence of the Duchess of Kent. The renovation, even transformation, of the Theatre Royal, would be overseen by Dick Condon, who had come to the theatre following its major refit in 1970. Applying for the job of general manager of the Royal, he had never been to Norwich until he arrived there for interview. On that day, he stood outside Debenhams store, a stone's throw from the Royal, and asked ten people where the Theatre Royal was. Only two knew. In March 1990 he told *Encore*:

> My upbringing in life always drummed into me that you should give, give, give. I like to see people satisfied and happy. That's what gives me the most pleasure in my job. I read on their faces a sense of anticipation when they step through the doors of the theatre, and when I see them go out I read satisfaction. There's a tremendous buzz in that.

His support and promotion and, hopefully, affection for the N&N stands as testament to the important role he played in its continuance and development. He had no unfulfilled ambitions.: 'I don't feel the need to strive for anything. I've never had anything in terms of worldly possessions. And yet – I have the one thing that eludes most people – peace.'

The mid-1990s saw one of the Society's greatest achievements in the Threshold Theatre Company created by John and Audrey Fiddes. This adjunct to the Society was set up to provide an introduction to all aspects of musical theatre both on and off stage. Its debut production was *West End Story* staged at the Hewett School's Walter Roy Theatre. In 2003 Threshold moved productions to Norwich Playhouse, allowing Threshold the facilities and expertise to grow in confidence, status and success, and enabling it to play to bigger audiences and critical acclaim. Its notable success has been recognised by nominations and awards from NODA (the National Operatic and Dramatic Association), the national body representing amateur theatre, establishing itself as a highly professional company.

At the Society's 1995 annual general meeting, the membership was 'generally in favour' of dropping the 'amateur' from the company's title, a view corroborated at the 1996 annual general meeting and finally ratified in 1997, when the Charity Commissioners agreed to the renaming. The agenda for the special general meeting of the Society of July 1997 stated:

> This amendment will in no way affect the principal charitable purpose of the Trust which will at all times be the education and training of persons with the object of furthering their careers in any one or more branches of the arts of the live theatre in all its forms, including cinema, radio, television and like forms of presenting the written word.

A note of dissension crept into the minutes of the committee in September 1995, when Keith Goodwin accepted the invitation to stage manage the 1996 show (*Meet Me in St Louis*), but explained that he would not undertake the duties of stage manager for the 1997 show (*Barnum*) if, as he believed, Mr Robert Marlowe was to be producer. He was not.

1990
ANNIE GET YOUR GUN

Norwich Theatre Royal, 12–17 February
Music and lyrics: **Irving Berlin**
Book: **Herbert and Dorothy Fields**
Director: **Robert Marlowe**
Musical Director: **David Kett**

It is one of those shows that demands a star performance where nothing else will do. Now, in the footsteps of Broadway's 1946 Ethel Merman, London's 1947 Dolores Gray and Norma Wick's N&N 1971 performance, came Susan Horton. Neville Miller considered the new production to be 'the Society's best show for several years' (a claim frequently made by critics through the years for many an N&N production), one of the reasons being an Annie who 'not only sings with a strong, clear voice that hits the notes smack in the middle but phrases the songs with considerable artistry. And, whatever she is doing, she stays firmly in the character of the spunky country girl who ain't had any learnin' but is no fool either.' For the *EDP*'s Ted Bell, Horton was 'A pocket-sized bubble of sparkling energy, she takes the show, and its other principals, by the scruff of the neck'. This was 'a simply adorable Annie'. For Miller, Robert Marlowe's 'beautiful looking production' had 'a satisfying discipline in the big dance numbers and a chorus sound that goes straight to the heart'.

There was success, too, for John Grimble and Caroline Fox, bringing 'outstanding finesse to youthful charm'. Miller's only reservations were that he wished 'the talented Pat Tabor did not go so far over the top' as Dolly Tate, and the singing of leading man Michael Mills. For Bell, the 'tanned and Gable-moustached' Michael Mills 'needed the first half to get fully in tune with Frank Butler' but went on to be 'a fine foil and adversary'; but the show belonged to Horton. One critic who reviewed Miss Gray's performance in the London production was upset by the fact that 'Miss Gray in particular is put to great disadvantage by being obliged to walk like a rheumatic platypus, this as a reminder of the Origins of Annie, and to assume the expression of a young heifer whenever her boyfriend comes in view'.[1] It is to be hoped that Miss Horton avoided this characterisation. The *New Statesman* critic wearily reported that the original London production contained 'an intolerable deal of talk', happily interrupted by Berlin's brilliant score.[2]

Cast
Charlie Davenport (David Rees), Mac (John Bill), Foster Wilson (Peter Mottram), Dolly Tate (Pat Tabor), Winnie Tate (Caroline Fox), Tommy Keeler (John Grimble), Frank Butler (Michael Mills), Annie Oakley (Susan Horton), Little Jake (Justin Wigg / Christopher Edwards), Nellie (Lucy Skitmore / Clare Summons), Jessie (Nicola Goodall / Nicola Middleton), Minnie (Rebecca Smith / Tahlia Baily), Col. Wm. F. Cody Buffalo Bill (John Fiddes), Mrs Littlehorse (Greta Carver), Mrs Blacktooth (Jean Sherlock), Train Conductor (David Joscelyne), Chief Sitting Bull (John Newell), Pawnee Bill (Alan Lee), Pawnee's Messenger (Paul Cray), Sylvia Potter-Potter (Jacqueline Annis)

Gentlemen of the Chorus John Bill, Martyn Bumstead, Mike Childs, Roger Cliffe, Paul Cray, Neil Freeman, Steve Hopkins, Chris Jeckells, David Joscelyne, Jim Lord, Peter Mottram, Geoff Payne, Alan Thwaites, Tony Welch

Ladies of the Chorus Jacqueline Annis, Susan Bailey, Christine Betts, Susan Booth, Yvonne Broady, Louise Brighton, Jenny Bugg, Linda Cockaday, Kate Deans, Penny Drew, Veronica Edwards, Ruth Hannant, Philippa Lee, Rachel Mockridge, Frances Rowell, Rebecca Scrutton, Jean Sherlock, Patience Tims, Lorna Turner, Joanne Wade, Kim Wright

Children Kerrie Hudson, Emma Kemp

There was no production in 1991 or 1992.

1993

THE MUSIC MAN

Norwich Theatre Royal, 1–6 February

***Music, book and lyrics*: Meredith Willson, from a story by Willson and Franklin Lacey**

***Director*: Ricky Price**

***Musical Director*: David Kett**

This was the first major N&N production since 1990, with the Theatre Royal undergoing major renovation. One of the most lovable Broadway shows from what we might see as the Golden Years of American Musical Theatre, Meredith Willson's brilliantly inventive *The Music Man* was something of a one-off. His first musical, it premiered in New York in 1957 and was followed by *The Unsinkable Molly Brown* (1960) and *Here's Love* (1963) of which most British theatregoers are blissfully unaware. The originality of much of *The Music Man* is too often overlooked, packed though it is with brilliant theatrical and musical adventure. The Broadway original had the advantage of the great Robert Preston as travelling salesman 'Professor' Harold Hill, fleecing money from parents who long to see their children in a band. Basically, Hill is a fast-talking con man, which makes for an interesting musical hero. When the show arrived in London in 1961 Preston stayed home, making way for Hollywood's Van Johnson to lead the West End company, capably but with less stellar quality.

On every level *The Music Man* succeeds. Willson's score is full of clever tricks: the opening 'Rock Island' performed by Professor Harold Hill's travelling salesmen colleagues to the rhythm of the locomotive taking them to Iowa; Marian's mother intruding into her daughter's 'Piano Lesson'; the male barbershop quartet of the town's worthies manipulated by Hill to break into song whenever he needs to evade closer scrutiny, tunefully evident in 'Sincere', 'Goodnight Ladies', 'It's You' and 'Will I Ever Tell You?'; the gossiping citizens of Iowa 'Pick-a-Little, Talk-a-Little' superbly characterised by Willson in a frenzied chicken-like gathering; Hill's gentle love song to 'Marian the Librarian' doing its best to observe the rule of silence in her workplace. As if such inventiveness were not enough, there are spankingly catchy company numbers in 'Wells Fargo Wagon' and 'Shipoopi'. What's more, it has a literary awareness, thanks mainly to Marian, battling with the small-minded citizens of Iowa who protest that she advocates 'dirty books' (Chaucer, Rabelais and Balzac!) as she dreams of her imaginary 'White Knight'.

> And if occasionally he ponders
> What makes Shakespeare and Beethoven great
> Him I could love till I die
> Him I could love till I die

The London production (as its blazingly effective original cast recording proves) had much to offer, most brilliantly Patricia Lambert as Marian the Librarian, with some of the score's most thrilling items: try 'Goodnight My Someone' (its melody is simply a slowed-down 'Seventy-Six Trombones'), the gorgeous aria 'My White Knight' and, surely one of the most craftily deceptive and simple lyrics from any major American musical, 'Till There Was You'. The last named is stunningly sung by Lambert against the background of the original London company orchestra, much augmented here for the recording. It is doubtful that London audiences heard such breath-taking sounds coming from the theatre pit at the Adelphi. Mr Johnson (who must have been aware of Lambert's brilliance) creeps into the song to join his leading lady for a few final bars, but we have Lambert to thank for this intensely moving contribution to British musical theatre. The lyric's simplicity is remarkable, with its rhyming of 'singing', 'bringing', 'winging', but the cumulative effect, especially in the superb original orchestrations by Don Walker and Laurence Rosenthal, is magical.

For some, those Seventy-Six Trombones may be a little too much, moving the song into the 'irritating' category, but its honest exuberance is commendable. Vigour seems to have been at the heart of Price's £43,000 production for the N&N, with David Rees' bright-as-a-button Harold Hill, and Andrea Ferguson (according to Roberts 'a real find') as Marian. Rees 'gives everything he has', with 'every last member of a very large cast (63) responding splendidly to Price's inspiration'. For Roberts, Ferguson 'not only looks enchanting and shows off her lovely costume with utter naturalness, but sings with a voice which makes one want to hear her far more than the score allows'. One wonders if something was missing here, for the score generously provides for Marian's role. The music was directed by David Kett with 'the warmth and care and pacey momentum which are the hallmarks of this hugely popular conductor'.

Cast
Travelling Salesmen (Roger Cliffe, John Fiddes, Christopher Penn, Martin Wilson, Gareth Woodcock), Charlie Cowell (Jim Lord), Conductor (Tony Welch), Harold Hill (David Rees), Mayor Shinn (John Newell), Ewart Dunlop (John Bill), Oliver Hix (Mike Childs), Jacey Squires (Christopher Penn), Olin Britt (Peter Russ), Marcellus Washburn (Peter Mottram), Tommy Djilas (Max Hogden), Marian Paroo (Andrea Ferguson), Mrs Paroo (Audrey Fiddes), Amaryllis (Claire Louise Eames), Winthrop Paroo (Christopher Edwards), Eulalie Mackecknie Shinn (Norma Wick), Zaneeta Shinn (Lucy Skitmore), Gracie Shinn (Rachel Bond), Alma Hix (Colleen Harris), Maud Dunlop (Nona Gray), Ethel Toffelmier (Jacqueline Brightman), Mrs Squires (Rosemary Stringer), Constable Locke (Gareth Woodcock)

Gentlemen of the Chorus Peter Brown, Roger Cliffe, Martin Coleman, John Fiddes, Neil Freeman, Jim Lord, Christopher Penn, Alan Thwaites, Peter Watson, Tony Welch, Martin Wilson, Gareth Woodcock

Ladies of the Chorus Brenda Atteron, Linda Bolton, Catherine Chalu, Suzanne Creamer, Elaine Dixon, Nicola Lyon, Christine Robertson, Melanie Russell, Joan Syrett, Susan Turner, Helen Welch, Kim Wright

Town Children Sophie Horlick, Lucy Martin, Heidi Nuthall, Emma Parker, Tommy Brown, Benjamin Harold, Mark Norman, Thomas Punt, Tristan Sanders

Dancers Emily Dennis, Georgina Fisher, Kate Freebury, Debbie Lawes, Kirsty Lewis, Nicola Middleton, Zena Stone, John Eastoe, Neil Freeman, Matthew Simpson

1994
OLIVER!

Norwich Theatre Royal, 31 January–5 February
Music, book and lyrics: Lionel Bart
Director: Ricky Price
Musical Director: David Kett

It seems extraordinary that *Oliver!* had to wait 34 years before making its debut at the N&N. Three decades later it is probably the only one of Lionel Bart's musicals that most of the British public remembers. Bart emerged in the late 1950s as one of the most promising home-made practitioners of musical theatre. In 1959 he was lyricist for the rumbustious *Lock Up Your Daughters* (a work that seems to have lapsed) and followed up that year with his music and lyrics for the 'kitchen sink' *Fings Ain't Wot They Used t'Be*, very much the sort of British musical that the N&N would never have given a second glance to.

Oliver! reached the West End in June 1960, but it almost never happened. Its producer Donald Albery had seriously considered cancelling its London opening, but the opening night was a sensation: suddenly, Bart's extraordinarily effective adaptation of Dickens' novel was a copper-bottomed critical and commercial success. On the face of it, it seemed an unlikely candidate for worldwide popularity: here was a musical that involved domestic violence and murder (Sikes killing of Nancy); robbery with GBH (Sikes' occupation); child exploitation by many of the principal characters including Fagin, Sikes, the Sowerberrys, the Beadle and Widow Corney, and corruption and malfeasance in public office. There was, too, the suggestion that Nancy might be working as a prostitute under Fagin's control. Perhaps Moody was flippant when he once described Fagin as 'a crazy old Father Christmas gone wrong'. In years to come, Fagin would probably be called on by social services.

Bart made two more important contributions to British musical theatre with the 1962 *Blitz!*, a sort of tribute to Londoners facing up to Hitler, and the Liverpudlian *Maggie May* in 1964. Neither of these have enjoyed enduring revival. He sealed his career as one of Britain's major creators of musical theatre with *Twang!!* in 1965, remembered as a notoriously chaotic occasion that effectively put an end to his career. Through the various misfortunes that dogged his later years, *Oliver!* has endured as a model of its kind, constructed with consummate skill. Indeed, it is a wonder that Bart had no assistance in its writing and composition. In his catalogue of works his immortality depends on *Oliver!*, although it was a work born of squabbling and dissent. Only two days before opening night, choreographer Malcolm Clare walked out because his routines had been altered by director Peter Coe, who wanted no dancing in the show. Its two stars, Ron Moody and Georgia Brown, did not 'get on', at loggerheads throughout the rehearsal period, with Moody (as we know from the diary entries included in his autobiography) obsessed with professional mistrust of his leading lady.

Critical reaction to the N&N's production was a little muted, with little evidence of hats being thrown into the air. For Charles Roberts, 'this production overall never really does ignite. There is a lack of electricity, of theatrical oomph, about it. Most of the potentially splendid characters hardly take on flesh.' Colin Harris' Fagin suggested 'an amiable, genteel Dr Coppelius'. For Neville Miller, Harris' skill showed in the musical numbers, but his characterisation was achieved 'without quite believing in the sleazy side'. Miller praised Kett's orchestra ('the best I have heard playing for the Society') but 'Admirable qualities are brought to other major roles without a final authoritative stamp' on the whole, and Paul Gray's Bill Sikes 'lacked deep evil'. Helen Welch's Nancy was one of the strongest components (Miller's opinion of her was glowing), although Roberts would have preferred 'some Piaf-like gustiness and angst against the sweetness', and her standout number 'As Long as He Needs Me' was not well-directed. Nevertheless, Welch was 'one of the strongest pillars in the show. Her Nancy has strength of character and real presence, backed by a lovely voice.'

Cast
Oliver Twist (Mark Norman, Timothy Bell), Workhouse Boys and Fagin's Gang (Lee Allan, Daniel Amis, Tommy Brown, Joseph Burley, Ben Carpenter, Gary Crowe, Ross Cullum, Christopher Edwards, Ian Fletcher, Alex Foxton, Nicholas Harding, Benjamin Harold, Giles Heap, Ashley Jackson, Matthew Jones, Thomas Punt, Tristan Sanders, Aaron Sillis, Mark Turner, Tom Walmsley, Timothy Winters, Jacob Wyatt), Mr Bumble (John Fiddes), Widow Corney (Audrey Fiddes), Mr Sowerberry (John Newell), Mrs Sowerberry (Margaret Elliott), Charlotte (Suzanne Chapman), Noah Claypole (Matthew Simpson), Artful Dodger (Shaun Aquilina / Joseph Crowley), Fagin (Colin Harris), Nancy (Helen Welch), Bet (Mandie Barnett), Mr Brownlow (Jim Lord), Bill Sikes (Paul Cray), Mrs Bedwin (Jean Barratt), Dr Grimwig (David Rees), Old Sally (Zelda Rolfe), Bulls-Eye (dog) Polar

Gentlemen of the Chorus Ian Chisholm, Gordon Clarke, Roger Cliffe, Neil Freeman, Peter Mottram, Brian Newell, Christopher Penn, Julian Read, Peter Russ, Matthew Simpson, Peter Watson, Tony Welch

Ladies of the Chorus Jacqueline Brightman, Jenny Bugg, Linda Campbell, Suzanne Chapman, Elaine Dixon, Andrea Ferguson, Colleen Harris, June Harrison, Debbie Lawes, Christine Robertson, Zelda Rolfe, Melanie Russell, Gillian Tichbourne, Glynis Tipple, Kim Wright

1995
42ND STREET

Norwich Theatre Royal, 30 January–4 February
Music: Harry Warren
Lyrics: Al Dubin
Book: Michael Stewart and Mark Bramble, based on the novel by Bradford Ropes
Director: Robert Marlowe
Musical Director: David Kett

Robert Marlowe's production of *42nd Street* was a stage adaptation of the 1933 Warner Bros film of which Leslie Halliwell wrote 'The clichés are written and performed with great zest, the atmosphere is convincing and the numbers when they come are dazzling.'[3] The N&N's production sold out two and a half weeks before curtain-up; the last show to have sold out was the 1976 *South Pacific*. Neville Miller thought it 'the most exciting first night that I can remember in the twenty or more years I have watched them'. Recalling Busby Berkeley's brilliant choreography for the film, Miller praised the N&N's 'huge vitality and style ... There is so much colour, sparkle and personality that the comparison does the show no harm at all.' Among the outstanding moments was the 'superb' dramatic scene between the ageing star and her replacement.

As the fading star Dorothy Brock, Nona Gray gave a memorable performance, praised by Charles Roberts as 'powerfully projecting the image – and a singing voice with smoke in its throat which catches at your heart-strings'. Gray's numbers included 'You're Getting to be a Habit with Me', 'I Know Now' and 'About a Quarter to Nine'. Among those sharing congratulations was David Rees as Julian Marsh, raising the roof in the title song and 'Lullaby of Broadway' and performing with 'great authority'. For Roberts, Rees had 'a role which has been waiting for him – and he gives it the best I've ever seen from him'. The validity of the product was all-encompassing: 'Every principal, and the fine reeds, brass and rhythm band directed by David Kett, all deserve accolades. All round, it's a congratulatory night.' Others mentioned in despatches included Pat Tabor ('irresistibly OTT as greasepaint-in-her-bloodstream Maggie'), 'deliciously bubbly comedienne' Susan Turner as Anytime Annie, Helen Welch's 'adorable' Peggy (Roberts compared her to Doris Day), and stalwart Christopher Penn 'radiating the persona of a likeable young guy' as Billy Lawlor.

A highlight in the company's portfolio, *42nd Street* suggested a new, younger vigour that promised well for the Society's future audience. Its publicity officer

50. *42nd Street* (1995) © Peter King Photography.

Melanie Russell told the press 'We are conscious that in choosing our next production we must keep them with us.'

Cast

Andy Lee (Mark Lane), Maggie Jones (Pat Tabor), Bert Barry (Ian Chisholm), Mac (John Fiddes), Anne Reilly (Susan Turner), Lorraine Fleming (Linda Campbell), Phyllis Dale (Andrea Ferguson), Ruby Smith (Justine Kerry), Billy Lawlor (Christopher Penn), Peggy Sawyer (Helen Welch), Julian Marsh (David Rees), Dorothy Brock (Nona Gray), Abner Dillon (Peter Mottram), Pat Denning (John Newell), Oscar (John Barnett), Doctor (Jim Lord), 'Wardrobe' (Brenda Atterton)

Gentlemen of the Chorus David Chapman, Roger Cliffe, Chris Floyd, Ian Freeman, Colin Harris, Jim Lord, Lorbreck Palmer, David Pulling, Peter Russ, Nick Sparkes, Alan Willoughby

Ladies of the Chorus Jane Arthurton, Susan Bailey, Jacqueline Brightman, Jenny Bugg, Nicola Butterfield, Gemma Caldicott, Rachel Colley, Elaine Dixon, Sue Duxbury, Veronica Edwards, Sue Gurney, June Harrison, Carolyn Johnston, Wendy Knipe, Melanie Russell, Glynis Tipple, Cheryl Turmaine, Claire Watts, Kim Wright

Boys David Chapman, Roger Cliffe, Chris Floyd, Ian Freeman, Colin Harris, Jim Lord, Lorbreck Palmer, David Pulling, Peter Russ, Nick Sparkes, Alan Willoughby

Offstage Chorus Brenda Atterton, Vanessa Andrews, Jean Barratt, Zelda Rolfe, Gill Tichbourne, Barry Allen, James Clayton, Brian Newell, Peter Russ, Tony Welch, Alan Willoughby, Peter Winter

1996
MEET ME IN ST LOUIS

Norwich Theatre Royal, 29 January–3 February
Music and lyrics: **Hugh Martin and Ralph Blane**
Book: **Sally Benson, based on Sally Benson's Kensington stories and the MGM film *Meet Me in St Louis***
Director: **Ricky Price**
Musical Director: **David Kett**

Following the hugely successful *42nd Street* of 1995, there was less enthusiasm for another theatrical adaptation of a much-loved Hollywood movie. MGM's charming account of a loving family in the 1944 *Meet Me in St Louis*, rated by Halliwell as 'Patchy but generally highly agreeable musical nostalgia with an effective sense of the passing years and seasons.'[4] An obvious disadvantage in its theatrical form was the absence of the incomparable Judy Garland. Neville Miller loved the film but on stage 'the piece is longer and the charm diluted' while 'Additional songs leave me thinking that Rodgers and Hammerstein and Lerner and Loewe did the same kind of thing better and that although the number of young people in the cast is encouraging, several need a good deal more vocal training before they can take command of a song'. Miller singled out Helen Welch and Andrea Ferguson as 'accomplished'.

The film critic Dilys Powell described MGM's film as having 'everything a romantic musical should have', but Charles Roberts' crushing review for the *EDP* ('Rendezvous with N&N gives painful birth to St Louis Blues') told its story. Here was a show 'not so much a musical, more a pastiche of a bad turn-of-the-century play with several unremarkable songs plus a few good ones'. Roberts' opinion chimes with John Douglas Eames description of the movie in his gargantuan history of MGM:

> Despite the fact that it contained fine songs including Martin and Blane's 'The Trolley Song', 'The Boy Next Door' and 'Have Yourself a Merry Little

Christmas', it wasn't so much a musical as a charming family album brought to life by director Vincente Minnelli.[5]

Roberts was in no doubt that, 'with a handful of exceptions, its singing, dancing and playing are disappointing, with scenery dull and repetitive and orchestral playing which is frequently embarrassing' although the show 'lifted' after the interval, with some full company scenes such as 'Banjos' led by Mark Lake.

Cast

Tootie (Georgina-Jane Leslie / Genevieve Raghu), Mr Smith (David Rees), Mrs Smith (Colleen Harris), Agnes (Emma Harte / Faye Liddle), Katie (Gillian Tichbourne), Esther (Andrea Ferguson), Rose (Helen Welch), Lon (Mark Lake), Grandpa Prophater (John Newell), Douglas Moore (David Chapman), John Truitt (Andy Lofthouse), Lucille Ballard (Linda Campbell), Chet (Christopher Penn), Frank (David McCaffrey), Peewee Drummond (Ian Chisholm), Miss Rockwell (Wendy Knipe), Doctor Bond (John Fiddes)

Gentlemen of the Chorus Darren Brooks, Ian Chisholm, Roger Cliffe, Adrian Fennell, Mark Fiddy, Clive Hoar, Jim Jenkinson, David McCaffrey, Peter Mottram, Lorbreck Palmer, Christopher Penn, David Pulling

Ladies of the Chorus Gillian Atterson, Susan Bailey, Kerrie Barnett, Jenny Bugg, Wendy Knipe, Jo Maud, Nicola Middleton, Alison Peck, Sarah Pryde, Glynis Tipple, Cheryl Turmaine, Claire Whiley, Juliet Williams, Kim Wright

1997

BARNUM

Norwich Theatre Royal, 28 January–1 February
Music: **Cy Coleman**
Lyrics: **Michael Stewart**
Book: **Mark Bramble**
Director: **Ray Jeffery**
Musical Director: **David Kett**

Gerald Bordman, a distinguished chronicler of American musical theatre, considered *Barnum* 'Diverting theatre rather than a contribution to our lyric literature' and the score was 'lively as all get out but had non sticking power'.[6]

For Stanley Green, the authors had decided to simply 'offer the show as a total circus concept with the entire cast constantly in motion tumbling, clowning, marching, twirling and flying through the air' in the original Broadway production of 1980.[7] Reviewing the London revival of 2017, Susannah Clapp reported: 'Cy Coleman's music – lots of brass oompah – and Michael Stewart's merry but undistinguished lyrics are entertaining but not strong enough to make the story vivid.'[8] Coral Newell's programme note for the N&N *Barnum* identified the show as 'the most challenging and costly production we have ever attempted'.

Norwich had substantial links with one of Barnum's greatest associates the 'Swedish Nightingale' Jenny Lind, a close friend of Hans Christian Andersen (he wanted to marry her) and favourite of Queen Victoria, Mendelssohn and Chopin, who explained: 'This Swede does not show herself in the ordinary light of day but in the magic rays of the aurora borealis.'[9] Lind frequently visited Norwich, generously donating money for the establishment of the Jenny Lind Childrens' Ward in Pottergate in 1854. When the building deteriorated, Jeremiah Colman donated a site at Unthank Road, where a new Jenny Lind hospital was opened in 1900. In later years Lind wrote: 'Of all the money God allowed me to give away when my poor throat could call an audience to listen to its production none has borne a nobler or genuine fruit than the Jenny Lind Hospital in Norwich.'[10]

For Roberts, one of the strengths of the N&N production was that 'the company is largely a young one, responding to the demands of a complex show, zestfully enjoying their hard-won circus tricks, moving with the pace and momentum of youth – and every face vibrantly alive and involved'. As Melanie Russell explained: 'The whole cast have had to learn to walk the tightrope and other circus tricks.'

As Barnum, Chris Darnell enjoyed a personal triumph. Miller thought he painted 'an extraordinary portrait that blends convincingly the bombast of the Prince of Humbug' with 'sincerity in his love for his wife, athleticism and musicality'. In fact, 'If there were Oscars for amateur performers Mr Darnell would deserve more than one'. Here was 'the N&N Society right back to the life-enhancing form that made its tap-dancing *42nd Street* an eye-opener two years ago'.

Charles Roberts was equally enthusiastic, finding the company 'at its resounding best' in a piece 'full of the glow of living and the warmth of loving', creating 'a radiant joyfulness'. Darnell displayed 'masterly showmanship and technique, a whipcord outline of relentless energy and drive which activates all around him' in 'a notable performance at the heart of an uplifting evening'. Helen Welch as Barnum's wife was an 'endearing presence, a personality to fall in love with, a lovely singing voice and an actress's command of timing'. Among the prominent curiosities were The Blues Singer (Christine Mullord), Tom Thumb (Andy Lofthouse) and Heth (Gillian Tichborne).

In October 1997 the American musical *Side Show*, which centred on the real lives of conjoined Siamese twins Daisy and Violet Hilton, opened in New York to mixed reviews. The opening number invited the audience to 'Come look at the freaks, Come gape at the geeks, Only pennies for peeks'. *Side Show* had more regard than *Barnum* for the darker aspects of circus, with Coleman and Stewart seemingly content on taking a ringside seat for a celebration of high energy capers with little regard for the self-appointed Greatest Showman on Earth's exploitation of humankind. Tod Browning's deeply disturbing 1932 American film *Freaks* suggested that some P. T. Barnum-inspired exploitation of the physically malformed might thrive still, its performers including valiant Violet and Daisy, Randion ('The Human Torso'), 'Pinheads', 'Half Boy' Johnny Eck, and 'The Human Skeleton' Peter Robinson. Nothing could be closer to the truth of much of Barnum's activities, assiduously avoided by the creators of the musical. As a horror movie, Browning's film has as disturbing a finale as any that ever came out of Hollywood. *Side Show* produced one of the most emotionally surging moments in American musicals of the 1990s in the Hiltons' roof-raising duet 'I Will Never Leave You', a tribute to the sisters' bravery and endurance. Their careers ended, they worked at a local convenience store in North Carolina. They died within a few days of each other in 1969.

Barnum's exploitation of such disadvantaged people should not be forgotten. Diminutive 'General' Tom Thumb was only four years old and 25 inches tall when Barnum presented him on stage as a curiosity; aged six, he was presented to Queen Victoria at Buckingham Palace. Her Majesty seems to have been fascinated by small people, meeting the 'Royal American Midgets' troupe in 1880. Another of Barnum's curiosities was the supposedly 116-year-old Joice Heth, billed as 'The Oldest Woman Alive', a 'marvellous relic of antiquity' and a 'living skeleton'. In collaboration with James Anthony Bailey from 1881, Barnum promised 'The Greatest Show on Earth: Peerless Prodigies of Physical Phenomena and Great Presentation of Marvellous Living Human Curiosities' in 'The World's Largest, Grandest, Best Amusement Institution'. The difficulty of revisiting the phenomenon of the Victorian freak show for musical theatre material seems obvious.[11]

Cast

Phineas Taylor Barnum (Chris Darnell), Charity Barnum (Helen Welch), Ringmaster (Ian Chisholm), Chester Lyman (Peter Mottram), Joice Heth (Gillian Tichborne), Amos Scudder (Mark Lake), White Faced Clown (James Saunders), Sherwood Stratton (Tony Wilds), Mrs Sherwood Stratton (Linda Campbell), Tom Thumb (Andy Lofthouse), Julius Goldschmidt (John Fiddes), Jenny Lind (Andrea Ferguson), Concertmaster (Philip Barley), Wilton (Chris Penn), The Blues Singer (Christine Mullord), Hubert Morrissey (John Newell), Edgar Templeton (Roger Cliffe), James A Bailey (David Rees), Emporium Lady

(Audrey Fiddes), Drag Clowns (Mark Lake, Andy Lofthouse, Chris Penn, Tony Wilds)

Gentlemen of the Chorus Trevor Bailey, Trevor Burgess, David Chapman, Joe Crowley, Colin Harris, Robert Laycock, Stephen Laycock, David Pulling, Crispin Rolfe, John Russell, Stephen Wiley

Ladies of the Chorus Jane Arthurton, Gillian Atterson, Sue Bailey, Rachel Bond, Sarah Boyd, Jenny Bugg, Niamh Church, Sara Crowley, Sue Duxbury, Sue Gardiner, Susan Gurney, Colleen Harris, Justine Kerry, Alison Ley, Caroline Laycock, Jo Maud, Nicola Middleton, Fiona Mitchell, Vicky Reynolds, Tessa Riddell, Angela Rowe, Esther Thirkettle, Glynis Tipple, Cheryl Turmaine, Emma Walters, Claire Whiley, Kim Wright

Special appearance Chermond Gymnastic Display Team

1998
HELLO, DOLLY!

Norwich Theatre Royal, 26–31 January
Music and lyrics: **Jerry Herman**
Book: **Michael Stewart, based on Thornton Wilder's play** *The Matchmaker*
Director: **Ray Jeffery**
Musical Director: **John Roper**

The second opportunity for the N&N to say 'Hello' to Dolly following Ricky Price's 1974 production proved to be another winner, with Christine Mullord as the irrepressible busybodying matchmaker Dolly Gallagher Levi. *Hello, Dolly!* had struggled to reach New York in 1964, with radical changes *en route* to Broadway. New writers were brought in, four songs dropped and three new numbers added, including the first act closer 'Before the Parade Passes By'. Gower Champion's original production triumphed, despite the fact that 'The show was in no way innovative and made not the slightest pretence to artistic merit'. But it had what it took to be a smash hit, 'and in its title song presented the most popular melody to come out of a Broadway musical in many seasons'.

This is a show that always found a sympathetic home at the N&N, now reproduced by Ray Jeffery with Christine Mullord as the Society's second incarnation of Mrs Levi. It was a performance that Roberts wanted 'both to hug and to cheer'. Mullord was 'Dolly to the life', with 'the sock-it-to-'em gravelly voice of Ethel Merman, the wit and style of a Yonkers Hermione Gingold and the American comic essence of The Golden Girls. It is her night, and one celebrates it with her.'

It was not a one-woman show. In all, this was the N&N 'at the top of its form and a continuing example of how talent, commitment and gritty hard work (powered by the continuing influx of young blood which the Society has introduced in recent years) create a show to send home its audiences happy, smiling and singing as they go'. Miller described how

> Director and choreographer Ray Jeffery has moulded his company into a show which flows without a single gap; in which visual comedy is as bright as the spoken variety; and in which the sparkling dance routines and stage patterns (set off by the gorgeous costumes and attractive sets) delight the eye with their precision and pace and have us all beaming with sheer pleasure and good humour.

The reviews did not overlook John Fiddes' supportive Vandergelder, Philip Barley as Cornelius (Roberts thought Barley had 'everything – looks, smile, agility, comedy and a thoroughly pleasing singing voice'), with Joe Crowley's Barnaby proving him to be 'a natural and endearing comedian'.

For Miller in the *EEN*, Mullord was 'a super actress who finds every nuance of meaning in the wit and worldly wisdom'. She was 'not a honey and cream singer like Barbra Streisand ... more a sock-it-to-them belter in the style of Ethel Merman'. Ultimately, 'whatever she does comes over with huge vitality, conviction and a sense of American optimism.'

The N&N once again said 'Hello' to Dolly in 2012.

Cast

Dolly Gallagher Levi (Christine Mullord), Ambrose Kemper (Mark Fiddy), Horace Vandergelder (John Fiddes), Ermengarde (Sarah Pryde), Cornelius Hackl (Philip Barley), Barnaby Tucker (Joe Crowley), Minnie Fay (Nicola Middleton), Irene Molloy (Andrea Ferguson), Mrs Rose (Colleen Harris), Ernestina (Gillian Tichborne), Rudolph (Jim Lord), Judge (David Rees), Court Clerks (Christopher Penn, David Pulling), Policemen (Greg Fitch, John Newell)

Gentlemen of the Chorus Martin Coleman, Greg Fitch, Ian Freeman, Colin Harris, Peter Mottram, John Newell, Simon Rumsey, John Russell, Tony Welch

Ladies of the Chorus Kate Arthur, Penny Brown, Niamh Church, Donna Collier, Sue Duxbury, Sue Gardiner, Julie Hewitt, Wendy Knipe, Dawn Moore, Tessa Riddell, Ann Stockwell, Katie Wilkinson, Kim Wright

Dancers Gillian Atterson, Sue Bailey, Jenny Bugg, Sara Crowley, Sue Gurney, Liz Ireland, Cheryl Turmaine, Claire Whiley, Ian Chisholm, Roger Cliffe, Ian

Freeman, Christopher Penn, David Pulling, Jonathan Rist, Khan Robinson, James Saunders, Peter Webb

Children Sophie Allen, Chelsea Halliday, Harriet Ventham, Julie Wainwright / Catherine Frost, Jessica Fullwood-Thomas, Gemma Holland, Hannah Wilson

1999
CAROUSEL

Norwich Theatre Royal, 26–30 January
Music: **Richard Rodgers**
Book: **Oscar Hammerstein II, based on Ferenc Molnar's play *Liliom*, as adapted by Benjamin F. Glazer**
Director: **Ray Jeffery**
Musical Director: **Geoff Oxley**

Previously performed by the N&N in 1972, with Coral Newell as Julie and John Dunsire as Billy, Ray Jeffery's production breathed new life into the Rodgers and Hammerstein tearjerking masterpiece. Charles Roberts saluted the display of 'huge vitality, colour and movement; terrific dance and splendidly arresting groupings and tableaux' with

> much beautifully-judged lighting, and sets and costumes which together give real pleasure. Call *Carousel*'s emotional philosophies trite and superficial if you will but Philip Barley's Billy Bigelow and Andrea Ferguson's Julie Jordan have much to recommend them. This is a Billy with matinee looks, an excellent natural stage presence, a proper swagger, a pleasing voice and an essential belief which carries the audience with him.

Under Jeffery's hand, Ferguson 'comes over initially in this interpretation as a frothy young miss in massed blonde tresses. But as unhappy wife and then grieving widow, the authority and depth one was looking for surface and take control.'

Cast
Billy Bigelow (Philip Barley), Julie Jordan (Andrea Ferguson), Carrie Pipperidge (Sarah Pryde), Nettie Fowler (Jean Barratt), Mrs Mullin (Tina Moore), Jigger Craigin (David Rees), Enoch Snow (Chris Darnell), Enoch Snow Jnr (Adam Carpenter), Louis Bigelow (Nicola Brooks), Starkeeper / Dr Seldon (Peter Mottram), David Bascombe (Geoffrey Hedger), Mrs Bascombe (Ann

Stockwell), Heavenly Friend (Ruth Saxton), Arminy (Kim Wright), Policemen (Greg Fitch, Ian Chisholm), Captain (Roger Cliffe), Principal (John Newell), Carnival Boy (Jonathan Rist)

Gentlemen of the Chorus John Bramley, Roger Cliffe, Martin Coleman, John Fiddes, Greg Fitch, Colin Harris, Darren Hill, Peter Mottram, John Newell, Simon Rumsey, Tony Welch

Ladies of the Chorus Jane Arthurton, Jacqueline Brightman, Marie-Louise Brooks, Penny Brown, Donna Collier, Sue Duxbury, Susan Gurney, Colleen Harris, Julie Hewitt, Wendy Knipe, Dawn Moore, Ann Stockwell, Katie Wilkinson, Maria Wilson, Kim Wright

Dancers Gillian Atterson, Susan Bailey, Rachel Bond, Tommy Brown, Jenny Bugg, Jo Chapman, Ian Chisholm, Niamh Church, Jo Crowley, Sara Crowley, Darren Hill, Liz Ireland, Justine Kerry, Christopher Penn, David Pulling, Jonathan Rist, Andrew Shipp, Lisa-Marie Whall, Claire Whiley

Snow Children Siobhan Allen, Sophie Allen, Cassie Brooker, George Crowley, Katie Suffling, Richard Suffling, Amy Wood / Nicholas Collier, Scott Collier, Victoria Collier, Jessica Fullwood-Thomas, Chelsea Halliday, Laura Miller, Harriet Ventham

Bascombe Children Michaela Medler, Hannah Wilkin / Emma Dyball, Gemma Knowles

Carnival and Graduation Children Megan Bradsworth, Ellie Brooker, Emma Cannell / Sarah Temple, Sharmayne Tuttle, Hannah Wilson

Beach Children Rachel Chiarotti, Laura Harvey, Lindsay Neish / Sarah Burton, Amy Ellis, Antony Moore

Gymnasts Susan Clarke, Anneka Hatch, Joanne Jarvis, Laura Mantripp

Juggler Stephen Wiley

Stilt Walker Trevor Bailey

The 2000s

The new decade found the Society in good shape, with the popular director Ray Jeffery taking up residence at the N&N from 1997 to 2006, with Geoff Davidson settling in as musical director between 2000 and 2009. A reworking of the popular 1930s Cockney spree *Me and My Girl* provided a bright start to the new regime, followed by Jerry Herman's tribute to the early black and white and frequently silent Hollywood *Mack and Mabel*, now making its debut at Norwich Theatre Royal. The year was notable for its solidly dependable crowd-pleasers that included the second N&N *South Pacific* (previously 1976) and second *Oklahoma!* (previously 1983), Cole Porter's sophisticated Shakespearean frolic *Kiss Me, Kate* (previously 1981) and Lerner and Loewe's evergreen *My Fair Lady* (previously 1986). Good reviews helped validate the choices made, closing the decade with one of the most complex and compelling productions ever mounted by the company, *Titanic*, a work made from the most tragic elements. Vibrancy sliced through Leonard Bernstein's score for *West Side Story*, an ideal showcase for the younger actors in the Society, and there was acknowledgement of Andrew Lloyd Webber's contribution to the British musical in his *Jesus Christ Superstar*.

2000
ME AND MY GIRL

Norwich Theatre Royal, 24–29 January
Music: Noel Gay
Book and lyrics: L. Arthur Rose and Douglas Furber, revised by Stephen Fry, with contributions to revisions by Mike Ockrent
Director: Ray Jeffery
Musical Director: Geoff Davidson

Few British musicals have enjoyed such theatrical longevity than this apparently irresistible Cockney celebration with its attractive Noel Gay score. Its original London production of 1937 ran 1,646 performances starring the remarkably athletic Lupino Lane. This was no passing glory: London revivals followed in 1941, 1945 (when the show had been greeted with 'uproarious delight') and 1949, all with Lane as chirpy Londoner Bill Snibson. At the show's heart was a 'walking' dance, 'The Lambeth Walk'. Lane conceived it as a sort of walking dance. He described it simply as 'just an exaggerated idea of how the Cockney struts'.[1] The dance was taken up by Adele England, an associate of the nationally recognised Locarno Dance Circuit,

> with the intention of devising movements which everyone could dance without instruction. Her special contributions were knee-slapping in place of the original skirt-raising, and the very important addition of the characteristic Cockney 'Oi' at the end of each verse, an invocation which became 'Och aye' in Glasgow and 'Ee by gum, it's champion' in Blackpool. When Miss England had done her best, 'The Lambeth Walk' was truly 'free and easy; do as you darn well pleasey, and therefore fitted for public consumption on a grand scale.[2]

Among her other achievements Miss England had turned 'The Lambeth Walk' into the natural successor to 'Knees Up Mother Brown'. There was no doubting the show's appeal; the King and Queen went to see it three times. It was 'The Lambeth Walk' that in 1946 undoubtedly prodded the desperate producers of the Sid Field musical *London Town* into offering the British public 'The 'Ampstead Way', a preposterously choreographed attempt at topping Lane's tribute to Lambeth. In fact, *Me and My Girl* refused to fade away, and a film version appeared in 1939.

The British public took to Sibson, the friendly Cockney, who unknowingly is the 17th Baron and eighth Viscount of Hareford. Suddenly enveloped by the wealthy upper-class, Bill at last returns to his faithful Lambeth sweetheart Sally.

In 1985 a refreshed version of the old piece was warmly welcomed, reaching 3,303 performances, and even more surprisingly lasted for 1,420 performances on Broadway. The opportunity was taken by Fry and the producers to smarten and enliven the original with a clutch of different Noel Gay songs. Ray Jeffery's N&N production for the Society's 75th anniversary was warmly welcomed by Ken Hulme in the *Norwich Evening News*, recommending that the public should 'Step out with this slick show ... You could pay London prices and not see a show as stunningly colourful, as full of movement and as enthusiastically performed. There is nothing amateurish about this show, tightly produced and slickly performed.' Nick Bird's Snibson was a worthy successor to Lupino Lane's interpretation, 'moving' in his George Formby number 'Leaning on a Lamp Post' and deserving a medal 'for very tricky leg-work with chairs and several comic scenes.' Watching Lane playing opposite the incandescent Lillian Roth performing 'Let's be Common' in Ernst Lubitsch's 1929 film *The Love Parade* is a revelation, reminding us of what a brilliant gymnastic dancer he was, a genius of physical comedy and perfectly partnered by Roth.

In Norwich, Sally ('wonderful' Sarah Pryde) shared honours with Christine Mullord's 'hilarious' Duchess of Dene and Christopher Penn's Honourable Gerald Bolingbroke, praised in Kirsty Rhodes' review for the *EDP* for his 'triple jointed legs which made my eyes water every time he flexed them.' The dance routines were 'slick' and the tap dancing devised by Jenny Bugg 'a triumph.' We cannot know if the Norwich audiences found themselves doing the Lambeth Walk in the aisles, but it must surely have joined in the Oi!s. Ray Jeffery's programme note remarked on Gay's 'talent for writing popular songs that were stylish and accessible. His instinctive abilities were enhanced by absorption of the secrets of successful hymn tunes and a loving study of Gilbert and Sullivan.'

Cast
Lord Battersby (John Fiddes), Lady Battersby (Audrey Fiddes), Sir Jasper Tring (Geoffrey Hedger), Lady Jacqueline Carstone (Holly Graham), Hon. Gerald Bolingbroke (Christopher Penn), Charles (Peter Mottram), Herbert Parchester (Colin Harris), Maria Duchess of Dene (Christine Mullord), Sir John Tremayne (David Rees), Bill Snibson (Nick Bird), Sally Smith (Sarah Pryde), May Miles (Julie Hewitt), Mrs Worthington-Worthington (Ann Stockwell), Lady Brighton (Colleen Harris), Sophia Stainsley-Asherton (Niamh Church), Pearly Queen (Jenny Bugg), Pearly King (David Pulling), Telegraph Boy (Jonathan Lofty), Anastasia Brown (Alison Cunnell), Bob Barking (Ian Chisholm), Constable (John Newell)

Gentlemen of the Chorus Darren Chapman, David Clay, Roger Cliffe, Martin Coleman, Stephen Gedge, John Lofty, James Lord, John Millward, John Newell, Tony Welch, Mick Wright

Ladies of the Chorus Penny Brown, Linda Campbell, Donna Collier, Alison Cunnell, Sue Duxbury, Sue Gurney, Colleen Harris, Julie Hewitt, Wendy Knipe, Dawn Moore, Ann Stockwell, Maria Wilson, Kim Wright

Dancers Gillian Atterson, Sue Bailey, Rachel Bond, Nicola Brooks, Jenny Bugg, Jayne Cator, Richard Chilvers, Ian Chisholm, Niamh Church, Sara Crowley, Andrea Ferguson, Kevin Harvey, Liz Ireland, Justine Kerry, David Knights, James Lofty, Jonathan Lofty, David Pulling, Andrew Shipp, Nicholas Sparkes, Cheryl Turmaine, Stephanie Walpole, Peter Webb

2001

MACK AND MABEL

29 January–3 February
Music and lyrics: Jerry Herman
Book: Michael Stewart
Director: Ray Jeffery assisted by Mark Lake
Musical Director: Geoff Davidson

Jerry Herman's tribute to silent Hollywood did not run long on Broadway in 1974 and had to wait until 1995 for its short-lived London production. As Gerald Bordman has pointed out: 'Whenever Broadway has sought to have fun at the expense of silent movies, it has fallen flat on its face.' Herman's musical was 'lively but not memorable.'[3] The relationship between Mack Sennett and actress Mabel Normand inspired Herman to write a brilliant score that included two magnificent torch songs, Mack's 'I Won't Send Roses' and Mabel's 'Time Heals Everything'. The show itself is one of those in the Society's history that Norwich audiences otherwise might not have had the chance of seeing, and Herman's shows were always worth getting to know. His *Hello, Dolly!* was a box-office success for the N&N with three productions (1974, 1998 and 2012), but his *Mame*, modelled very much on the *Hello, Dolly!* formula (Mame was another strong-minded woman with a title song that set Broadway and London and eventually Hollywood alight) would not be seen at the N&N.

Neither has the N&N ever turned to Herman's 1983 *La Cage aux Folles*. This was 'The first Broadway musical to have homosexual characters in the major roles, the musical otherwise was a very conventional crowd pleaser with plenty of glitter and hummable songs.'[4] Perhaps this underrates the significance of a piece that possesses a profundity way beyond 'glitter and hummable songs'. Bordman reminds us: 'Of course, homosexuals had fluttered across musical stages for decades, but only as passing comic figures, and their sexual preferences remained unmentioned.'[5]

Indeed, gay characters fluttered at the N&N throughout its productions of *The Producers* (2010), and *Top Hat* (2018), when Adrian Wright's playing of Roger de Bris and Bates left nobody in doubt about the character's sexuality.

The N&N's 2023 *Kinky Boots* seemed to offer a discussion on gay issues without ever satisfactorily developing its themes. In 2003 Norwich Theatre Royal and Buxton Theatre collaborated in producing a new musical *The Land of Might Have Been* using the songs of Ivor Novello. The show followed the love between two young homosexuals (indeed, its same-sex couple was more prominent than its heterosexual couple). Norwich audiences responded with huge enthusiasm to its emotional pull. After 100 years, perhaps it is time for the N&N to consider *La Cage aux Folles*, to which the local audience would surely flock. What audience could not be moved by such of its numbers as 'Song on the Sand' and 'Over There' and the defiant 'I Am What I Am'. Anyway, *La Cage aux Folles*'s songs reach deeper than anything in *Mack and Mabel*. Indeed, *La Cage* is a musical that 'succeeded in pleasing not merely hardened Broadway regulars but even little old ladies from Dubuque and, just possibly, anti-homosexual evangelists from Cornpone, Alabama'. There is no reason why little old ladies from Wymondham or Seething would not be equally entranced.[6]

Meanwhile, the brief reviews for the N&N *Mack and Mabel* lacked pungency. Ken Hulme in the *Evening News* made no mention of any performers, but had 'no doubt that the N&N's standards have risen beyond measure in recent years' as here in 'a truly exciting and exhilarating production' of 'this marvellous musical'. The *EDP*'s critic Michael Drake thought 'the whole cast look as if they are enjoying themselves' but his response only reached lukewarm. The leads played by Greg Fitch and Sarah Pryde 'tell the story poignantly without, it has to be said, having top-class vocal talents. All have a reasonable stab at American accents and are backed by the large chorus whose footwork is splendid.' Along the way there was some 'excellent comedy' as in the Keystone Cops sequence and 'few unplanned gaps'.

Cast

Mack Sennett (Greg Fitch), Mabel Normand (Sarah Pryde), Lottie Ames (Andrea Ferguson), Ella (Ann Stockwell), Frank (Ian Chisholm), Freddy (Huw Jones), Harry (Alan Syder), Fatty Arbuckle (David Rees), Jerry (Ben Glover), Charlie (Julie Hewitt), Bob (Roger Cliffe), Andy (Christopher Penn), Max (John Newell), Ford (Nick Sparkes), Mary-Lou (Alison Cunnell), Buzz (Peter Mottram), Phyllis (Linda Campbell), Iris (Niamh Church), Lucy (Wendy Knipe), Joanne (Penny Brown), Gertie (Christine Mullord), Kleiman (Colin Harris), Fox (John Fiddes), William Desmond Taylor (John Millward), Night Watchman (Geoffrey Hedger)

Gentlemen of the Chorus Richard Chilvers, Matt Clark, Martin Coleman, David Knights, Mark Lake, Jim Lord, Mark McCormack, Christopher Penn, David Pulling, Nick Sparkes, Tony Welch

Ladies of the Chorus Sue Bailey, Rachel Bond, Penny Brown, Jenny Bugg, Linda Campbell, Jayne Cator, Niamh Church, Donna Collier, Sara Crowley, Kirsty Cutting, Sue Duxbury, Sue Gurney, Colleen Harris, Julie Hewitt, Liz Ireland, Justine Kerry, Dawn Moore, Carol North, Pat Tabor, Stephanie Walpole, Maria Wilson

2002
SOUTH PACIFIC

Norwich Theatre Royal, 28 January–2 February
Music: **Richard Rodgers**
Lyrics: **Oscar Hammerstein II**
Book: **Oscar Hammerstein II and Joshua Logan, adapted from James A. Michener's** *Tales of the South Pacific*
Director: **Ray Jeffery**
Musical Director: **Geoff Davidson**

Following *Mack and Mabel* the Society turned back to Rodgers and Hammerstein's middle-aged (the show was now more than 50 years old) romance between a Navy nurse and older French planter Emile Becque. Ricky Price's 1976 production for the N&N had Audrey Chapman and Brian Goodfellow as the lovers. The relationship of an older man with a younger woman would reappear in Rodgers and Hammerstein's *The King and I* and *The Sound of Music*. Rodgers' biographer Meryle Seacrest notes:

> A woman's asset was her youth and a man's, his social and economic status. Her value faded with the colour of her hair, but his wrinkles just made him seem more interesting.
>
> What might have made the story look especially attractive to the musical's creators was the undeniable fact that they themselves [Rodgers and Hammerstein and their collaborators] were getting older. When *South Pacific* opened, Hammerstein was 54 and Rodgers, at 47, too close to 50 for comfort.[7]

Beyond *South Pacific*, several other Rodgers and Hammerstein musicals never found their way into the Society's repertoire, including the 1947 *Allegro* (a folksy celebration of an American family, very much in the voice of Hammerstein), *Me and Juliet* (1953), *Pipe Dream* (1955) and the underrated *Flower Drum Song* (1958), a piece difficult to stage because it needed genuine Chinese-Americans. Once again, as in *South Pacific* and throughout the writers' cannon, the conflicting views of the young and old and racial difficulties were prominent. One of the least performed of any of the Rodgers and Hammerstein musicals, *Flower Drum Song* has one of their finest scores, although 'I Enjoy Being a Girl' with its welcoming lyric 'When I hear a complimentary whistle that greets my bikini by the sea, I turn and I glower and I bristle, But I'm happy to know the whistle's meant for me' may not chime to modern taste.

John Lawson's *EDP* review for this second helping of *South Pacific* enthusiastically approved how 'Jeffery uses his huge cast to superb effect – they are never still and there are lovely little vignettes taking place all over the stage'. Furthermore, there was 'as dynamic a collection of principals as you could find – headed by the marvellous Sarah Pryde and Greg Fitch as Nellie Forbush and Emile de Becque'. Ultimately, 'The National Theatre is currently reviving *South Pacific* in London – but I cannot believe they are doing a better job than this. Quite simply, I don't think you will see a better show at the Theatre Royal this year'.

Cast
Nellie Forbush (Sarah Pryde), Emile de Becque (Greg Fitch), Luther Billis (Nick Bird), Bloody Mary (Tina Vanston), Liat (Rachel Bond), Lt Joseph Cable (Huw Jones), Jerome (Alex Munford / Shaun Taylor), Ngana (Chloe Christou / Laura Dale), Capt. George Brackett (John Fiddes), Cmdr William Harbison (Peter Mottram), Lt Buzz Adams (Andy Lofthouse), Bloody Mary's Assistant (Ann Stockwell), Radio Operator McCaffrey (Nick Sparkes), Stewpot (David Rees), Professor (Ian Chisholm), Quale (Christopher Penn), Henry (Geoffrey Hedger), Marine Officer Steeves (Andy Boesen)

Nurses Sue Bailey, Penny Brown, Jenny Bugg, Jayne Cator, Niamh Church, Donna Collier, Sara Crowley, Alison Cunnell, Nicola Dodds, Andrea Ferguson, Sarah Fish, Laura Green, Sue Gurney, Julie Hewitt, Justine Kerry, Wendy Knipe, Dawn Moore, Sue Ridge, Ann Stockwell, Cheryl Turmaine, Maria Wilson, Kim Wright

Seebees Lee Chapman, Richard Chilvers, Matthew Clark, Roger Cliffe, Martin Coleman, Liam Gentry, Mark McCormack, John Newell, David Pulling, Phil Ridge, Simon Rumsey, Tony Welch, Mick Wright

Island Children Lorren Bailey, Lucy Cook, Charlene Folds, Nicola Gray, Georgia King, Georgia Livock, Michael Medlar, Sandy Ni'man, William Norton, Michelle Webb

2003
MY FAIR LADY

Norwich Theatre Royal, 27 January–1 February
Music: Frederick Loewe
Book and lyrics: Alan Jay Lerner
Director: Ray Jeffery
Musical Director: Geoff Davidson

All tickets were sold before opening night for the second N&N production of the Lerner–Loewe–George Bernard Shaw musical that had opened on Broadway in 1956 and was first produced at the N&N in 1986. It had taken the Society 30 years to catch it. From contemporary accounts, this second edition of the piece seems to have been more artistically successful than the first, 'another sensational achievement from director and choreographer Ray Jeffery and his stunning company' in which 'No movement is wasted, no move superfluous'. The new Eliza Doolittle, Sarah Pryde, 'bursts into the action like a hurricane and goes on to devastate our senses with a performance of passion and power. Every scene, as lady or flower girl, is beautifully judged.' Pryde was perfectly matched with David Hawkins as Higgins and strong performances from Christine Mullord as Mrs Higgins (according to John Lawson's *EDP* review 'as fine a portrayal of the role as I have ever seen') and John Fiddes' Colonel Pickering. On the other hand, Liam Gentry's Freddy Eynsford-Hill was 'more seaside postcard than unworldly toff'. As Alfred Doolittle, with two of the show's most rumbustious numbers 'With a Little Bit of Luck' and 'Get Me to the Church on Time', the always dependable Peter Mottram enjoyed one of his most prominent roles. Lawson also contributed the brief review in the *Evening News*, assuring readers that 'you won't want to miss a moment of a simply stunning night out' watching 'this sensational company' with its 'chorus of Hollywood proportions'.

Cast

Mrs Eynsford-Hill (Linda Campbell), Eliza Doolittle (Sarah Pryde), Freddy Eynsford-Hill (Liam Gentry), Colonel Pickering (John Fiddes), Henry Higgins (David Hawkins), Bartender (Roger Cliffe), Harry (Simon Rumsey), Jamie (Andy Lofthouse), Alfred P. Doolittle (Peter Mottram), Mrs Pearce (Ann Stockwell), Mrs Hopkins (Alison Cunnell), Mrs Higgins (Christine Mullord), Lord Boxington (Alan Syder), Lady Boxington (Debbie Johnson), Zoltan Karparthy (Roy Preston), Major Domo (Geoffrey Hedger), Queen of Transylvania (Colleen Harris), Prince of Transylvania (David Knight), Mrs Higgins' Maid (Dawn Moore)

Gentlemen of the Chorus Lee Chapman, Ian Chisholm, Matt Clark, Roger Cliffe, Martin Coleman, Andy Cowan, John Ducker, Colin Harris, David Knights, Jason Lambert, Andy Lofthouse, John Newell, Chris Penn, Peter Pepper, David Pulling, Simon Rumsey, Steven Scase, Nick Sparkes, Alan Syder, Rob Waller, Andrew Williams

Ladies of the Chorus Sue Bailey, Penny Brown, Sarah Browne, Jenny Bugg, Jayne Cator, Niamh Church, Rebecca Cockaday, Sara Crowley, Alison Cunnell, Janette Davidson, Andrea Ferguson, Sarah Fish, Susan Gurney, Colleen Harris, Liz Ireland, Debbie Johnson, Justine Kerry, Dawn Moore, Sue Ridge, Alli Robson, Melissa Sampson, Stephanie Taylor, Cheryl Turmaine, Maria Wilson, Kim Wright

Cockney Quartet Ian Chisholm, Matt Clark, Chris Penn, Rob Waller

Servants Janette Davidson, Geoffrey Hedger, Chris Penn, Simon Rumsey, Nick Sparkes, Melissa Sampson, Esther Thirkettle, Andrew Williams, Kim Wright, Mick Wright

Busker Dancers Liz Ireland, Stephanie Taylor, Andy Lofthouse, Nick Sparkes

2004
KISS ME, KATE

Norwich Theatre Royal, 26–31 January
Music and lyrics: **Cole Porter**
Book: **Sam and Bella Spewack, based on William Shakespeare's** *The Taming of the Shrew*
Director: **Ray Jeffery**
Musical Director: **Geoff Davidson**

Ahead of opening night, Derek James in the *Evening News* reassured the public that the 'Operatic Group has gone from success to success – Still Hitting All the Right Show Notes'. For the last two years the productions had sold out at the box office. Indeed, 'It's the hottest show in town. Tickets sell quicker than for a Daniel O'Donnell concert. So what is the secret behind this extraordinary success story?' Desmond Elliott, a former president of the Society, explained: 'We do have a very good and loyal following. We put on a full-scale musical and we always keep our prices as low as possible.'[8]

Helen McDermott went to a rehearsal:

The director, a flamboyant fellow called Ray Jeffery, is merciless, coaxing and shoving them into giving their best. He works as hard as if they were getting money for it instead of them actually paying for the pleasure. They practice the finale with last orders from Ray about how to bow, first to the audience and then to 'the blowers, scrapers and bangers' in the orchestra pit. There's advice, too, for the chaps. 'Gentlemen,' says Ray, 'never stand with your legs together when you're wearing tights.' He should have his own show.[9]

Previously seen at the N&N in Ricky Price's 1981 production, Jeffery's edition of the Porter classic was well received. David Porter for the *EDP* applauded its casting: 'Peter Howell as Fred Graham and Sarah Pryde, playing Katharine, merit a mention for quality renditions'. In the soubrette role of Lois 'Amanda Howell gives us a non-irritating airhead'. Airhead she may be, but she has two of the show's best numbers, the soulful 'Why Can't You Behave?' and the delightfully capricious, 'Always True to You in My Fashion'. The two gangsters, Ian Chisholm and Andy Boesen, had the wittiest turn of the night in their 'Brush Up Your Shakespeare' which 'with their sure comic touches would steal the show if it wasn't such a strong cast'.

Ken Hulme's *Evening News* review suggested:

> It's not a faultless presentation of course. There are times when the orchestra is too loud. Vocal projection suffers too when the performers are too deep on the stage. Tight direction allows for gracefully flowing movement without hesitation but when the occasion demands, as in the more stylised sequences, there is wonderful control.

Perhaps a little of *Kiss Me, Kate* goes a long way. Somehow, it gives the impression of being the sort of musical that will be most appreciated by an already cultured audience. Perhaps it deserves a reinvention to give it an up to the moment twist. And is not 'Wunderbar' a dreary love song? Yes! And then you realise it is supposed to be!

The critic for the kindly old monthly magazine *Theatre World* (much missed) enjoyed the songs in the original London production of 1951 but,

> I think the authors of *Kiss Me, Kate* are asking a good deal of their cast, by expecting them to be able not only to sing these gems of Porter's but also to play scenes from *The Shrew* with equal conviction. We have too high a Shakespearean standard in this country and, as a result, these scenes are sometimes lame and laboured and one awaits the next musical number impatiently.[10]

Cast

Fred Graham (Peter Howell), Harry Trevor (David Hawkins), Lois Lane (Amanda Howell), Lilli Vanessi (Sarah Pryde), Hattie (Niamh Church), Paul (David Pulling), Pops (Martin Coleman), Bill Calhoun (Nick Bird), First

51. Handover of Presidency from Desmond Elliott to Charles Roberts, July 2000. Courtesy of NNOS Archive.

Gangster (Ian Chisholm), Second Gangster (Andy Boesen), Ralph (Huw Jones), Harrison Howell (John Fiddes)

The Taming of the Shrew Players Bianca (Amanda Howell), Baptista (David Hawkins), Gremio (Nick Sparkes), Hortensio (Christopher Penn), Lucentio (Nick Bird), Katharine (Sarah Pryde), Petruchio (Peter Howell)

Gentlemen of the Chorus Nick Bird, Lee Chapman, Matt Clark, Roger Cliffe, Liam Gentry, Gary Hall, John Newell, Bruce Parker, Christopher Penn, Peter Pepper, David Pulling, Andrew Shipp, Nick Sparkes, Tony Welch, Andrew Williams, Paul Woodhouse

Ladies of the Chorus Sarah Browne, Jenny Bugg, Rebecca Cockaday, Natalie Crisp, Sara Crowley, Alison Cunnell, Gaynor Egan, Georgina Fielder, Sarah Fish, Sue Gurney, Clair Jordan, Justine Kerry, Dawn Moore, Sue Ridge, Melissa Sampson, Ann Stockwell, Esther Thirkettle, Cheryl Turmaine, Helen van der Veldt, Maria Wilson, Hayley Wright

2005

JESUS CHRIST SUPERSTAR

Norwich Theatre Royal, 24–29 January
Music: Andrew Lloyd Webber
Lyrics: Tim Rice
Director: Ray Jeffery
Musical Director: Geoff Davidson

Following their collaboration for *Joseph and the Amazing Technicolor Dreamcoat* (yet to be produced at the N&N), Tim Rice and Andrew Lloyd Webber's *Jesus Christ Superstar* fulfilled Rice's ambition to write a show about Judas Iscariot,

> whom I thought was a slightly maligned character. The story of a man who betrayed Christ seemed to me to be much more relevant to what goes on today, if the guy who turned Christ in was portrayed as an ordinary bloke and therefore much easier to relate to being not entirely evil [...] What we are trying to do is bring Christ home to the people, to make him more real and bring him down from the stained glass windows.[11]

Chairman Coral Newell welcomed 'a show I've always wanted the N&N to perform', 'the largest-vast production ever attempted by the company'. The show 'has brought together all our existing members, as well as a wealth of new, young talent, which is always so welcome, for without these the Society would, in time, go out of existence'.[12]

The three young principals were all making their debuts with the company: Chris Dilley, a student at the University of East Anglia, as Jesus, Steve Jones, a land surveyor from Halesworth making his debut on any stage, as Judas, and 17-year-old college student Stephanie Moore as Mary. John Lawson, sometime theatre critic for the *EDP*, joined the company as Eighth Leper. In the pit was the Norwich Pops Orchestra.

There was no doubting the strong gust of new winds blowing through the company, the feeling that a new vitality might influence the Society's future. Visually, the production (with its impressive hired set) was stunningly effective, but the critical reaction was a little muted. Sound issues affected the first night. For Christopher Smith in the *Evening News*:

> The balance is not always kind to the soloists, and Stephanie Moore as Mary was apparently the victim of a microphone glitch early on. Steve Jones brought anguish, though not very clear diction, to the role of Judas, while Chris Dilley's Jesus was both of this world and of the other.

52. Steve Jones, Stephanie Moore and Chris Dilley, *Jesus Christ Superstar* (2005). Courtesy of David Pulling.

For the *Evening News* Rowan Martell reported that the ending was 'stark and dark with a brutality more *The Passion of Christ* than *Jesus Christ Superstar*'. It seems to have been an anxious night in which Judas was 'anguished and angry, sometime staking his incomprehension at what was happening to him to the point of incomprehensibility'. Unfortunately, Andy Shipp suffered a costume malfunction: 'it was something falling from his costume which spoilt poor Herod's big moment. Despite catastrophic microphone failure he still carried it off fabulously.' Such blips were not uncommon throughout the Society's history, reminding us of the intense pressures the company was under when it only moved into the theatre the day before the show opened to the public. Those pressures were alleviated when opening night for a production was moved to the Tuesday.

The spirit of the old company begun by Lady Ballance and her coterie was reinvigorated by the Society already having promised a £1,000 donation to an appeal to build a family cancer information and support centre at the N&N Hospital. As Melanie McDonald, the Society's publicity office, explained 'We felt this year that because of the subject matter of *Jesus Christ Superstar* and the fact that it is a very emotive performance, it would be appropriate to choose a charity to benefit.'

Would the new blood that now seemed to be coursing through the company's veins take it forward? Choosing *Oklahoma!* as the next production may not have been the company's most imaginative decision. This, after all, would be the third time the Surrey with the fringe on top had trundled into view.

Cast
Jesus (Chris Dilley), Judas (Steve Jones), Mary (Stephanie Moore), Annas (Martyn Rolfe), Caiaphas (Greg Fitch), Priests (Neil Chapman, Andy Cowan, Ian Chisholm), Simon (Chris Carroll), Pilate (Jack Halpert), Peter (Stephen Pickess), Herod (Andy Shipp), 9 Apostles (Chris Carter, Huw Jones, Andy Lofthouse, Thomas Monument, David Pulling, Jamie Saunders, Nick Sparkes, Ed Wilson, Paul Woodhouse), Soul Singers (Linda Campbell, Jayne Cator, Niamh Church, Tracey Evans, Dawn Moore, Esther Thirkettle), Maid by the Fire (Sarah Browne), Old Man (Roger Cliffe)

Gentlemen of the Chorus Mark Bird, Lee Chapman, Matt Clark, Roger Cliffe, Mark Downes, Ian Doughty, Lawrence Kemp, John Lawson, John Newell, Bruce Parker, Peter Pepper, Kevin Ward, Andrew Williams

Ladies of the Chorus Sarah Browne, Jenny Bugg, Linda Campbell, Jayne Cator, Hayley Cawthorne, Niamh Church, Emily Clark, Zara Crowley, Gaynor Egan, Tracey Evans, Karen Ewing, Deborah Goddard, Sue Gurney, Liz Ireland, Clair Jordan, Wendy Knipe, Dawn Moore, Sue Ridge, Rebecca Rowe, Melissa Sampson, Ann Stockwell, Esther Thirkettle, Cheryl Turmaine, Helen van der

Veldt, Selina White, Caroline Wilkinson, Maria Wilson, Jeannie Woods, Kim Wright

Roman Soldiers Andy Boesen, David Chapman, David Paternoster, Phil Ridge, Mick Wright

Children Meredith Bell, Jack Daly, Alice Fitt, William Griffiths, Charlotte Knowles, Jessica Knowles, Justin Leon, Emily Moore, Molly-Jo Norman / Frank Brown, Kyle Cattee, Aimee Huggins, David Jarvis, Ryan Livermore, Robyn Nash, Danielle Norman, Alice Ross, Michelle Webb

2006
OKLAHOMA!

Norwich Theatre Royal, 23–28 January
Music: **Richard Rodgers**
Book and lyrics: **Oscar Hammerstein II**
Director: **Ray Jeffery**
Musical Director: **Geoff Davidson**

How to recapture that reaction to the first night of *Oklahoma!* at Drury Lane in April 1947. The actor Edward Fox was taken by his parents and remembered his father telling him 'This is exactly what we needed. This will lift the country's spirits and we can begin again.' In 1950, the idiosyncratic critic Beverley Baxter M.P. reminded the readers of *Everybodys* 'how dreary and disillusioned we were at that time. We had passed from the war of the scorched earth to a parched peace.'[13] In fact, 'the timing of the British *Oklahoma!* was perfect, as if something brilliant and startling had strolled uninvited into a room crammed with dullness.'[14]

Now, that Surrey with the fringe on top rounded the hill for the third time at the N&N, refreshed by some of the younger performers retained from *Jesus Christ Superstar*, among them Chris Dilley, Huw Jones and Stephanie Moore. Susannah Leigh's *EDP* review reported that 'a slightly over-exuberant Dilley' had a 'fine voice'; Sarah Pryde delivered 'a beautifully pitched' Laurey, and Moore's Ado Annie was 'delightfully kooky'. Christine Mullord was 'in commanding form' as Aunt Eller, while Jones' Jud Fry 'with his marvellously rich voice brings a malicious undercurrent to the role.' For the *Evening News*, Jacqueline Briggs praised Dilley as 'energetic and believable' while the choreography was 'superb' and everything 'gorgeously costumed'. Tony Joslin won praise for his 'wonderful turn as Ali Hakim; he's a natural and very funny comedian'.

At the time of writing (August 2022) a new London production of *Oklahoma!* has found new success in a radically refreshed concept. Just as we have come to expect and hopefully accept that operas are revived in imaginative and transforming ways that would seem strange to their authors, why should that principle of rethinking the original concept not be applied to musical theatre? Why, indeed, should it not be applied to revivals staged by amateur operatic societies? There would of course be impediments galore. The rigid conditions of licensing a show puts an immediate obstacle in the way of the innovative director who might want to supplant *Oklahoma!* on to a building site. The hands of the director and choreographers are bound to conform. Why not take *Oklahoma!* out of the outdoors, make the characters dream of the corn as high as an elephant's eye? Turn Oklahoma into a utopia longed for but unattainable? Turn the land known as Oklahoma into an illusion for which the characters are yearning? Allow the amateur operatic societies to bring new life and understanding to these works. They are sturdy enough to survive all sorts of treatment, and liberating the conditions under which amateur operatic societies work can only reawaken and possibly refresh our understanding of them.

Cast

Curly (Chris Dilley), Laurey (Sarah Pryde), Aunt Eller (Christine Mullord), Ado Annie (Stephanie Moore), Will Parker (Paul Woodhouse), Jud Fry (Huw Jones), Ali Hakim (Tony Joslin), Andrew Carnes (John Fiddes), Gertie Cummings (Zara Crowley), Ike Skidmore (Alan Syder), Slim (Dave Montgomery), Cord Elam (Greg Fitch), Fred (Peter Pepper), Annie Pigtail (Elizabeth Futter), Fall-Down Girl (Charlene Ledgard)

Gentlemen of the Chorus William Baker, Lee Chapman, Neil Chapman, Roger Cliffe, Jon-Paul Court, Peter Dear, Mark Downes, Greg Fitch, William Fitt, Matthew Hardy, John Lawson, Peter Pepper, Nick Sparkes, Kevin Ward, Ed Wilson

Ladies of the Chorus Sue Bailey, Sarah Browne, Jenny Bugg, Jayne Cator, Niamh Church, Zara Crowley, Hannah Davidson, Gaynor Egan, Tracey Evans, Elizabeth Futter, Deborah Goddard, Liz Ireland, Clair Jones, Wendy Knipe, Charlene Ledgard, Dawn Moore, Melanie Platten, Sue Ridge, Rebecca Rowe, Melissa Sampson, Ann Stockwell, Pat Tabor, Cheryl Turmaine, Helen van der Veldt, Maria Wilson, Jeannie Woods

Dancers Laurey (Liz Ireland), Curl (Nick Sparkes), Jud (Huw Jones), Elizabeth Futter, Charlene Ledgard

2007
42ND STREET

Norwich Theatre Royal, 29 January–3 February
Music: Harry Warren
Lyrics: Al Dubin
Book: Michael Stewart and Mark Bramble, based on the novel by Bradford Ropes
Director: Jeremy Tustin
Musical Director: Geoff Davidson

Previously seen at the N&N in Robert Marlowe's 1995 production, this popular tribute to 1930s Hollywood was refreshed by Jeremy Tustin's new interpretation. According to the *EDP* review by Robert Wright, Linda Campbell did 'a wonderful job of being the self-opiniated star but she had a great singing voice to throw in' in 'an exciting and spectacular show', whose company included Hannah Wilson as Hannah and Greg Fitch. Neither Wright's review, or the *Evening News* review by Ken Hulme (positive but mentioning no names), bore comparison with reviews of Marlowe's production written by the *Evening News*'s Neville Miller and the *EDP*'s Charles Roberts. Agree or argue about their critical conclusions as you might, both were writers who treated amateur theatre with just as much gravitas as they awarded to the professional. They wrote with authority. They enticed the reader's interest. They observed what was happening on stage from the watch tower of theatrical experience.

Comparing Miller and Roberts' reviews for the 1995 *42nd Street* with those by Hulme and Wright, the all too obvious *degringolade* in the quality of criticism in the local press (vitally important to the amateur movement) is all too obvious. Comparisons, as too often in life, are odious. Hulme tells us that 'the large cast – most of whom apparently take a week off from their normal occupations – can feel justifiably pleased with their efforts'. This effectively has 'amateur theatre' stamped all over it. What is more, the company 'looked not only thoroughly at home on stage, but enjoying themselves'.

Cast
Peggy (Hannah Wilson), Dorothy (Linda Campbell), Maggie (Laura Marvell), Annie (Gaynor Egan), Lorraine (Elizabeth Futter), Phyllis (Andrea Ferguson), Diane (Tracey Evans), Gladys (Sarah Browne), Ethel (Justine Kerry), Julian (Greg Fitch), Bert (Ian Chisholm), Billy (Nick Sparkes), Andy (Christopher Penn), Mac (John Newell), Pat (Alan Syder), Abner (John Fiddes), Two Thugs

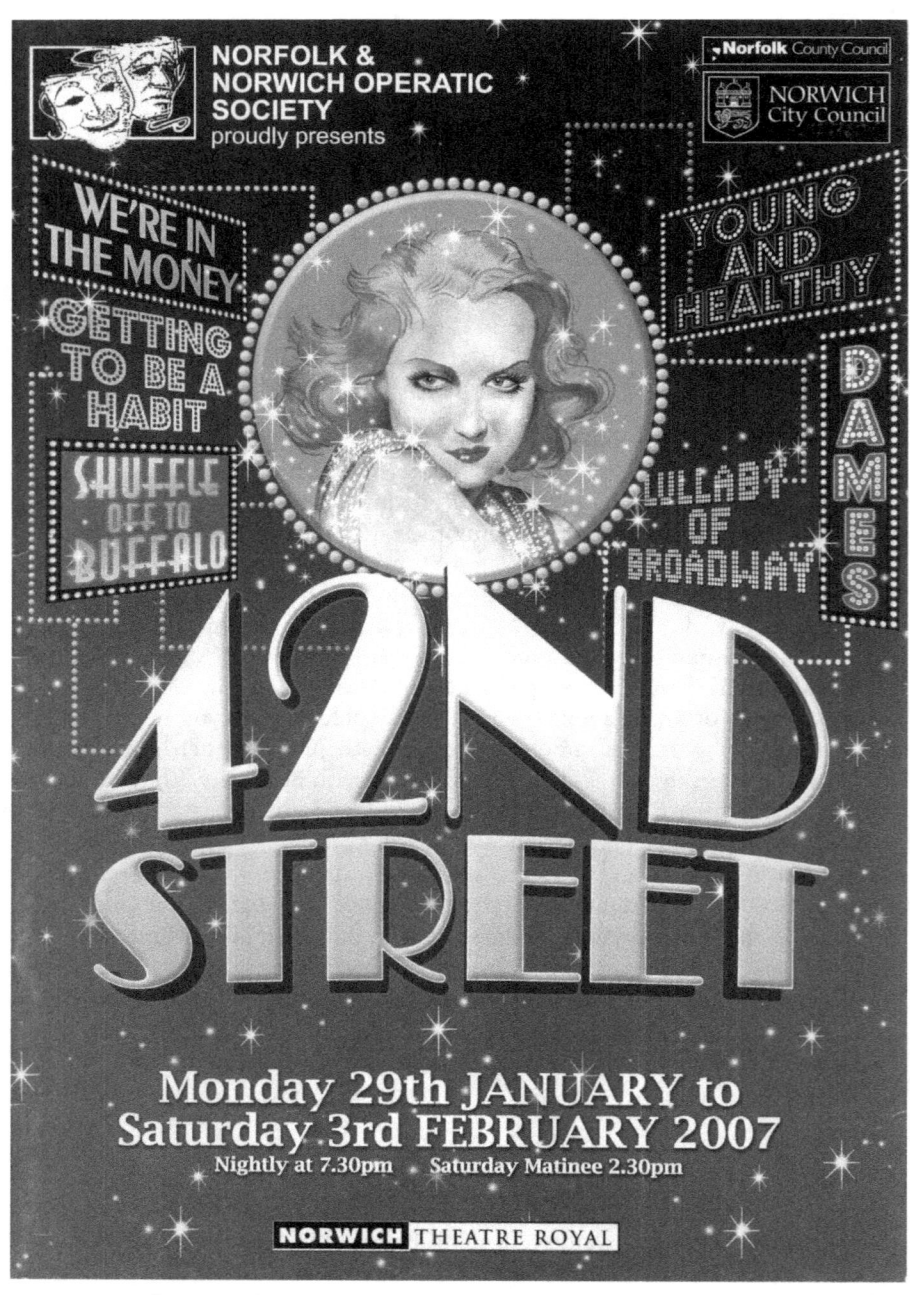

53. *42nd Street* Theatre programme cover (2007). Courtesy of NNOS Archive.

(Andy Cowan, Jon Paul Court), Doctor (Peter Mottram), Oscar (Matthew Hardy)

Chorus Joanna Carr, Neil Chapman, Niamh Church, Andy Cowan, Nia Howe, John Lawson, Dawn Moore, Peter Mottram, Sue Ridge, Helen van der Veldt, Kevin Ward, Jeannie Woods

Girl Dancers Megan Bradsworth, Jenny Bugg, Jayne Cator, Natalie Crisp, Alex Fielding, Deborah Goddard, Sue Gurney, Liz Ireland, Clare Rhodes, Rebecca Rowe, Melissa Sampson, Debbie Whomes, Maria Wilson

Boy Dancers William Baker, Michael Catling, Sam Clarke, Jon Paul Court, Ian Doughty, David Knights, Thomas Monument, William Norton, Stephen Pickess, David Pulling, Ed Wilson

2008
TITANIC

Norwich Theatre Royal, 28 January–2 February
Music and lyrics: **Maurey Yeston**
Book and story: **Peter Stone**
Director: **Jeremy Tustin**
Musical Director: **Geoff Davidson**

Unquestionably one of the Society's greatest achievements was Jeremy Tustin's production of a musical that seemed unlikely to find popular approval. At its 1997 Broadway premiere The *New Yorker* expected as much.

> It seemed a foregone conclusion that the show would be a failure; a musical about history's most tragic maiden voyage, in which fifteen hundred people lost their lives, was obviously preposterous [...] Astonishingly, *Titanic* manages to be grave and entertaining, sombre and joyful; little by little you realise that you are in the presence of a genuine addition to American musical theatre.[15]

The Norwich critics applauded. David Porter for the *EDP* recognised 'a minor masterpiece of musical theatre. [Your author would promote his "minor" to "major".]. It's a major hit for the Norfolk and Norwich Operatic Society' during which 'Geoffrey Davidson conducts a magnificent orchestra that swells the revamped Theatre Royal just beautifully'. Tustin had recaptured 'the sense of tragic destiny against the folly of people believing the largest moving object

54. Ian Chisholm, Josh Lincoln, Sarah Browne and Christine Mullord set sail on the ill-fated *Titanic* (2008). Courtesy of David Pulling.

on earth couldn't sink'. An extraordinary effect of the treatment was to emphasise the ultimate and devastating meaningless of class differentiation.

Ken Hulme's warm appreciation spilled into his review for the *Evening News*, saluting

> a brave and ambitious production [...] On the face of it an entertainment depicting a major catastrophe cannot possibly work – and yet the show is hugely successful. What you have is a brilliant set with occasional overhead projection, superb costumes, exciting routines with slick movement and a kaleidoscope of colour when most of the large cast are on stage together.

Essentially, this was an ensemble piece that has the capacity to deeply move the spectator, as in 'The Proposal' when stoker Barrett (played here by Steve Jones) sends a telegraph wire to his sweetheart, and radioman Harold Bride (Scott Collier) reveals his soul in 'The Night Was Alive'. *Titanic* is a work full of such brilliant moments.

Cast
Thomas Andrews (Andrew Burgess), J. Bruce Ismay (Martyn Rolfe)

Ship's Personnel Captain E. J. Smith (John McInnes), 1st Officer W. Murdoch (William Drew-Batty), 2nd Officer C. Lightoller (Ed Wilson), 3rd Officer H. Pitman / Musician Hartley (Andy Lofthouse), 4th Officer J. Boxball / Musician Taylor (Tim Kelly), Quartermaster R. Hitchens / Musician Bricoux (Lee Chapman), Radioman H. Bride (Scott Collier), Senior Stoker F. Barrett (Steve Jones), Chief Engineer J. Bell (Peter Mottram), Stokers (Ron Eaglen, Peter Pepper), Stevedore (Peter Pepper), Lookout F. Fleet (William Fleet), Senior 1st Class Steward H. Etches (Christopher Penn), 1st Class Steward A. Latimer (Ian Doughty), Stewardess Hutchinson (Rebecca Rowe), Stewardess Robinson (Nia Howe), Bellboy (Callum Bicknell / Philip Poole), 2nd Class Steward (Ron Eaglen), 3rd Class Steward (Christopher Penn)

1st Class Passengers John J. Astor and Madeleine Astor (Alan Syder, Kristina Dalzell), Madame Aubert (Laura Marvell), Charlotte Cardoza (Niamh Church), Edith Corse Evans (Ann Stockwell), Benjamin Guggenheim (John Fiddes), The Major (David Hawkins), J. H. Rogers (Colin Harris), Ida Strauss and Isador Strauss (Coral Newell and John Millward), John B. Thayer and Marion Thayer (David Pulling and Jenny Bugg), Jack Thayer (Frank Brown / Jack Daly), George and Eleanor Widener (John Newell and Val Lofthouse), Frank Carlson (John Newell), Passengers (Michelle Gothard, Colleen Harris, Liz Ireland, Jenni Medlock, Clare Rhodes, Maria Wilson, Roger Cliffe, Ian Doughty, William Norton, Tony Welch)

2nd Class Passengers Alice Beane and Edgar Beane (Christine Mullord and Ian Chisholm), Charles Clarke (Josh Lincoln), Caroline Neville (Sarah Browne),

Other Passengers (Jacqualyn Aitken, Donna Collier, Claire Harper, Carole Lloyd, Joanne Madden, Sue Ridge, Melissa Sampson, Helen van der Veldt, Ian Doughty, William Drew-batty, Ron Eaglen, Ed Wilson)

3rd Class Passengers Jim Farrell (Sam Clarke), Kate McGowan (Elizabeth Futter), Kate Mullins (Sharon Aitken), Kate Murphey (Sinead Merron), Other Passengers (Megan Bradsworth, Hayley Carter, Nia Howe, Charlotte Litten, Keira Long, Melanie Patten, Rebecca Rowe, Rose Williams, Lee Chapman, Neil Chapman, Tim Kelly, Nick King, Andy Lofthouse, Jim Lord, Peter Mottram, Peter Pepper, Tyler the Pekinese)

2009
WEST SIDE STORY

Norwich Theatre Royal, 26–31 January
Music: **Leonard Bernstein**
Lyrics: **Stephen Sondheim**
Book: **Arthur Laurents, based on a conception by Jerome Robbins**
Director: **Jeremy Tustin**
Musical Director: **Geoff Davidson**

There is some justification for claiming that *West Side Story*

> was probably the first almost guaranteed star-resistant musical of our time, and has remained in the repertory as such. The demands of its libretto, dances and vocal numbers make it star-resistant: how many stars can act, sing and dance at the same time? That takes a trouper, and *West Side Story* is made for them.[16]

The original London production of 1958 had a mixed critical reaction, the *Daily Mail* suggesting that 'many will recoil from the knuckle-duster impact of this Teddy Boy musical'.[17] *The Times* thought that 'the show increases enormously the pressure on classical ballet, pinnacle of the dance world, to abandon the supernatural and to confront life as it is lived in the middle of the twentieth century', but had Arthur Bliss and Robert Helpmann not already fused ballet with modernity in their 1944 ballet *Miracle in the Gorbals*? Furthermore, the characters in *West Side Story* were mostly 'morons' and 'self-pitying teenagers [...] in language and social context elusively alien'.[18]

This was a changing time for the N&N. *Jesus Christ Superstar* had prised open a door for a younger company, a shift of emphasis. Now, Coral Newell's

55. The Jet Boys and Jet Girls of *West Side Story* (2009). Courtesy of David Pulling.

56. The Shark Boys and Girls of *West Side Story* (2009). Courtesy of David Pulling.

programme note seemed to reach out to a new generation: 'As you will see, the show has attracted many new, young and talented members, some of whom are appearing in this theatre for the first time.' A corner had been turned, as if the Society was at last turning its back on an earlier epoch of operettas. It had, after all, staged a whole battalion of them throughout the 1960s and spasmodically throughout the 1970s. It was at the company's annual general meeting in September 2009 that Newell decided to step down as chairman: 'I saw all these young faces and decided that they needed a younger Chair.'

Two brief and somewhat similar reviews welcomed the fresh air blowing through the company. For Ken Hulme in the *Evening News* 'Overall, there are times when it's hard to accept that here we have an amateur production. You could pay London prices and not see better.' Michael Drake's *EDP* review reported that Josh Lincoln as Tony and Liz Futter as Maria

> work well as believable characters. Riff (Shane King) and Anita (Holly Graham) have a real presence, vocally and physically, while the dance scenes are slick and colourful – 'America' is one of the best sequences – lively and disciplined [...] Overall, it is often difficult to believe this is an amateur cast.

This was musical director Geoff Davidson's tenth and final production for the Society.

Cast

The Jets Tony (Josh Lincoln), Riff (Shane King), Action (Lee Chapman), Arab (Matthew Cara), Baby John (Alex Green), Snowboy (Laurence Guymer), Big Deal (Paul Woodhouse), Diesel (Joe Ringer), G-Tar (Scott Collier), Mouthpiece (Ed Wilson), Tiger (Daniel Waite)

The Sharks Bernardo (Christopher Penn), Chino (Will Norton), Pepe (Adam Roberts), Indio (Chris Harvey), Jose (Andrew Williams), Luis (Callum Bicknell), Anxious (Peter Pepper), Nibbles (Tim Kelly), Moose (Ian Doughty), Juano (Gabriel Mokake), Toro (John Paul Court)

The Jet Girls Anybodys (Carole Weeds), Velma (Andrea Ferguson), Graziella (Tracey Evans), Martha (Clare Rhodes), Minnie (Justine Kerry), Ellie May (Jenny Bugg), Clarice (Liz Ireland), Mary-Anne (Bethany Bugg), Pauline (Rebecca Rowe), Alice (Rebecca Molloy), Betsie (Gemma Bain)

The Shark Girls Maria (Elizabeth Futter), Anita (Holly Graham), Rosalia (Sharon Aitken), Consuela (Sinead Merron), Francisca (Sarah Browne), Carmen (Jacqualyn Aitken), Tereseta (Claire Harper), Estella (Maria Wilson), Juanita (Abigail Kingsley-Parker), Josephina (Chloe Cousins), Margarita (Niamh Church), Gloria (Helen van der Veldt), Lucia (Amelia Goymer)

The Adults Doc (John McInnes), Lt Shrank (Peter Mottram), Office Krupke (John Newell), Gladhand (David Pulling)

The 2010s

On hearing that the N&N's 2010 production was to be *The Producers*, the president of the Society Helen McDermott wrote that she

> wasn't alone in thinking that this might be tempting fate. After all, Zero Mostel and Gene Wilder laid down the marker in Mel Brooks' hysterically brilliant film so, for a lot of people, comparisons would be inevitable. We needn't have worried. The N&N laid down a marker of its own, and the audience responded with tears of laughter and warm applause.

For Christine Mullord, then assistant to director Jeremy Tustin, 'I think it was the best thing the Society ever did. I had friends who never ever went to see amateur productions. I told them they must not miss this one.'

Some solid classics of American musical theatre found their place in the new decade: a revival of *Fiddler on the Roof* (originally done by the Society in 1980), and another *Hello, Dolly!* (previously 1974 and 1998) and another *Guys and Dolls* (previously seen in 1987). Of operetta there was no sign, and by now the make-up of the company was such that it would probably have struggled to satisfactorily cast such a work. The company seemed vibrant, and eager for the challenges offered by Stephen Sondheim in the wonderfully dark melodrama of his *Sweeney Todd* and Andrew Lloyd Webber's *Sunset Boulevard*. There was no doubting the quality of *Top Hat* and the audience's fondness for such as *Sister Act*, another critical and commercial success in the modern vein. One of the company's finest achievements had been the 1980 *Fiddler on the Roof*, now repeated in 2011. Sadly, its tragic story was no less (and probably more) relevant than it had seemed two decades before.

In November 2010 the Society moved into Douro Place Chapel in the heart of Norwich, its change of use from a Place of Worship to the Society's rehearsal studio having been officially registered.

2010
THE PRODUCERS

Norwich Theatre Royal, 1–6 February
Music and lyrics: **Mel Brooks**
Book: **Thomas Meehan and Mel Brooks**
Director: **Jeremy Tustin**
Musical Director: **Matthew Brown**

For the EDP's critic Keiron Pym:

> The only signs that this was the first night of an amateur production were the tardy scene-changing and a rather muted opening minute or two, but the cast quickly found their voices. Nick Bird was assured as Bialystock and Laurence Guymer was winningly energetic as the neurotic Bloom. Holly Graham's vocals were superb as the Swedish blonde bombshell actress Ulla and Adrian Wright was hilarious – first as DeBris, then by taking the 'star' role in Springtime for Hitler as a mincing Fuhrer with 'a song in his heart'. It is a show better known for its humour than for sing-along songs, but numbers such as 'Along Came Bialy' and 'Keep it Gay' are certainly memorable. The ensemble cast totalled almost 50 and as ever with the N&N had a live orchestral backing. Together they more than did *The Producers* justice: it was well sung, danced and acted and, most of all, very funny indeed.

Cast
Max Bialystock (Nick Bird), Leo Bloom (Laurence Guymer), Ulla (Holly Graham), Franz Liebkind (Andy Lofthouse), Roger DeBris (Adrian Wright), Carmen Ghia (Luke Owen), Hold Me, Touch Me (Laura Watling), Lick Me, Bite Me (Val Lofthouse), Kiss Me, Feel Me (Niamh Church)

Gentlemen of the Chorus David Chapman, Lee Chapman, Neil Chapman, Matthew Hardy, Tim Kelly, Peter Mottram, John Newell

Accountants Ian Chisholm, Pete Cummins, Shane King, Josh Lincoln, Christopher Penn, Peter Pepper, Joe Ringer, James Sessa, Ed Wilson

Ladies of the Chorus Jenny Bugg, Donna Collier, Sara Crowley, Elizabeth Futter, Abigail Kingsley-Parker, Daisy Merrick, Clare Rhodes, Sue Ridge, Rebecca Rowe, Ann Stockwell, Deborah Ward

Follies' Girls Sharon Aitken, Jayne Andrew, Kristina Dalzell, Meryl Dempsey, Tracey Evans, Liz Ireland, Danielle Warne, Debbie Whomes, Ann Stockwell (The Not You Girl)

57. Little old ladies out on their zimmers in *The Producers* (2010)
Courtesy of David Pulling.

58. Roger de Bris (Adrian Wright) and his team 'Keep it Gay' in *The Producers* (2010).
Courtesy of David Pulling.

59. Roger de Bris overcome by finding stardom in 'Springtime for Hitler' in *The Producers* (2010). Courtesy of David Pulling.

60. Hatching a plot: Lawrence Guymer, Holly Graham and Nick Bird in *The Producers* (2010). Courtesy of David Pulling.

61. Holly Graham as Ulla in *The Producers* (2010). Courtesy of David Pulling.

2011
FIDDLER ON THE ROOF

Norwich Theatre Royal, 24–29 January
Music: Jerry Bock
Lyrics: Sheldon Harnick
Book: Joseph Stein
Director: Jeremy Tustin
Musical Director: Matthew Brown

The revival of the Bock–Harnick–Stein *Fiddler on the Roof* had been one of the Society's most outstanding productions in 1980, with Gordon Canwell and Norma Wick heading the company with, according to Neville Miller, its 'remarkable degree of commitment in the playing'. At the time of writing (2023) 12 years after the N&N revival of 2011, the show's tragic theme of racial persecution still thrives, with the desperate plight of those suffering such devastation forever in the headlines. Stanley Green, writing in 1976, reminds us that here is a musical that 'had neither attractive costumes nor scenery. Yet its theme of a people vainly trying to preserve tradition in an alien, hostile and changing world turned out to be one with which large numbers could readily identify'.[19] There is and can be no happy final curtain.

The brilliant construction of the piece owes much to Joseph Stein, 'a specialist in turning modern literary classics into musical librettos, responsible for such works as Marc Blitzstein's often dazzling *Juno* (1959) and Bob Merrill's *Take Me Along* (1959). Its original Broadway director Jerome Robbins urged Stein to dramatise the story of Tevye as that of a man in the state of transition. He wrote Bock and Harnick that 'This is the story we are telling; without it our show is just a touching Jewish *Cavalcade*. There is a much more vital, immediate and universal one to tell, i.e. the changing of the times ... and the conflicts and tensions made by these changes'.[20] Larry Stempel recognises that here is a piece of work that 'had astonishingly wide cultural resonance despite what some feared would be 'too Jewish' a show to play outside New York. 'That it negotiated deftly between the particularity of its subject and the universality of its theme accounts in large measure for its success'.[21]

For the N&N, *Fiddler on the Roof* again displayed the effectiveness of its ensemble's commitment to performance, now headed by John McInnes Tevye and Linda Campbell's Golde. Retained from the company's 2010 production of *The Producers*, musical director Matthew Brown appreciated 'There was a spirit among the cast and a great camaraderie within the group'. He noticed that in *The Producers* 'there were a lot of people who come in and are really good people who can all perform and sing. But this year is entirely different people which does show the depth of the Society and the depth of friendships that exist within the Society.'[22]

Cast

Tevye (John McInnes), Golde (Linda Campbell), Tzeitel (Marie Wilson), Hodel (Elizabeth Futter), Chava (Kate Smith), Shprintze (Emelia Campbell), Bielke (Eleanor Dolman), Perchik (Joe Redmond), Motel (Luke Owen), Fyedka (Alex Green), Lazar Wolf (Nick Bird), Yente (Tina Vanston), Avram (Ed Wilson), Rabbit (Colin Harris), Mendel (Daniel Herman), Nachum (John Newell), Fruma-Sarah (Niamh Church), Granma Tzeitel (Lavinia Pirret),

Mordcha (Greg Fitch), Constable (David Chapman), Shaindel (Ann Stockwell), Sasha (Ian Chisholm), The Fiddler (Matt Coulton)

Gentlemen of the Chorus Neil Chapman, Roger Cliffe, Sven Herrmann, Tom Monument, Peter Mottram, Peter Pepper, Ryan Young

Ladies of the Chorus Jenny Bugg, Kristina Dalzell, Liz Ireland, Bonnie Jerman, Emma Nuule, Clare Rhodes, Sue Ridge, Rebecca Rowe, Maria Wilson, Rose Williams

Bottle Dancers Frank Brown, Alex Green, Daniel Herman, Sam Wheeler-Brown, James Wilsher, Ed Wilson

Village Boys Frank Brown, Thomas Monument

2012
HELLO, DOLLY!

Norwich Theatre Royal, 23–28 January
Music and lyrics: Jerry Herman
Book: Michael Stewart, based on Thornton Wilder's play *The Matchmaker*
Director: Ray Jeffery
Musical Director: Matt Brown

'And what do you do for a living?' Ambrose Kemper asks of Dolly Levi. 'Some paint, some sew' she replies, 'I meddle'. Succeeding the N&N's previous Dollies (Norma Wick in Ricky Price's 1974 production, and Christine Mullord in Ray Jeffery's 1998 edition) the baton was passed to Gloria Dashwood, well known to various local societies, her roles having included Anna in *The King and I* and Nancy in *Oliver!* She told Tony Mallion:

> I've always loved the show, but it's never been done locally in my time – and I've never been the right age for the part. I love the comedy, she's so funny. I felt I had to audition. [Seven would-be-Dollies were auditioned.] I really didn't think I stood a chance so I suppose I wasn't as nervous as I would be normally. I just went for it.

Dashwood responded eagerly to Jeffery's careful tuition. 'I'm learning so much. He gives such detailed direction. Dolly's not a singer, she's a belter.'

For the *EDP*'s Christopher Smith, Dashwood 'confidently takes the role of the meddling Mrs Dolly Levi, the main spring of the plot and the focus of every eye when she chooses to command attention in situations where looks count for a lot'. 'The creative team putting on this complex production is strong', displaying 'inexhaustible energy. Set pieces like the Waiters' Gallop lift the action on to another plane, with the stage full of movement in a show that 'sparkles with love, laughter and a cheeky cheerfulness.'

Jeffery reminded the public that 'Local audiences are very lucky that they have a company of this standard. There are very few companies that play such a big venue as Norwich Theatre Royal and have such a big reputation. The reputation of the N&N is second to none.'[23] To recapture some of the blatant splendour of this hugely likeable piece, we can do nothing better than turn to the original London cast recording with the great Mary Martin. It is stonkingly brilliant. Never mind that by this time Miss Martin's voice had plenty of gruff. Her performance fizzles with delight, and the title song has a brilliance that takes us absolutely to the heart of this gorgeous old warhorse of a show, hopefully now, at least for a few years, laid to well-earned rest in the N&N graveyard of beloved memory.

Cast

Mrs Dolly Levi (Gloria Dashwood), Horace Vandergelder (Peter Howell), Cornelius Hackl (Joe Phelps), Irene Molloy (Andrea Ferguson), Barnaby Tucker (Gary Higgs), Minnie Fay (Claire Doughty), Ambrose Kemper (Will Arundell), Ermengarde (Kristina Dalzell), Rudolph (David Chapman), Ernestina Money (Niamh Church), Judge (Colin Harris)

Gentlemen of the Chorus Sean Bray, Frank Brown, Will Chapman, Ian Chisholm, Roger Cliffe, Colin Harris, David Knights, Duncan Peach, Nick Sparkes

Ladies of the Chorus Jenny Bugg, Linda Campbell, Niamh Church, Donna Collier, Abi Dennington-Price, Amanda Howell, Katie Hunt, Rebecca Jillings, Laura Marvell, Sue Ridge, Beth Smith, Ann Stockwell

Boy Dancers Will Arundell, David Chapman, Lee Chapman, Sven Hermann, Alex Kubiesa, Jonathan Lawson, Christopher Penn, Peter Pepper, Ed Wilson, Ryan Young

Girl Dancers Kristina Dalzell, Meryl Dempsey, Liz Ireland, Clair Jones, Katrina Porter, Clare Rhodes, Rebecca Rowe, Rose Williams, Maria Wilson, Marie Wilson

The Chermond School of Gymnastics and Dance, Circus Chermond Branch

2013
SWEENEY TODD

Norwich Theatre Royal, 4–9 February
Music and lyrics: **Stephen Sondheim**
Book: **Hugh Wheeler, from an adaptation by Christopher Bond**
Director: **Ray Jeffery**
Musical Director: **Matthew Brown**

It was inevitable that through the almost 100 years of the N&N's activity it would occasionally collide with a masterpiece. Tony Mallion's programme note described Sondheim as

> the musical equivalent of Marmite. There are those who are total devotees and who hail him as a genius (legendary Broadway director Hal Prince says he is simply the best in the world) while others beg to differ, summed up in the words of a Sondheim number 'You Could Drive a Person Crazy'.[24]

His astonishingly theatrical musicalisation of the fabled *Demon Barber of Fleet Street* was greeted by a considerable barrage of critical repulsion when it opened on Broadway. One such review appeared in *Harper's Magazine*. For Sondheim, 'it was part of an essay propounding the thesis that I represented the death of the American musical having taken all the joy and spontaneity out of this beloved, exuberant American art form and infused it with an impotent sourness.' Understandably, Sondheim gave up reading reviews of his work. He admitted that *Sweeney Todd* was 'a resounding commercial failure both on Broadway and in the West End, the latter reception particularly disheartening, since I had written the show as my love letter to London, a city I treasure above all except for New York'.[25]

To some, it manifested as semi-operatic, and has proved itself as such in several opera houses, although as Thomas Hischak reminds us 'the ghoulish

62. Andy Gledhill and Stephanie Moore: *Sweeney Todd* (2013). Courtesy of David Pulling.

story of the mass murderer Sweeney Todd put off many Broadway theatregoers in 1979.' Hugh Wheeler's libretto based on a nineteenth-century tale most recently dramatised by Christopher Bond in London 'was sly and entertaining, never falling into camp and yet always remaining on a stylised Grand Guingol level'.[26] Hischak parcels up the piece as 'a challenging blend of Victorian melodrama, English operetta, Brechtian music drama, and a ghoulish sense of humour'. We wonder if Sondheim was ever made aware of the 1936 British film *Sweeney Todd the Demon Barber of Fleet Street*, with the industrious gentlemen's hairdresser played by the utterly irreplaceable Tod Slaughter. Less grisly than Wheeler and Sondheim's adaptation (there is no hint, for example, of Mrs Lovett's pies being filled with body parts sent three times through the grinder), we urgently recommend Mr Slaughter's brilliant and frequently hilarious film to the reader.

The musical marked a fitting end to Ray Jeffery's tenure as the N&N's director. His strong directorial intervention into the performances was obvious. One of his undoubted techniques was to encourage highly credible performances out of individuals who may not have been natural actors. Attention to detail was never overlooked. The casting was strong. Andy Gledhill's Sweeney Todd had an operatic approach that dignified the role and made the most of the emotional peaks. Without exception, this was a memorable company in what is essentially an ensemble piece to be played up to the hilt by all. Especially touching was Gary Higgs as Sweeney's boy assistant Tobias (beautiful in his 'Nothings Going to Harm You' sung to Mrs Lovett), Genevieve Plunkett was perfectly in trilling birdsong-like tune as the captive Johanna, and Andrea Ferguson as the deranged beggar woman revealed as Sweeney's lost wife. Ian Chisholm as Pirelli, Huw Jones as the self-flagellating Judge, John Mangan as the Beadle, and Matt Willcock (with obvious direction on stance and

63. Stephanie Moore and Gary Higgs in *Sweeney Todd* (2013). Courtesy of David Pulling.

movement from Mr Jeffery) adding nautical and romantic flavour as Johann's luckless lover Anthony.

If one performance stood out, it was Stephanie Moore's brilliantly skilful and moving reincarnation of Mrs Lovett, one of the most inventive cooks known to history, even more terrifying then Fanny Cradock. For this alone Moore deserves to be remembered as one of the finest of the Society's many leading ladies. Matthew Brown's conducting of the orchestra revealed one of the most distinguished and professional ever heard at the N&N. The company was in very fine fettle.

Cast
Sweeney Todd (Andy Gledhill), Mrs Lovett (Stephanie Moore), Anthony (Matt Willcock), Beggar Woman (Andrea Ferguson), Judge (Huw Jones), Beadle (John Mangan), Johanna (Genevieve Plunkett), Pirelli (Ian Chisholm), Tobias (Gary Higgs), Bird Seller (Bob Sharman), Fogg (David Chapman), Three Tenors (Joseph Betts, Bob Sharman, Charles Tweed), Quintet (Joseph Betts, Ian Chisholm, Katie Hunt, Bob Sharman, Beth Smith)

Gentlemen of the Chorus Joseph Betts, Sean Bray, Frank Brown, David Chapman, Jack Harper, Timothy Littlejohns, David Pulling, Bob Sharman, Daniel Smith, Alan Syder, Charles Tweed, Ryan Young

Ladies of the Chorus Megan Bradsworth, Jenny Bugg, Lisa Chapman, Niamh Church, Donna Collier, Maria Cutting, Claire Doughty, Tracey Evans, Rachell Folley, Louise Harper, Katie Hunt, Rebecca Jillings, Charley Little, Kathryn Loveday, Sue Ridge, Melissa Sampson, Beth Smith, Kyanna Sutton, Rose Williams

2014
ANYTHING GOES

Norwich Theatre Royal, 27 January–1 February
Music and lyrics: **Cole Porter**
Original book: **P. G. Wodehouse, Guy Bolton, Howard Lindsay and Russel Crouse**
New book: **Timothy Crouse and John Weidman**
Director: **Jeremy Tustin**
Musical Director: **Matt Brown**

P. G. Wodehouse's idea of a musical comedy built around a shipwreck foundered when in September 1934 the ocean liner *SS Morro Castle* was wrecked with the loss of 134 lives. Ultimately, Lindsay and Crouse's new book revolved around cabaret singer Reno Sweeney's adventures on board. This was the work that propelled that powerhouse of musical theatre talent Ethel Merman to stardom in the 1934 Broadway production. With Merman unwilling to travel, the 1935 London Remo was the less-known Jeanne Aubert.

The N&N was heartily welcomed by James Goffin, describing how:

> A strong cast, headed by Andrea Ferguson as Reno, powers the farcical goings-on aboard the *SS American*, mixing some of Porter's songs with

great dance and charming wit [...] Ferguson's voice is strong and she is an eye-catching presence on stage.' There was strong comedy from Joseph Betts ('a joy to watch: Brilliant facial expressions and a real talent for physical comedy'), Christopher Penn (more 'great comedy'), and Ian Chisholm ('a reliable note of humour from start to finish: silly, over the top and a lot of fun'). Claire Doughty was 'under-used' as Hope Harcourt but 'entranced' when given a chance. Standing in for Stephanie Moore as Erma, Kathryn Jones was 'definitely one to watch for future productions'.

Porter's score delivered a strong dash of wry sophistication in a string of memorable numbers. Walter Clemons has defined any Porter song as a 'luxury item'. 'In a way no other songs of the period quite did, Porter created a world. It was a between-the-wars realm of drop-dead chic and careless name-dropping insouciance', not least in 'You're the Top'. His approach to song-writing seemed almost formulaic:

> First, I think of the idea and then I fit it to a title. Then, I go to work on the melody, spotting the title at certain moments in the melody, and then I write the lyric – the end first – that way, it has a strong finish. I do the lyrics like I'd do a crossword puzzle.[27]

For Merman, 'You're the Top' 'brought audiences to their feet because it was a new kind of love song. There had never been a song like it before. So I wasn't surprised that at the peak of its popularity Cole received 300 parodies a month.'[28] One such parody was the duet 'You're Absolutely Me' in Sandy Wilson's 1964 British musical *Divorce Me, Darling*.

Just before curtain-up on the opening night, the N&N company of *Anything Goes* was informed of the death of 23-year-old Gary Higgs who had been cast as John. He had previously played Barnaby Tucker in the 2012 *Hello, Dolly!* and Tobias in the 2013 *Sweeney Todd*, especially notable for his moving performance of 'Nothing's Going to Harm You' with Stephanie Moore's Mrs Lovett. He had withdrawn from *Anything Goes* and married Stephanie Moore in hospital a few days before his death. David Pulling told the *EDP* 'He was constantly dedicated and committed to the roles that he took on and never once failed us [...] everybody could see how theatre was a huge part of his life'.

Cast

Reno Sweeney (Andrea Ferguson), Billy Crocker (Andy Gledhill), Evangeline Harcourt (Linda Campbell), Evelyn Oakley (Christopher Penn), Hope Harcourt (Claire Doughty), Moonface Martin (Joseph Betts), Erma (Stephanie Moore), Elisha Whitney (Ian Chisholm), Captain (David Chapman), Purser (Jason Ames), Henry Dobson (Nick Bird), Fred (Joshua Egirani), Old Lady in Wheelchair (Audrey Fiddes), Luke (Sean Bray), John (Gary Higgs), Boy in Bar (Charles Tweed), Girl in Bar (Rachel Bird), Cheeky (Renwar's Tinker Tyler)

Reno's Angels Tracey Evans, Liz Ireland, Kathryn Jones, Debbie Whomes

Crew Quintet Jason Ames, Frank Brown, Joshua Egirani, Charles Tweed, Ryan Young

Gentlemen of the Chorus Frank Brown, Joe Keeley, David Knights, Charles Tweed, Ryan Young

Ladies of the Chorus Nicola Brooks, Niamh Church, Lorna Cracknell, Meryl Dempsey, Kate Evans, Millie Evans, Tracey Evans, Megan Frosdick, Liz Ireland, Nicci Mills, Berni Necchi, Sam Parker, Genevieve Plunkett, Lesley Rix, Connor Roper, Lisa Rowe, Melissa Sampson, Jo Weston, Debbie Whomes, Rose Williams

2015
SISTER ACT

Norwich Theatre Royal, 26–31 January
Music: Alan Menken
Lyrics: Glenn Slater
Book: Cheri and Bill Steinkellner, based on the film written by Joseph Howard
Additional book material: Douglas Carter Beane
Director: Jeremy Tustin
Musical Director: Geoff Davidson

A crowd-pleaser made even more popular by its 1992 film version starring Whoopi Goldberg, *Sister Act* was described by David Pulling as 'our most adventurous project yet', presenting a considerable challenge. As Pulling explained 'Finding a suitable black actress who could sing, dance and carry the huge role of Deloris was always going to be difficult in Norwich, and several months of searching were fruitless. Stretching the boundaries has meant that we've been able to find our Deloris' (Trenetta Jones, a Suffolk teacher of drama and English, who happened to be auditioning for a Threshold production of *Hairspray*). An online review praised Jones who 'brilliantly balances the comedy moments and the emotional impact of Deloris's journey. She riffs excellently with Linda Campbell, who is hilarious as the traditional, dry-witted Mother Superior, and some of the best and funniest moments in the show occur as these two butt heads.' Ultimately, 'it is within the walls of the convent that *Sister Act*'s heart truly lies'. The strong supporting company included Joseph Betts, Jessica Stewart and Laura Marvell-James. Jones returned to the role for Chris Cuming's production at Cambridge Arts Theatre by the Cambridge Operatic Society in November 2015.

Cast

Deloris Van Cartier (Trenetta Jones), Mother Superior (Linda Campbell), Sister Mary Patrick (Laura Marvell-Jones), Sister Mary Robert (Jessica Stewart), Sister Mary Lazarus (Judi Daykin), Sister Mary Theresa (Lesley Rix), Monsignor O'Hara (Nick Bird), Sister Mary Martin (Jenny Bugg), Eddie Souther (Joseph Betts), Tina (Andrea Ferguson), Michelle (Michelle Clark), Curtis Shank (Andy Gledhill), Pablo (Jason Ames), Joey (Ryan Young), TJ (Frank Brown), Ernie (David Chapman)

Gentlemen of the Chorus Jason Ames, Frank Brown, David Chapman, Paul Greathead, Colin Harris, David Mills, Robert O'Sullivan, Christopher Penn, Connor Roper, Bob Sharman, Ryan Young

Ladies of the Chorus Christina Allcock, Holly Allton, Niamh Church, Michelle Clark, Rowena Croston-Clegg, Lucie Curtis, Janette Davidson, Meryl Dempsey, Andrea Ferguson, Hayley Hubbard, Liz Ireland, Heather Jones, Genevieve Plunkett, Nicola Robinson

2016
SUNSET BOULEVARD

Norwich Theatre Royal, 25–30 January
Music: **Andrew Lloyd Webber**
Book and lyrics: **Don Black and Christopher Hampton, based on the film by Billy Wilder**
Director: **Jeremy Tustin**
Musical Director: **Rob Goodrich**

'Great sets and superb performances' was the headline for the *EDP*'s brief review. It suggested that the more analytical and detailed critical assessments of the Society's past (compare it to the *EDP* reviews of the 1925 *Dorothy* and more recently the well-considered criticisms by Neville Miller and Charles Roberts) were things of the past. They had been reviews that somehow reflected the importance of what was happening on stage, the sort of reviews that now seemed in danger of receding into the theatrical mist.

Billy Wilder's 1950 film *Sunset Boulevard* retains its reputation as one of the great Hollywood movies, personified by Gloria Swanson's extraordinary performance as the fading movie star Norma Desmond. The American film critic James Agee wrote: 'Miss Swanson, required to play a hundred per cent grotesque, plays it not just to the hilt, but right up to the armpits, by which I mean magnificently.' The British film critic Dilys Powell recognised: 'In a truly outstanding performance she shows us a woman to whom playing a part has become second nature, and an actress to whom acting is life: here is the star of the days when a face had to speak without words.'[29]

Richard Kislan unarguably realises that audiences love Andrew Lloyd Webber's shows and 'appreciate the songs that speak to them directly and without complication. His productions bind sound to spectacle at a time of unprecedented demands for special effects, over-design, and lavish adornments that seem to assure audiences more accustomed to movies that they are getting the biggest bang for their money.' For Kislan, 'The critical consensus falls far below the level of his commercial success', while the *Sunday Times* critic Robert Hewison argues that 'Lloyd Webber has developed a way of writing music which is familiar before you have heard it.'

The *EDP* reviewer for the N&N described how the Society's production 'revels in the big numbers that gave the original show its grandeur'. There was space for mentioning the 'sumptuous sets' and that 'Desmond's dazzling vintage outfits are enough to entertain in themselves'. Linda Campbell's Norma had 'fine emotional intensity', and Joe Edwards as Joe Gillis 'turns in a superbly judged performance, with a voice that seems effortlessly perfect'. 'Show-stealing, however, is the 29-strong orchestra that brings out the best in this lush imaginative score'. The reviewer overlooked the contribution of the talented small-part players that included skilled veterans Peter Howell, Adrian Wright, Ian Chisholm and Samuel Fletcher, and neglected the appearances of the always welcome John McInnes as Norma's devoted companion Max von Mayerling, and Jessica Stewart as an assured Betty Schaefer.

It may be that the reviewer found little else of interest about the musical adaptation of *Sunset Boulevard* about which to write. This may equally be true of this modest essay. There are those who simply cannot get excited about certain works or come up with anything interesting to say about them.

Cast

Norma Desmond (Linda Campbell), Joe Gillis (Joe Edwards), Max von Mayerling (John McInnes), Betty Schaefer (Jessica Stewart), Cecil B DeMille (Peter Howell), Artie Green (Sam Fletcher), Sheldrake (Ian Chisholm), Manfred (Adrian Wright)

64. Linda Campbell as Norma Desmond in *Sunset Boulevard* (2016)
© Jaz Instone-Brewer.

Gentlemen of the Chorus Louis Aves, David Chapman, Joshua Gould, David Mills, Peter Mottram, Joseph Reed, Dominic Sands, Alan Syder, George Wilson, Ryan Young

Ladies of the Chorus Niamh Church, Michelle Clarke, Lucie Curtis, Meryl Dempsey, Andrea Ferguson, Lauren Hewitt, Jasmine Instone-Brewer, Laura Marvell-James, Demi Mayne, Tracy Melton, Phillipa Nortcliffe, Jennifer Pallister, Lesley Rix, Fritha Roberts, Melissa Sampson, Rebekah Watts

2017
THE WITCHES OF EASTWICK

Norwich Theatre Royal, 31 January–4 February
Music: **Dana Rowe**
Book and lyrics: **John Dempsey, based on the novel by John Updike and the Warner Bros Motion Picture**
Director: **Jeremy Tustin**
Musical Director: **Geoff Davidson**

Peter Walsh's modest *EDP* review may not have sent the box office into a frenzy with his comment that Terry Boast's performance was

> more Jim Carey than Jack Nicholson, with the emphasis on the comic rather than the charismatic. But that is not to belittle Boast's turn which, although sometimes awkward, was strangely mesmerising in a can't take your eyes off him kind of way. He, like the rest of the cast, did not take himself too seriously in a production that was filled with light as well as shade, even in its darkest moments.

There was widespread praise for the trio of witches, Andrea Ferguson, Claire Reynolds Chandler and Kathryn White.

Amie Croxton's review for *justregional.co.uk* alerted patrons to 'Keep an eye out for the little girl played by Alisha Hart, and Fidel played by Joshua Gould . Their smaller but hilarious parts in the show really made it for me. Subtle but brilliantly executed and had the whole crowd laughing.' Furthermore, 'Harriet Chambers as Felicia and David Chapman as Clyde were brilliantly cast – they performed the roles perfectly and hilariously.'

Holly Byrne's review for *concrete-online.co.uk* was refreshingly observant, noting the polished professionalism of Kathryn White, Claire Reynolds Chandler, Andrea Ferguson and Isabelle Anderson. Ultimately, Byrne thought the production 'successful in terms of its casting and individual performance, however, this was sadly overshadowed by the lack of a strong story-line, which unfortunately left me feeling unsatisfied at points'. Byrne considered that 'The focus seemed to lay more in the song and dance of each scene, rather than the overall plot. As a consequence of this, much of what I felt should have been the main part of the play was crammed into the latter part of the second act which made it seem extremely rushed and clumsy.'

The first act closer 'I Wish I May' had the leading ladies taking to the air as if Kirby's Flying Ballet had taken flight. In Norwich, this highlight of technical magic was something of an anti-climax, lacking the sensation of the trio flying above the auditorium as they had at the Theatre Royal Drury Lane.

Cast

Darryl Van Horne (Terry Boast), Alexandra Spofford (Claire Reynolds Chandler), Jane Smart (Kathryn White), Sukie Rougemont (Andrea Ferguson), Felicia Gabriel (Harriet Chambers), Clyde Gabriel (David Chapman), Jennifer Gabriel (Isabelle Anderson), Michael Spofford (Joseph Reed), Little Girl (Alisha Hart), Fidel (Joshua Gould), Rebecca Barnes (Phillipa Nortcliffe), Cassie Barnes (Sophie Chapman), Toby Bergman (Tom Mack), Eudora Bryce (Karen Cockrill), Rose Hallybread (Melissa Sampson), Curtis Hallybread (James Bell), Mavis Jessup (Olivia Dolman), Franny Lovecraft (Liz Ireland), Gina Marino (Jasmine Instone-Brewer), Joe Marino (Dominic Sands), Ralph Nader (Ryan Young), Clara Nader (Lucie Curtis), Greta Neff (Sarah Cubitt), Raymond Neff (Mark Stoyle), Heidi Neff (Alexandra Hever), Mabel Ogden (Lesley Rix), Harriet Osgood (Meryl Dempsey), Deborah Osgood (Demi Mayne), Ed Parsley (Alan Syder), Brenda Parsley (Jenny Bugg), Marge Perley (Niamh Church), Dawn Polanski (Rebecca Maitland), Gus Stevens (Harrison Elvin), Marcy Willis (Fritha Roberts)

2018
TOP HAT

Norwich Theatre Royal, 22–27 January
Music: **Irving Berlin**
Book: **Matthew White and Howard Jacques, based on the RKO film**
Director: **Chris Cuming**
Musical Director: **Kevin Bell**

James Goffin's *EDP* review had no doubt about the production's quality; here was 'an all-singing, all-dancing gem':

> Mistaken identity, love, and mad dashes across Europe – *Top Hat* is a frothy, fun journey that features some of Irving Berlin's finest tunes and sharpest lyrics. Norfolk & Norwich Operatic Society's production of this

65. *Top Hat:* Christopher Penn, Linda Campbell, Adrian Wright, Ian Chisholm and Alex Green (2018). Courtesy of David Pulling.

film adaptation has a mass of talent on stage. Alex Green as leading man is going to be left with very sore feet by the end of the run: he taps, dances, and sings his way through the show with unbounded energy. Female lead Kathryn White is in great voice and holds a perfect line throughout, flexing between wit and vulnerability as her character's fortunes shift. Together the two are captivatingly cinematic as they glide through 'Cheek to Cheek 'and 'Let's Face the Music'. Adrian Wright is a comic star as valet Bates, with great support too from Ian Chisholm, Linda Campbell, and Christopher Penn. The ensemble lack discipline in some early sequences, but deliver a barnstorming all-tap version of 'Top Hat, White Tie and Tails' that could pass muster in the West End. Some minor technical trips on the first night were not enough to detract from the triumph of such a big show; I take my hat off to them.

Cast

Jerry Travers (Alex Green), Dale Tremont (Kathryn White), Horace Hardwick (Ian Chisholm), Madge Hardwick (Linda Campbell), Alberto Beddini (Christopher Penn), Bates (Adrian Wright)

Gentlemen of the Chorus Terry Boast, David Chapman, Harrison Elvin, Nic Gordon, Joshua Gould, Lewis Rogers, Mark Stoyle, Charles Tweed, Ryan Young

66. *Top Hat*: Alex Green and Kathryn White in *Top Hat* (2018). Courtesy of David Pulling.

Ladies of the Chorus Jayne Andrew, Jenny Bugg, Millie Catlin, Karen Cockrill, Sara Crowley, Annabelle Culley, Meryl Dempsey, Olivia Dolman, Andrea Ferguson, Claire Ford, Alisha Hart, Ellis Keeler, Rebecca Maitland, Sharon Morter, Katrina Porter, Emma Rogers, Phillipa Nortcliffe, Melissa Sampson, Bethany Tuckwood, Rose Williams, Emmie Wright, Charlotte Wyndham

Off-Stage Singers Matt Ashley, Lewis Aves, Emilia Campbell, Sara Cubitt, Tracy Melton, Joseph Reed

2019
GUYS AND DOLLS

Norwich Theatre Royal, 22–26 January
Music **and lyrics: Frank Loesser**
Book: **Jo Swerling and Abe Burrows, based on Damon Runyon's story 'The Idyll of Miss Sarah Brown'**
Director: **Chris Cuming**
Musical Director: **Kevin Bell**

Liz Ireland's programme note succinctly identified the Runyonesque quality of the piece.

> Based on his links with the real criminal world, Runyon took ruthless, murderous counterfeiters and used his whimsical literary style to add comedy and rueful wisdom to their escapades. Nobody in a Runyon tale is murdered, only eliminated; guns are not lethal weapons, only equalisers. The world of the criminal set to music and allowed to dance. Thankfully

for us, Swerling and Burrows saw the appeal in this world and, using Sarah and Sky as inspiration, created arguably the most unlikely yet enduring love story in musical theatre history.

Chris Cuming was especially conscious that

> for this production colour is very important. We've chosen to move away from traditional stage sets this year and will be using colour in the video projection that is being designed specifically for us. Costume colour is therefore more important as it needs to work in conjunction with the video projection to pop when we need the costumes to stand out and also to match at other moments. We're aiming to match the vibrancy yet also the naturalism of the time and locations.

Considering the costuming, one of his aims was 'that we look at the women beyond their stereotype. They are strong women with opinions and we're trying to represent this in the characterisation. The costumes should demonstrate that. Some of our costumes are not what audiences might expect for this reason.'[30]

This revival seems to have been much better received than the N&N's 1987 production. The *EDP* sent Bethany Whymark ('I am a big musicals fan, but not a very active one') as its reviewer. She was impressed by Holly Graham's 'stunning vocals, and the effortless way she commanded the stage made her captivating to watch', while her leading man Phil Ormerod was 'smooth and charismatic'. Their duetting was 'mesmerising'. Several other critical bouquets fell at the supporting cast's feet. Other special moments included Joseph Betts and ensemble's roof-raising 'Sit Down, You're Rocking the Boat', and Arvide's Salvation Army aria 'More I Cannot Wish You', an unexpected moment of reflection among the ensuing hubbub.

Cast

Sky Masterson (Phil Ormerod), Nathan Detroit (Nick Bird), Miss Adelaide (Andrea Ferguson), Sarah Brown (Holly Graham), Nicely-Nicely Johnson (Joseph Betts), Benny Southstreet (Craig Loxston), Rusty Charlie (Chris Davidson), Arvide Abernathy (Adrian Wright), General Cartwright (Linda Croston), Lt Brannigan (Ray Tempesta), Harry the Horse (Alex Glenn), Big Jule (Mark Wells), Society Max (Josiah Blake), Liverlips Louis (Zak Poll), Angie the Ox (David Van Den Bergh), Scranton Slim (Ryan Young), Cuban Dancers (Nicola Brooks and Zak Poll)

Hotbox Girls Lena (Nicola Brooks), Irene (Claire Ford), Peggy (Jenny Hutchins), Ruth (Rebecca Maitland), Mimi (Kezia Dunham), Nancy (Rose Williams)

Mission Girls Laverne (Niamh Church), Agatha (Rowena Croston-Clegg), Betty (Sharon Morter), Calvin (Lavinia Pirrett), Lorraine (Lesley Rix), Martha (Cassie Woolley)

The 2020s

In 2020 the Society explained:

> The wonderful support our audiences have given our productions over many years enabled a Trust Fund to be set up with the object of assisting local talented people to train for a career in professional theatre. Since 1970, over £80,000 in grants has been awarded and we have supported over 100 students who have graduated from theatre schools and colleges, many going on to perform or work in the performing arts.

This was a decade that found the company on good form, and with a programme of musicals that clearly demonstrated how the Society had progressed. A strong sense of ensemble playing, with standout performances, contributed to the success of the British musical *Made in Dagenham*. Plans to present *The Sound of Music* (originally produced by the Society in 1989) were abandoned when theatres nationwide were closed down in March 2020, as David Pulling explained: 'Little did we know that our production of *Made in Dagenham* in January 2020 would be the last for so long. How fortunate we were to complete our run before Covid struck. Many societies across the country were not so fortunate.'

The Sound of Music, one of the most consistently popular classic Broadway musicals and first performed by the Society in 1989, was announced for February 2021. It was not to be. When restrictions were lifted, rehearsals for Chris Cuming's inventive production were fraught with difficulties. Strict protocol and stringent home-testing for Covid (a worrying procedure) constantly threatened the proceedings. Up to the very last week or so of rehearsals there remained the possibility that the show would falter. Ultimately, only one of the many nuns (Cuming had a battalion of them, all in wonderful voice) had to withdraw from the run after testing positive for Covid. As it happened, there could hardly have been any better choice of show than *The Sound of Music* at this moment of public fear and anxiety. The idea of climbing that mountain had a special resonance in January 2022.

2020
MADE IN DAGENHAM

Norwich Theatre Royal, 28 January–1 February
Music: David Arnold
Lyrics: Richard Thomas
Book: Richard Bean
Director: Chris Cuming
Musical Director: Kevin Bell

British (and American) musicals have long had a fascination with industrial strife, with striking workers withdrawing their services and joining picket lines with a song in their hearts. One of the most striking British examples was Peter Wildeblood and Peter Greenwell's *The Crooked Mile*, one of the 'New Wave' musicals that opened in London in 1959. Central to its plot was a strike by Soho's working girls.

That same year Jerry Bock and Sheldon Harnick's *Fiorello!*, a musical biography of New Yorker Fiorello LaGuardia, was a substantial Broadway success, incorporating his support for female shirtwaist strikers in 1909. Probably the largest strike in American history, it involved 20,000 Yiddish-speaking immigrants who downed tools for 11 weeks at the Triangle Shirtwaist Factory. Although the Broadway *Fiorello!* won the Pulitzer Prize for Drama, it did not long survive an all-British London production in 1962, perhaps because most British people had not the faintest idea what the title meant.

There was almost a luxuriance of strikes in West End musicals in 1966. *The Matchgirls* dealt with the strike by female workers at London's Bryant and May Factory in 1888 (the dockers subsequently came out in sympathy). Astonishingly, another British musical about the Bryant and May industrial dispute (*Strike a Light!*) quickly followed *The Matchgirls* into London, and was an even faster flop. Most successful of all was the hugely successful *Billy Elliot*, a work that literally went around the world.

Made in Dagenham was a musical retelling of the 1968 strike for equal pay by Ford Motor Company's female sewing machinists in Essex, adapted from the successful 2010 film. For the *Guardian* 'this stage version of the film suffers from its caricatures, relentless jokiness and functional score'. Furthermore, 'the show has mislaid the quality that made the film so good: a real heart'. There is no doubting the potency of *Made in Dagenham*. Theatrically effective, it brought out the best of the Society working as an ensemble. David Pulling described the piece as an uplifting musical comedy about friendship, love and the importance of fighting for what is right: 'It is important when we select a show to make it both appealing for the cast to perform as well as for the audience to watch. *Made*

67. *Made in Dagenham*, yet another musical about striking workers (2020). Courtesy of David Pulling.

in Dagenham is not your traditional musical, so it is exciting and challenging when one of the more modern productions becomes available.'

Perhaps the political edge was weakened by the writers lampooning the then prime minister, Harold Wilson (distinctly played by Nick Bird), and there was the uneasy feeling that the big closing number 'Stand Up' was too much of a blatant signal for the audience to give the inevitable (sometimes almost obligatory) standing ovation. Nevertheless, there was no doubting the sincerity of the performances, not least those of Craig Loxston and Holly Graham, and this is a musical that deserves its place in the proud history of musicals involving industrial unrest.

For some reason we have yet to be presented with a musical about the Music Hall strike of 1907. Led by major stars such as Marie Lloyd and Gus Elen, the music hall artistes demand for better pay, a minimum wage and reduced hours of work was met after a mere two weeks. A musical version could use the vast immensely overlooked archive of music hall songs. An interesting project for the more adventurous amateur societies who could withstand the risk.

Meanwhile, Liz Ireland's programme note pointed out that, although the film version was 'based on real events, it is not completely accurate. There was no real Rita O'Grady – the writers based her character on a combination of several of the female Ford workers.' The original London production of 2014 had received 'mixed but generally positive reviews. Quentin Letts deemed it "witty fun fitfully inventive and distinctly British"'.

Cast

O'Grady Family Rita (Holly Graham), Eddie (Craig Loxton), Graham (Korben White), Sharon (Lottie Lake)

Featured Roles Harold Wilson (Nick Bird), Barbara Castle (Sara Crowley), Civil Servants (Samuel Fletcher, James Ford, Alex Glenn), Lisa Hopkins (Andrea Ferguson), Cortina Man / Mr Buckton (Ric Gardner-Collis), Chubby Chuff (Steven Melton)

Ford Factory Workers Beryl (Michelle Unstead), Connie Riley (Tracy Melton), Sandra Beaumont (Matilda Chitty), Clare (Rowena Croston-Clegg), Cass (Emmie Wright), Sid (James Ford), Bill (Alex Glenn), Stan (John Ducker), Barry (Samuel Fletcher), Monty (Ian Chisholm)

Ford Factory Management Mr Hopkins (Ray Tempesta), Mr Tooley (Alex Green), Ron Macer (Mark Wells), Gregory Hubble (Steven Melton)

Gentlemen of the Chorus Ric Gardner-Collis, Steven Melton, Joseph Newport, Lewis Rogers, Kieran Shooter, Ed Wilson, Ryan Young

Ladies of the Chorus Niamh Church, Judi Daykin, Jasmine Harvey, Samantha Elmhurst, Georgina Farrow, Anna Fehr-Foote, Jessica Lovelock, Rebecca Maitland, Demi Mayne, Sharon Morter, Lavinia Pirret, Louise Smith, Bethany Tuckwood, Hannah Walmesley-Browne

2022
THE SOUND OF MUSIC

Norwich Theatre Royal, 18–22 January
Music: **Richard Rodgers**
Lyrics: **Oscar Hammerstein II**
Book: **Howard Lindsay and Russel Crouse, suggested by** *The Trapp Family Singers* **by Maria Augusta Trapp**
Director: **Chris Cuming**
Musical Director: **Kevin Bell**

There was no production in 2021, with theatres closed worldwide because of Covid restrictions. Inevitably, the fear that Covid would rage on into the New Year overshadowed rehearsals for the 2022 production. Almost up until the last week of rehearsals it seemed that the show might not yet go on but, with the advertised cast intact, it took to the Theatre Royal stage on 18 January. In the circumstances it seemed utterly appropriate that Rodgers and Hammerstein's seemingly

68. *The Sound of Music* 2022: The von Trapp Family. Courtesy of David Pulling.

69. *The Sound of Music* The escape to the mountains (2022). Courtesy of David Pulling.

immortal piece had been selected. The hope and determination to survive of that old piece of musical theatre with its urging to 'Climb Every Mountain' caught the moment perfectly. There was not a dry eye from those in the wings as Maria and her Captain and his children climbed those mountains to freedom.

James Goffin's review for *cultivated.org.uk* could not have been more welcoming:

> Musicals can often be a bit frustrating – a few catchy numbers and then a lot of dreary musical exposition padding out the rest of the story, but this is one of my favourite things: the sheer joy of *The Sound of Music*. It also sneakily pulls on the heartstrings with the seven-strong Von Trapp family brood, and this Norfolk and Norwich Operatic Society production features as cute a coterie of kids as any: Sophie Chapman, Archie Heather, Tallulah Godfrey, Archie Woodward, Beth Buckley, Eden Chan, and especially the youngest, the scene-stealing Florence Martin as Gretl. Next to them, the adult cast has a job capturing your attention, but Michelle Unstead is a bold and likeable Maria, a ball of energy next to a straight-laced Captain von Trapp, played by Sam Greig. Kathryn White and Adrian Wright enjoy themselves and entertain as the hedonistic Elsa and Max, with just the right amount of eye rolling to be this side of panto season. Sara Cubitt demonstrates her vocal prowess as Mother Abbess, including when surrounded by members of an extremely talented 40-strong ensemble. The acapella opening of religious choral singing sets the bar extremely high, and it never really falters. Chris Cuming's production uses video projection for most of the scenery, which largely works but lacks the power of the few pieces of physical stage furniture – for example, the charm of the benches that turn into a bed, or the shock of seeing Nazi flags unfurl in the final scene. You really do have to pinch yourself to remember that, even allowing for the Society and its members' years of experience, this is an amateur production: Kevin Bell leads a 24-piece live orchestra, costumes and stage management for an extensive cast are slick, and the whole enterprise has the crisp perfection of the Alpine snow in the distance. The dark undertones of the story are inescapable, but this production is a life-affirming joy.

Cuming made cuts in the two numbers 'How Can Love Survive?' and 'No Way to Stop It' for the second leads Elsa and Max. Both songs were probably unknown to most of the Norwich audience as they were not included in the film version. It was nevertheless a delight to have them reinstated; among all that Rodgers and Hammerstein sweetness the cynicism and world-weariness was allowed to break through. As Cuming's programme note explained:

> *The Sound of Music* is such an iconic musical loved and known by so many. This makes my job as the director a little easier as your audience has an idea of what they're watching. We wanted to ensure that audiences get the full visual of the movie and transport them to some of those stunning locations. Video designer Sam Jeffs and I have been able to do just that whilst also hitting on some of the darker aspects of the show. Nowhere in theatre do you get to hear *The Sound of Music* played by a 24 piece orchestra anymore

[not to mention the ample supply of nuns which no professional production could afford] so it's fully worth a visit to the Norwich Theatre Royal.

Cast

Maria Rainer (Michelle Unstead), Captain Von Trapp (Sam Greig), Liesl Von Trapp (Sophie Chapman), Friedrich (Archie Heather), Louisa (Tallulah Godfrey), Kurt (Archie Woodward), Brigitta (Beth Buckley), Marta (Eden Chan), Gretl (Florence Martin), Elsa Schraeder (Kathryn White), Max Detweiler (Adrian Wright), Mother Abbess (Sara Cubitt), Rolf Gruber (James Bell), Sister Berthe (Lesley Rix), Sister Margaretta (Sarah Browne), Sister Sophia (Ruby Bardwell-Dix), Franz (Samuel Fletcher-Browne), Frau Schmidt (Tracy Melton), Admiral Von Schreiber (Paul Clark), Herr Zeller (Ray Tempesta), Frau Zeller (Philippa Nortcliffe), Baron Elberfeld (Alex Telling), Baroness Elderfeld (Meryl Dempsey)

Gentlemen of the Chorus Neil Chapman, Paul Clark, John Ducker, Gabriel Jones, Joseph Newton, Ed Wilson, Ryan Young

Ladies of the Chorus Rebecca Ayers, Ruby Bardwell-Dix, Kizzy Beckett, Sarah Browne, Caroline Caldecott, Niamh Church, Meryl Dempsey, Georgina Farrow, Hannah Fletcher-Browne, Georgia Folkard, Claire Ford, Jasmine Harvey, Katie Hewson, Debs Hulbert, Lottie Lake, Jessica Lovelock, Rebecca Maitland, Kimberley Mason, Liberty McCrohon, Sharon Morter, Philippa Nortcliffe, Jade North, Catherine Oaten, Rachel Pannell, Lavinia Pirret, Lesley Rix, Amy Rose, Melissa Sampson, Eleanor Sanders, Darci-Rose Sayer, Caitlin Woolrich

2023
KINKY BOOTS

Norwich Theatre Royal, 31 January–4 February
Music and lyrics: **Cyndi Lauper**
Book: **Harvey Fierstein, based on Geoff Deane and Tim Firth's film**
Director: **Chris Cuming**
Musical Director: **Kevin Bell**

As David Pulling explained:

> The casting of Lola was a particular nightmare. Needing a 'triple threat' of dancing, acting and singing, along with the need to perform in heels, proved difficult and we had little interest from the wider community of Norfolk. As a result, for the first time in our history, we've cast this role with a professional actor – Akeem Ellis-Hyman. Akeem has recently

70. 'I'm Not My Father's Son': Dominic Sands and Akeem Ellis-Hyman from the 2023 *Kinky Boots* © Richard Jarmy Photography.

played the part of Seaweed in the UK tour of *Hairspray* and has been a delight to work with.

James Goffin's notice for *cultivated.org.uk* was wholly congratulatory, recognising Dominic Sands' achievement in giving 'a confident performance while keeping true to his understated character' (indeed, Sands' portrayal had a fine emotional edge throughout), with Kathryn White as his ambitious fiancée Nicola ('sassy and on form').

Ellis-Hyman 'has a tough role and is definitely captivating stage presence, but his vocals faltered occasionally on this opening night production'. Alex Green was especially notable in 'the beautifully-staged boxing match – possibly the strongest set piece of the show', with Emmie Wright 'lifting the later part of the first half with great physical comedy and strong vocals'. Elsewhere, 'Steve Melton as factory foreman was a subtle delight' and Adrian Wright's cameo was 'deliciously exaggerated'. The work itself was 'a good yarn and an entertaining watch; undoubtedly a strong cast and the production values are every bit the professional show'.

Sophie Skyring was equally enthusiastic in the *EEN*, highlighting Emmie Wright's 'extreme vocal talent, which was apparent to everyone – but it was her comic timing that really put the entire audience in the palm of her hand'. Skyring acknowledged the effective supporting players that included 'Norwich favourites such as Alex Green, Kathryn White and even a cameo appearance from NNOS royalty Adrian Wright (Milan Stage Manager). This whole cast really does pack a punch. The factory girls seemed to reunite some of the Society's *Made in Dagenham* girls 'getting a laugh on almost everything they said'.

Cast
Charlie Price (Dominic Sands), Lola / Simon (Akeem Ellis-Hyman), Lauren (Emmie Wright), Nicola (Kathryn White), Don (Alex Green), George (Steven Melton), Pat (Michelle Unstead), Trish (Rowena Croston-Clegg), Madge (Tracy Melton), Gloria (Emma Venier), Harry (James Bell), Richard Bailey (Paul Clark), Milan Stage Manager (Adrian Wright), Mr Price (Ian Chisholm), Simon Senior (Delon Commosioung), Young Lola / Simon (Terrel Taylor), Young Charlie (Archie Woodward)

The Angels Shane Balls, Luke Clare-Wrigley, Daniel Elliott, Jamie O'Sullivan, Aiden Pulford, Fletcher Thomson

Gentlemen of the Chorus Mathew Bangley, James Bell, Neil Chapman, Paul Clark, Charlie Collins, Alex Dewitt, John Ducker, Jasper Godfrey, Simon Godfrey, Gabriel Jones, Mark Stoyle, Ed Wilson, Ryan Young

Ladies of the Chorus Joanna Brown, Niamh Church, Georgia Folkard, Jasmine Harvey, Olivia Knight, Rebecca Maitland, Kimberley Mason, Sharon Morter, Katie Porter

Booth Singers Mathew Bangley, Joanna Brown, Alex Dewitt, Olivia Knight, Katie Porter, Ryan Young

2024
BETTY BLUE EYES

Norwich Theatre Royal, 23–27 January
Music: **George Stiles**
Lyrics: **Anthony Drewe**
Book: **Alan Bennett**
Director: **Chris Cuming**
Musical Director: **Matt Brown**

By any standards, and certainly by the ever-challenging aspirations of the 99-year-old N&N, this delightful piece must be considered one of the company's outstanding contributions to the joy of the county. The original London production had not been especially notable, with mixed notices. For the *Daily*

71. *Betty Blue Eyes* A Private Function (2024) © Richard Jarmy Photography.

Telegraph's Charles Spencer, here was 'popular entertainment at its very best', leaving him 'grunting and snorting with pleasure'. James Goffin warmly welcomed the occasion of its East Anglian premiere:

> The large ensemble cast from Norfolk and Norwich Operatic Society get it just right too, with Chris Cuming's direction and choreography bringing everything together. The Primrose Ballroom scene is perfectly presented, with a stage full of dancers and strong vocals from the 'Lionheart' trio (Ruby Barwell-Dix, Holly Graham, and Genevieve Plunkett) and Michelle Unstead as Joyce Chilvers and Will Mugford as Gilbert. The central two are impressive throughout, with Mugford's wide eyes believably innocent and a sweet counterpart to Unstead's iron will. Their 'fight' is a touching and beautifully-wrought moment.

Furthermore, Tracy Melton and Joseph Betts deserved 'praise for their comic props', while Alex Green 'hams it up as the villainous meat inspector Wormold'. Goffin appreciated the 'fully professional feel' of a show that was 'funny, and just a bit revolutionary; it's a choice cut, and definitely worth a taste'.

For *eatpod.co.uk* Mugford 'played with great skill and charm', while Tracy Melton as Mother Dear 'threatens to steal the show at times, such is her wonderful performance. Equally show-stealing was Alex Green as 'meat inspector Mr Wormold. His performance was a hilarious whirling virtuoso turn as the villain of the piece, where he was able to showcase his brilliant dance ability, alongside some booming quasi-operatic vocals.' Here was 'a slick, professional

72. The finale of *Betty Blue Eyes* (2024) © Richard Jarmy Photography.

performance' for 'this absolute stonker of a musical had absolutely everything: beautiful vocal performances and stunning arrangements, impressive, energetic choreography, superb comic acting, and a wonderful musical score performed with skill and precision by both the 10-strong band and the onstage actor / musicians'.

Cast

Gilbert Chilvers (Will Mugford), Joyce Chilvers (Michelle Unstead), Mother Dear (Tracy Melton), Alex Green (Mr Wormold), Henry Allardyce (Joseph Betts), James Swaby (Steven Melton), Gemma Bain, Metcalf (Mathew Bangley), Waiter (Luca Barrell), Veronica Allardyce (Beth Buckley), Mrs Turnbull (Sarah Browne), Nuttall (Paul Clark), Mrs Metcalf (Rowena Croston-Clegg), Sutcliffe (Chris Davidson), Barraclough (John Ducker), Francis Lockwood (Sam Fletcher-Browne), Mrs Allardyce (Holly Graham), Mrs Lockwood (Jessica Lovelock), Mrs Sutcliffe (Rebecca Maitland), Mrs Roach (Kimberley Mason), Sergeant Noble (Craig Mayne), Mrs Lester (Lesley Rix), Reg Bowen (Mark Stoyle), BBC Newscaster (Adrian Wright), Betty the Pig Puppeteer (James Bell)

Gentlemen of the Chorus Luca Barrell

Ladies of the Chorus Gemma Bain, Ruby Bardwell-Dix, Alexa Batterham, Carole Beatty, Niamh Church, Eloise Cubbin, Meryl Dempsey, Emily Johnson, Sharon Morter, Caitlin Woolrich

Lionheart Trio Ruby Bardwell-Dix, Holly Graham, Genevieve Plunkett

Envoi

Two things before we go looking forward. Two shows that nudged one another into the West End in December 1968, *Mr and Mrs* at the Palace Theatre and *The Young Visiters* at the Piccadilly Theatre. Both were commercial flops. Despite having disappointing runs, both were effectively rescued from oblivion by having original cast recordings. In many cases, all that was left of so many London flop musicals was a tatty theatre programme containing scant information and not offering so much as a whiff of the show's atmosphere. The original cast recording is our best evidence of a show that has evaporated into the arcane fog of British flops. Without an original cast recording so much of British musical theatre has been lost.

Let us first consider *Mr and Mrs*. Just as the reputation of *Betty Blue Eyes* was enhanced by having Alan Bennett's name among its credits, *Mr and Mrs* had no less a progenitor than Noël Coward, being a fusion of two of his 1936 one-act plays *Fumed Oak* (*Mr*) and *Still Life* (*Mrs*). In 1945 *Still Life* reappeared as David Lean's seminal film *Brief Encounter*, starring Celia Johnson and Trevor Howard. The score for *Mr and Mrs* was written by one of the least remembered British musical theatre composers of the period John Taylor, whose biggest West End success had been the 1965 *Charlie Girl* for which he co-wrote the score with David Heneker.

Mr and Mrs was something quite new in British musicals, explained as 'Two separate and complete one-act plays in which the three leading actors covered a total of six roles between them.' The theme of both 'halves' of the bill was married life: swinging young people with no time for it, lonely old people willing to try again (now played by Hylda Baker and Alan Breeze), happily married middle-aged people disrupting the lives of their families for the passions of extra-marital relationship (as in *Mrs*) and the hen-pecked husband who finally just ups and leaves the nagging wife, mother-in-law and daughter (*Mr*). John Neville and Honor Blackman (a fascinating combination) played the two leads. There remains the choice of any revival to have its principals double up for both plays or share the roles with different leads.

Coward was impressed when Taylor and Neville 'auditioned' the songs for him, noting in his diary that 'Some of the tunes are very good, I think. Whether the mixture of *Fumed Oak* and *Still Life* will really work or not remains to be seen. If enthusiasm is anything to go by – and it sometimes is – it ought to run for capacity for eleven years.' However, following the show's first night, his diary entry sighed 'Oh dear! It was all, I fear, a bit of a botch-up.'

But what a score! This must be one of the noisiest musicals ever, brimming with vigour and vitality. Charting their love for one another, *Mrs* has *four* superb duets for Laura and Alec, 'Father of Two, Mother of Three', 'Come Thursday', 'Before Today' and the glorious 'I'll Be Always Loving You' complete with heavenly chorus. But there is much more: the male ensemble gets together for two rowdy numbers 'Give Us a Kiss' and 'I Want To Wet My Whistle', there is the stonkingly exciting 'I Feel I Want To Dance', and a roof-lifting disco-thumping acknowledgement to swinging London in the pounding disco reverberations of 'The Electric Circus'. This is a show that swings like no other of its period. In its way much of this delightful, wonderfully catchy score epitomises that moment when London was swinging. Johnnie Spence's fabulous orchestrations were rescued from the Palace Theatre following the show's speedy closure and are rumoured to reside in Australia. This is a work that (any financial considerations aside!) would illuminate any operatic society, revisiting a piece that so deserves to be rescued from oblivion.

*

In December 1968 a Mrs Daisy Devlin from Norwich was at the Piccadilly Theatre for the first night of one of the brightest British musicals of this or any other decade, *The Young Visiters*. In 1889, Mrs Devlin (then nine-year-old Daisy Ashford) had written (in pencil) a novelette that eventually fell into the hands of J. M. Barrie, who arranged for its publication. Many thought Barrie had written it himself as a sort of literary joke. As Mrs Devlin recalled 'I adored writing and used to pray for bad weather so that I need not go out but could stay in and write'. The *Daily Mail* applauded Daisy's hugely enjoyable grammatical and literary curiosity, a book 'over which half of London is laughing, the other half having to wait while more copies are being printed'. Daisy's view of the social whirl of her elders captivated readers.

The distinctive atmosphere of Daisy's masterpiece pervaded the musical adaptation by composer Ian Kellam and libretto by Michael Ashford, as the audience was informed that:

> Daisy Ashford's written a book
> With a start and a middle and an end.
> She's put chapters in it, lots,
> She's put paragraphs and plots
> And a start and a middle and an end.
> There are one or two blots
> And some i's without dots
> And her writing don't exactly toe the line
> And the spelling's pretty gory
> But the glory's in the story
> Realism! Drama!
> And Miss Daisy only nine!

ENVOI

Michael Ashford's artful translation from book to musical is faithful to young Daisy's original scheme, following the amorous adventures of Mr Salteena ('not quite a gentleman' but eager to climb the social ladder) to choose as his partner 'the prettiest in the face'. He is ultimately unsuccessful in his pursuit of the shamelessly social-climbing Miss Ethel Monticue, eventually having to make do with the much less glamorous Bessie Topp who admits 'I'm not beautiful', one of the most touching numbers. There are moments when Kellam's score bursts with delight, and its last ten minutes reach far beyond the superficial artifice of the characters in a glorious final chorale of happiness. In this heart-stopping moment, something in Kellam's composition lifts the show way above its modest pretensions, and Daisy's characters seem visceral. The message is profound.

This is a wondrous musical, underrated at the time of its original production, a thing of gentle charm and quiet wit, with great opportunities for its performers. Of course, like almost every one of the shows performed by the N&N in the last 100 years, the curtain falls on smiling faces, as Daisy's childish perception of adults rounds off its tale.

So, before blowing out the candles on the old girl's birthday cake, let us look forward to a future where success, continuing quality and a dash of daring, is ready to step out of the wings to carry the old company into the new unknown. It is entirely appropriate that, in these closing moments, we should find a perfect expression of the endings of the majority of the Society's productions. Ultimately *The Young Visiters* confirms the universality and deeply moving message of young Daisy's scribbling.

> I am content to have married you
> I am content to wear your ring
> It's like a dream that is coming true
> For it is joy beyond imagining.
> Why should we sigh for a might have been
> When everythings well on the mend?
> Better by far than a might have been
> We come …
> To our happy end!

Appendix 1: Norwich Amateur Operatic Company

Taken from the theatre programme of *Dorothy* at Norwich Hippodrome, 31 March–5 April 1913:

The Opera Company: Its History

The Norwich Amateur Opera Company was formed in 1901, and its first production took place in April 1902, when Gilbert and Sullivan's *Yeomen of the Guard* was produced with conspicuous success at the Theatre Royal. During the period of its existence, the Company has, like many others in various parts of the Kingdom, had its ups and downs - its successes and its failures. In 1904, the Company made its first appearance at the Grand Opera House (now the Hippodrome), in that popular Comic Opera *The Mikado*. In this, another brilliant success was scored. Still greater were the successes of 1905 and 1906, when *Dorothy* and *Haddon Hall* were given respectively.

The personnel of the Company has changed much since its formation, but despite the opposition from many quarters the present Company is full of enthusiasm, and hopes to score a pronounced success. *Les Cloches de Corneville* was produced in 1910, and will long be remembered for its excellent representation. *Maritana* and *Yeomen of the Guard*, the two last productions, though splendidly given, showed serious loss, and the Company is faced with clearing off a large deficit.

It is very proud of its President [the Revd C. B. Lipscomb] for the staunch manner in which he served the Society last season, and the already hard work he is doing on its behalf this year. The Officers and committee are exceptionally keen, and an excellent feeling exists among them. Mr Jerrold Manville, who staged the Opera of *Dorothy* in 1905, has been specially engaged to produce it again this year. It should prove once again an excellent attraction, as it is one which admits of sumptuous dressing and staging, while the music is light and ear-haunting, and the fun is fast and furious. Though there have been many changes in the various offices of the Company, there is one which has remained unchanged, namely, the office of the Musical Director. In all the Company's vicissitudes, no stauncher supporter, nor harder worker, has it had than its Conductor [Mr G. E. Harris].

*

In Norwich, amateur performances of light opera thrived in the early years of the twentieth century, with the works of Gilbert and Sullivan (but only their most popular) well to the fore. *The Mikado* was performed at the

Theatre Royal in mid-May 1901, heightening expectations by announcing 'Our Grand Amateur Performance' in aid of the Princess of Wales's Fund. It seems that from the earliest days one of the central *raison d'être* for mounting such productions was to raise money for charity. In this case, the show was credited to 'Dr. Thomsons' Operatic Company', but perhaps also marks the beginning of the Norwich (as distinct from the Norfolk and Norwich) Amateur Operatic Company' formed in 1901. Its first show, *The Yeomen of the Guard*, was produced 'with conspicuous success' at the Theatre Royal in 1902.

In this, another brilliant success was scored.

Dr. Thomson's Amateur Operatic Company was at the Theatre Royal with 'the charming comic opera' *The Gondoliers* in April 1905. Rehearsals were helped by the theatre's stage being available for practice, 'an opportunity which will be of the utmost advantage to all concerned'. The many encores demanded by the audience speak of the show's success, and Thomson thanked the audience for supporting the fundraising 'to benefit local charities'.

Jerrold Manville directed the Norwich Amateur Operatic Company's production of *Dorothy* at the Hippodrome in May 1905 with Lilian Le Fevre in the title role and J. T. Harborne playing Geoffrey Wilder. J. J. Manning is believed to be the only man who performed with both the Norwich Amateur Operatic Company and the subsequent Norfolk and Norwich Amateur Operatic Society, now playing Harry Sherwood and getting the standout number of the show 'Queen of My Heart'.

The Norwich Company's staging of Sullivan and Sydney Grundy's *Haddon Hall* at the Hippodrome in 1906 promised 'Wonderful Atmospheric Effects, the Whole Setting on a scale of Magnificence never before attempted in Norwich'. It was certainly a financial success, making a profit of £123, the local critic remarking that 'practically the "high water mark" had been reached. Busily diversifying, in the same year the Company presented two operas and other musical selections in the Assembly Room of the Agricultural Hall in Charing Cross, on 5 December Isidore Legouix's comic operetta *The Crimson Scarf* and the following evening Michael William Balfe's now long forgotten 1864 opera-cum-cantata *The Sleeping Queen*.

April 1907 saw the Company's production of Gilbert and Sullivan's ghostly *Ruddigore*. The luxuriance of décor was accentuated in promoting the 1908 production of G&S's only three Act opera *Princess Ida*, with 'Full Band and Choir'. What was more, 'The Scenery, Costumes and Setting are on a Scale Magnifical'.

The Company's next choice was Edward German and Basil Hood's *Merrie England* at the Hippodrome in April 1909. Its publicity promised 'Special Scenery and Costumes. Sparkling Music, Clever Wit and Humour. No Flagging from start to finish'. The cast included Kate Storey as Queen Elizabeth I, Grace Stevenson as Jill-all-Alone, and J. T. Harborne as Walter

Raleigh, supported by a band and chorus of 120, musically directed by George Harris. By September the Company was advertising in the *EDP*, announcing 'Voice Testing' to be held for prospective performers at St. Peter's Parmentergate Institute in King Street.

In April 1910 advance publicity for the Hippodrome's *Les Cloches de Corneville*, catchily promoted as *The Bells! The Bells!*, trumpeted its 'Strong Cast' and 'Band of Chorus of 80' for 'Grand Fashionable Nights', with profits donated to the Jenny Lind Infirmary. In aid of local charities, William Vincent Wallace and Edward Fitzball's opera *Maritana* played the Hippodrome in April 1911, a very ambitious undertaking. In May 1912 the Company appeared in a 'Popular Concert' at Norwich's St. Andrews' Hall, accompanied by the Operatic Company's Orchestra and the String Band of the 16th (The Queen's) Lancers.

At the Company's AGM on 6 November 1912, the possibility of revisiting *Dorothy* as the next production sparked a discussion. What was the point of repeating a piece that the Norwich Amateur Operatic Company had presented in 1905? Some argued that what the public wanted was not opera or operetta but musical comedy; something more modern than Cellier's genteel valentine.

Harris was aware that Lowestoft's amateur Society had followed their *Dorothy* with *The Belle of New York*. This was, he suggested, a lowering of the tone. He insisted that *Dorothy* had always proved good box-office. As alternatives he proposed Robert Planquette's 1882 *Rip van Winkle* (a fascinating prospect) and Puccini's *Manon Lescaut*, both of which would undoubtedly have tested the Company's mettle. Harris also considered reviving the formidable *Maritana*, despite the fact that their 1911 production had been a financial failure. Some preferred the idea of *Haddon Hall* (one of the dreariest scores that Sullivan ever produced) and *The Gondoliers*. If they really wanted a musical comedy, Harris thought the only certain candidate was Franz Lehár's *The Merry Widow*.

Ultimately, the Company decided to revisit *Dorothy* for its booking at the Hippodrome in April 1913, involving 'Band and Chorus of 80 performers' conducted by the seemingly indefatigable Mr Harris. The theatre programme for that event told patrons that 'The Norwich public have much to thank the Company for, for not only has £700 been given to various charities, but the chances of seeing some Operas, namely *Haddon Hall, Ruddigore, Princess Ida* and *Merrie England* would have been very remote, but for their production by the Amateurs.' However, although *Merrie England* had been 'one of the most lavishly staged operas ever produced in Norwich', it left the Company with substantial debts. Weathering such setbacks, the programme explained that 'The personnel of the Company has changed much since its foundation, but despite the opposition from many quarters the present Company is full of enthusiasm'.

In fact, the 1911 *Maritana* and 1912 *The Yeomen of the Guard* 'though splendidly given, showed serious loss, and the Company is faced with clearing off a large deficit' ... in all the Company's vicissitudes, no stauncher supporter, nor harder worker, has it had than its Conductor'. The Norwich Amateur Operatic Company shut up shop in 1913.

Appendix 2: Directors and Musical Directors

Directors

1925–31	Henry Butcher
1932–34	Harry W. Briden
1935–39	T. G. Woolley
1940–46	No productions
1947	Woolley resumed
1948	Ross Hills
1949–54	Thomas J. Bell
1955	Maurice Dixon
1956–57	Alison MacClaren
1958	Maisie Griffiths
1959	Charles Ross
1960	Frank Rydon
1961	Frank Rydon and Frances Davis
1962	Frank Rydon
1963–65	R. D'Arcy Richards
1966–67	Willie Martin
1968–71	Frances Davis
1972–1987	Ricky Price
1988	Ray Jeffery
1989–90	Robert Marlowe
1991	No production
1992	No production
1993–94	Ricky Price
1995	Robert Marlowe
1996	Ricky Price
1997	Robert Marlowe
1998–2006	Ray Jeffery
2007–11	Jeremy Tustin
2012–13	Ray Jeffery
2014–17	Jeremy Tustin
2018–24	Chris Cuming

Musical Directors

1925–27	Henry Butcher
1928	B. K. Wilson
1929	No production
1930–39	R. J. Maddern Williams
1940–46	No productions
1947–50	Heathcote Statham
1951–53	W. H. Walden Mills
1954	Richard Butt
1955	George B. Bullen
1956–62	Maurice Illiffe
1963–67	Frederick J. Firth
1968	Maurice Illiffe
1969–77	David Kett
1978	Frederick J. Firth
1979	Colin Goodchild
1980	David Kett
1981–84	Colin Goodchild
1985–87	David Kett
1988	Adrian Connell
1989–97	David Kett
1998	John Roper
1999	Geoff Oxley
2000–09	Geoff Davidson
2010–14	Matthew Brown
2015	Geoff Davidson
2016	Rob Goodrich
2017	Geoff Davidson
2018–22	Kevin Bell
2023	Matthew Brown

Notes to the Text

Beginnings
1 p. 10 of minute book 1925–35. It is unknown whether this was a professional or amateur production, but seems to have been in Leeds.
2 Newspaper clipping uncredited 1925.
3 Letter from Desmond Elliott to Peter Bance, 5 May 2001.
4 As described for Chappell's published libretto.
5 The D'Oyly Carte Opera Company had played a week at Norwich Theatre Royal in 1924 and 1925, and were due again in April 1926.
6 Minute book 1925–35, p. 43.

The 1920s
1 J. C. Trewin, *The Gay Twenties: A Decade of the Theatre* (London: Macdonald, 1958), p. 9.
2 Kurt Ganzl, *The Encyclopedia of the Musical Theatre* (New York: Schirmer Books, 1994), p. 293.
3 Thomas S. Hischak, *The Mikado to Matilda: British Musicals on the New York Stage* (London: Rowman and Littlefield, 2020), pp. 78–80.
4 Richard Traubner, *Operetta: A Theatrical History* (London: Victor Gollancz, 1984), p. 197.
5 F. C. Burnand, whose many works included the libretto for Sullivan's one-act opera *Cox and Box*.
6 CD notes for recording of *Dorothy*.
7 *EDP*, 15 February 1881.
8 Gervase Hughes, *Composers of Operetta* (London: Macmillan, 1962), p. 82.
9 Ibid, p. 87.
10 Traubner, p. 86.
11 Ibid, p. 87.
12 Michael R. Booth, *English Melodrama* (London: Herbert Jenkins, 1965), p. 13.
13 *Play Pictorial*, no. 35.

The 1930s
1 Traubner, p. 331.
2 Ibid, p. 332.
3 Ibid.
4 Arthur Jacobs, *Arthur Sullivan: A Victorian Musician* (Oxford: Oxford University Press, 1984), p. 274.
5 'The Field for the Amateur', *EDP*, 26 November 1928.
6 Hughes, p. 227.
7 Committee report for year ending 30 June 1934.
8 *EDP*, 3 December 1935.

9 Leslie Baily, *The Gilbert and Sullivan Book* (London: Spring Books, 1966), p. 230.
10 Ibid, p. 129.
11 *EDP*, 26 April 1938.
12 Traubner, p. 193.
13 Hughes, pp. 210–11.

The 1940s

1 *EEN*, 2 November 1948.
2 Quoted in Baily.
3 *EDP*, 15 November 1949.

The 1950s

1 Audrey Williamson, *Gilbert and Sullivan Opera* (London: Marion Boyars, 1982), p. 61.
2 Ibid, p. 63.
3 *EDP*, 22 April 1952.
4 Baily, p. 181.
5 Williamson, p. 20.
6 Ian Bradley, *Oh Joy! Oh Rapture!* (London: Oxford University Press, 2005), p. 131.
7 Adrian Wright, *Must Close Saturday* (Woodbridge: Boydell Press, 2017), p. 97.
8 Ibid.
9 Hughes, p. 226.
10 Hischak, *The Mikado to Matilda*, pp. 146–7.
11 *EDP*, 27 April 1954.
12 Andrew Lamb CD notes for *Lionel Monckton: Songs from the Shows*.
13 *EDP*, 17 April 1956.
14 Theatre programme.
15 *EEN*, 25 February 1958.
16 Hughes, p. 152.
17 *EDP*, 7 April 1959.
18 *EEN*, 7 April 1959.
19 Colin MacInnes, *Sweet Saturday Night* (London: MacGibbon and Kee, 1977), pp. 127–9.
20 Tise Vahimagi, *British Television* (Oxford: Oxford University Press, 1994) p. 71.

The 1960s

1 *EDP*, 21 February 1961.
2 Hughes, p. 146.
3 *EDP*, 21 February 1961.
4 *EEN*, 21 February 1961.
5 *Sunday Times*, 2 June 1968.
6 Traubner, p. 386.

7   James Agate, *Immoment Toys* (London: Jonathan Cape, 1945), p. 118.
8   *EDP*, 27 February 1962.
9   *EEN*, 27 February 1962.
10 *EDP*, 26 February 1963.
11 *EEN*, 26 February 1963.
12 *EEN*, 25 February 1964.
13 *EDP*, 25 February 1964.
14 Traubner, p. 249.
15 Larry Stempel, *Showtime: A History of the Broadway Musical* (New York: Norton, 2010, p. 175.
16 *EDP*, 8 February 1966.
17 Steve James, *EEN*, 7 February 1966.
18 *EDP*, 8 February 1966.

The 1970s
1   Agate, p. 91.
2   Adrian Wright, *Cheer Up!* (Woodbridge; The Boydell Press, 2020), p. 142.
3   Adrian Wright, *West End Broadway* (Woodbridge: Boydell, 2012), p. 212.

The 1980s
1   Hughes, p. 126.
2   *EDP*, 14 February 1984.
3   Hughes, p. 248.
4   Wright, *West End Broadway*, p. 139.
5   Ibid.
6   Wright, *West End Broadway*, p. 170.

The 1990s
1   Unidentified newspaper clipping in Victoria and Albert Theatre and Performance Collections.
2   *New Statesman*, 14 June 1947.
3   Leslie Halliwell, *Halliwell's Film Guide* (London: Paladin, 6th ed., 1988), p. 367.
4   Ibid, p. 671.
5   John Douglas Eames, *The MGM Story* (London: Octopus, 1975), p. 192.
6   Gerald Bordman, *American Musical Theatre* (New York: Oxford University Press, 3rd ed., 2001), p. 761.
7   Stanley Green, *Broadway Musicals Show By Show* (New York: Applause, 2007), p. 256.
8   *Guardian*, 10 December 2017.
9   Maddy Shaw Roberts, *classicfm.com*.
10 Derek James, *EDP*, 4 August 2019.
11 Information extracted from John Woolf's *The Wonders* (London: Michael O'Mara, 2019).

The 2000s

1 Charles and Tom Harrisson, *Britain by Mass Observation* (London: Penguin, 1939).
2 Ernest Short, *Fifty Years of Vaudeville* (London: Eyre and Spottiswoode, 1946), p. 251.
3 Bordman, p. 740.
4 Thomas Hischak, *The Oxford Companion to the American Musical Theatre, Film and Television* (New York: Oxford University Press, 2008), p. 409.
5 Bordman, p. 772.
6 Ibid.
7 Meryle Secrest, *Somewhere for Me* (London: Bloomsbury, 2002), pp. 294–5.
8 Helen McDermott, *East Anglian Times*.
9 *East Anglian Times*, unidentified newspaper clipping.
10 Wright, *West End Broadway*, p. 71.
11 Programme note for N&N production.
12 Ibid.
13 *Everybodys*, 21 October 1950.
14 Wright, *West End Broadway*, p. 37.
15 Nancy Franklin, 'The Gem of the Ocean', *The New Yorker*, 12 May 1997, pp. 102–3.
16 Wright, *West End Broadway*, p. 143.
17 Edward Goring, *Daily Mail*.
18 *The Times*, 19 December 1958.
19 Stanley Green, *Encyclopaedia of the Musical* (London: Cassell, 1976), p. 121.
20 Stempel, p. 362.
21 Ibid, p. 363.
22 *EDP*, 21 January 2011.
23 Theatre programme.
24 Theatre programme.
25 Stephen Sondheim, *Finishing the Hat* (London: Virgin Books, 2010), pp. 375–6.
26 Hischak, *Oxford Companion to the American Musical*, p. 727.
27 Stempel, p. 267.
28 William McBrien, *Cole Porter: The Definitive Biography* (London: Harper Collins, 1998), pp. 171–2.
29 David Shipman, *The Great Movie Stars: The Golden Years* (London: Hamlyn, 1970), pp. 516–7.
30 *Norwich Resident*, January 2019, pp. 30–1.

Select Bibliography

Agate, James, *Immoment Toys: A Survey of Light Entertainment on the London Stage 1920–1943* (London: Jonathan Cape,1945)
Baxter, Beverley, *First Nights and Footlights* (London: Hutchinson, 1955)
Blackwell, Michael and Carole, *Norwich Theatre Royal: The First 250 Years* (Norwich: Connaught Books, 2007)
Bordman, Gerald, *Jerome Kern: His Life and Music* (New York: Oxford University Press, 1980)
Bradley, Ian, *Oh Joy! Oh Rapture!: The Enduring Phenomenon of Gilbert and Sullivan* (London: Oxford University Press, 2005)
Citron, Stephen, *Jerry Herman: Poet of the Showtune* (New Haven: Yale University Press, 2004)
Citron, Stephen, *Noël and Cole: The Sophisticates* (London: Sinclair Stevenson, 1992)
Citron, Stephen, *The Wordsmiths: Oscar Hammerstein II and Alan Jay Lerner* (New York; Oxford University Press, 1995)
Everett, William A., *Sigmund Romberg* (New Haven: Yale University Press, 2007)
Fordin, Hugh, *Getting to Know Him: A Biography of Oscar Hammerstein II* (New York: Da Capo Press, 1977)
Gänzl, Kurt, *The Encyclopedia of the Musical Theatre* (New York: Schirmer Books, 1994)
Green, Stanley, *Encyclopaedia of the Musical* (London: Cassell, 1976)
Harding, James, *Ivor Novello* (London: W. H. Allen, 1987)
Hischak, Thomas S., *The Oxford Companion to the American Musical* (New York: Oxford University Press, 2008)
Hughes, Gervase, *Composers of Operetta* (London: Macmillan, 1962)
Jablonski, Edward, *Alan Jay Lerner: A Biography* (New York: Henry Holt, 1996)
Kilgarriff, Michael, *Grace, Beauty and Banjos: Peculiar Lives and Strange Times of Music Hall and Variety Artistes* (London: Oberon, 1998)
Lambert, Philip, *To Broadway, To Life!: The Musical Theater of Bock and Harnick* (New York: Oxford University Press, 2011)
Lees, Gene, *The Musical Worlds of Lerner and Loewe* (London: Robson Books, 1991)
MacInnes, Colin, *Sweet Saturday Night* (London: MacGibbon and Kee, 1967)
McBrien, William, *Cole Porter: The Definitive Biography* (London: Harper Collins, 1998)
Mandelhaum, Ken, *Not Since Carrie: Forty Years of Broadway Musical Flops* (New York: St Martin's Press, 1991)
Maschwitz, Eric, *No Chip on My Shoulder* (London: Herbert Jenkins, 1957)

Mordden, Ethan, *Beautiful Mornin'; The Broadway Musical in the 1940s* (New York: Oxford University Press, 1999)
Mordden, Ethan, *Pick a Pocket or Two: A History of British Musical Theatre* (New York: Oxford University Press, 2021)
Plays and Players [periodicals]
Riis, Thomas L., *Frank Loesser* (New Haven: Yale University Press, 2008)
Seeley, Robert and Bunnett, Rex, *London Musical Shows on Record 1889–1989* (London: General Gramophone Publishers, 1989)
Short, Ernest, *Fifty Years of Vaudeville* (London: Eyre and Spottiswoode, 1946)
Short, Ernest, *Theatrical Cavalcade* (London: Eyre and Spottiswoode, 1942)
Theatre World [periodicals]
Theatre World Annuals
Traubner, Richard, *Operetta: A Theatrical History* (London: Victor Gollancz, 1984)
Trewin, J. C., *The Gay Twenties: A Decade of the Theatre* (London: Macdonald, 1958)
Williamson, Audrey, *Gilbert and Sullivan Opera: An Assessment* (London: Marion Boyars, 1982)
Wilson, Sandy, *Ivor* (London: Michael Joseph, 1975)
Wright, Adrian, *A Tanner's Worth of Tune: Rediscovering the Post-War British Musical* (Woodbridge: The Boydell Press, 2010)
Wright, Adrian, *Must Close Saturday: The Decline and Fall of the British Musical Flop* (The Boydell Press, 2017)
Wright, Adrian, *West End Broadway: The Golden Age of the American Musical in London* (The Boydell Press, 2012)

Index of N&N Productions

42nd Street   175–177, 201–203

Annie Get Your Gun   122–124, 169–170
Anything Goes   222–224

Barnum   178–181
Belle of New York, The   76–78
Betty Blue Eyes   241–243
Brigadoon   106–108, 160–162

Camelot   137–139
Carousel   124–126, 183–184
Cloches de Corneville, Les   8–11
Cox and Box   64–65

Desert Song, The   90–93
Dorothy   2–7
Dubarry, The   126–128

Fiddler on the Roof   146–147, 216–217
Fledermaus, Die   149–150

Gigi   140–141
Gondoliers, The   11–13, 40–42, 59–60
Guys and Dolls   159–160, 219–232
Gypsy Princess, The   93–95

H. M. S. Pinafore   43–45, 60–62
Hello, Dolly!   128–130, 181–183, 217–219

Iolanthe   38–39, 50–52, 71–73

Jesus Christ Superstar   196–199

King and I, The   155–156
King's Rhapsody   131–135
Kinky Boots   239–241
Kismet   113–116
Kiss Me, Kate   147–148, 193–195

Little Michus, The   14–17

Mack and Mabel   188–190
Made in Dagenham   234–236
Maid of the Mountains, The   67–71

Marriage Market, The   20–22
Me and My Girl   186–188
Meet Me in St Louis   177–178
Merrie England   45–48
Merry Widow, The   103–106, 142–144
Mikado, The   28–31, 52–53
Most Happy Fella, The   152–155
Music Man, The   170–172
My Fair Lady   157–158, 192–193

Oklahoma!   98–100, 151–152, 199–200
Oliver!   173–174

Pink Champagne   100–102
Pirates of Penzance, The   62–65
Producers, The   212–215

Quaker Girl, The   74–76

Rebel Maid, The   34–37
Rose Marie   111–113
Ruddigore   54–56

Show Boat   82–85
Sister Act   224–225
Song of Norway   109–111
Sound of Music, The   163–165, 236–239
South Pacific   136–137, 190–191
Student Prince, The   96–98
Sunset Boulevard   225–228
Sweeney Todd   219–222
Sybil   22–27

Titanic   203–206
Top Hat   229–231
Trial by Jury   42–44, 60–62

West Side Story   206–209
White Horse Inn   79–82, 118–122
Witches of Eastwick, The   228–229

Yeomen of the Guard, The   32–34, 65–67

www.ingramcontent.com/pod-product-compliance
Lightning Source LLC
Chambersburg PA
CBHW051605230426
43668CB00013B/1991